MANPOWER MOBILITY ACROSS CULTURAL BOUNDARIES

SOCIAL, ECONOMIC AND LEGAL ASPECTS

SOCIAL, ECONOMIC AND POLITICAL STUDIES OF THE MIDDLE EAST
ÉTUDES SOCIALES, ÉCONOMIQUES ET POLITIQUES DU MOYEN ORIENT

VOLUME XVI

R. E. KRANE (ED.)

MANPOWER MOBILITY
ACROSS CULTURAL BOUNDARIES

SOCIAL, ECONOMIC AND LEGAL ASPECTS

LEIDEN
E.J. BRILL
1975

MANPOWER MOBILITY ACROSS CULTURAL BOUNDARIES

SOCIAL, ECONOMIC AND LEGAL ASPECTS

The Case of Turkey and West Germany

EDITED BY

R. E. KRANE

With 42 Tables and 5 Maps

LEIDEN
E. J. BRILL
1975

Comité de rédaction—Editorial committee

F. BARTH (University of Bergen), E. GELLNER (London School of Economics),
C. ISSAWI (Columbia University), S. KHALAF (American University of Beirut),
M. F. AL-KHATIB (Cairo University), P. MARTHELOT (École Pratique des Hautes
Études, Paris), S. H. NASR (Arya-Mehr University of Technology, Tehran), M. SOYSAL
(Ankara University), M. ZGHAL (Université de Tunis).

Rédacteur—Editor

C. A. O. VAN NIEUWENHUIJZE

Le but de la collection est de faciliter la communication entre le grand public
international et les spécialistes des sciences sociales étudiant le Moyen-Orient, et
notamment ceux qui y résident. Les ouvrages sélectionnés porteront sur les phéno-
mènes et problèmes contemporains : sociaux, culturels, économiques et administratifs.
Leurs principales orientations relèveront de la théorie générale, de problématiques plus
précises, et de la politologie : aménagement des institutions et administration des
affaires publiques.

The series is designed to serve as a link between the international reading public
and social scientists studying the contemporary Middle East, notably those living
in the area. Works to be included will be characterized by their relevance to actual
phenomena and problems : whether social, cultural, economic, political or administrative. They will be theory-oriented, problem-oriented or policy-oriented.

ISBN 90 04 04008 0

Copyright 1975 by E. J. Brill, Leiden, Netherlands

TABLE OF CONTENTS

INTRODUCTION

In contemporary world demographic history there is undoubtedly no more outstanding example of large-scale international migration of the type motivated by economic incentives than that which has come to the fore in Western Europe since 1960. Not only have there been major movements of population between and among the Common Market countries themselves, but of even greater significance is the vacuum which the demand for labor there has created for drawing in manpower from the economically less developed nations on the peripheries of Western Europe.

Among the nations participating in this mass movement of manpower, perhaps no two have become more closely interdependent over the past decade than have Turkey and West Germany. Indeed, Turks have now become the largest single contingent of alien workers in the Federal Republic, and barring unforeseen developments, this situation will in all likelihood continue to prevail for quite some time into the future. This volume represents an essentially empirical case study of the social, economic and legal issues and aspects associated with the cyclical, cross-cultural migration of labor, using the experience of Turkey and West Germany as an example in point.

After the 1966-67 economic recession in Western Europe subsided and the revised labor agreement between the two nations became effective in early 1968, migration from Turkey to Germany accelerated rapidly. It was not only in business and governmental circles that this increasing flow of manpower attracted attention, but in academic circles as well. More and more, scholars began to recognize the far-reaching social, economic, political and legal implications of a movement of these dimensions.

When in 1971 it became apparent to this writer that a number of other researchers had launched empirical investigations complementary to that which he himself had completed just several years earlier, the idea for the present volume of articles was formulated. The forum at which the initial drafts of certain of the following chapters were aired was the 1972 annual meeting of the Middle East Studies Association of North America where a panel of papers on the general subject of Turkish migration was presented. Meanwhile, through the contribution of others who themselves were unable to participate in this original panel, the scope of the topic was widened to include other aspects and dimensions of the phenomenon under study.

The book is organized essentially in two sections with chapter five serving as the transitional chapter. While chapters one through four treat the subject first and foremost in the German context, chapters six through nine examine it primarily in the Turkish context. Chapter five studies differences in industrial learning behavior in both Germany and Turkey.

Chapters one and seven are intended as complementary chapters, the former treating the ramifications of migration policy with respect to the German economy, the latter examining the same from the point of view of the developing Turkish economy. Both authors weigh the pros and cons of current policy and both clearly point out that theoretical assumptions often made about the economic advantages of migration are not necessarily upheld by the empirical evidence nor by effects which are likely to accrue in the long run to the economies in question.

After examining the effects of Germany's importation of labor upon income, wealth, wages, prices, employment, balance of payments and infrastructure, Völker concludes that ultimately the disadvantages of labor migration may well outweigh its advantages. A preferable alternative, he suggests, may be the substitution of capital export for labor import, especially if threats of nationalization in labor-surplus countries can be offset by Common Market guarantees.

To assess the impact of migration policy upon Turkish economic development, Miss Kolan studies the indices of GNP, capital formation, employment, labor productivity and per capita income by testing theoretical considerations against what empirical data is available on the actual performance of the Turkish economy during the period an active migration policy has been operative. Of major concern to this author is a consideration common to several other contributors as well—namely, that the uncontrolled export of skilled labor from Turkey takes its toll in one form or another upon labor productivity in that country and that this situation will continue to prevail until a more systematic effort is made to control migration in the nation's best interests and to coordinate the skills of returning migrants with appropriate job openings. A further concern strongly emphasized in this chapter also repeatedly brought out elsewhere in the book is the urgent need for essential data in Turkey with which to scientifically study the migration phenomenon. Finally, both Völker and Miss Kolan provide valuable perspective on pre-1960 developments which led up to the adoption of active migration policies by both nations during the sixties.

Closely allied in subject matter with chapter seven is chapter six which focuses on the comparative earning capacities of Turkish workers at home and abroad, the hypothetical distribution of these earnings, and the potential which hard currency remittances have for providing capital investment funds for the developing Turkish economy. Among the more crucial considerations which Miller and Çetin bring out is the fact that remittances from workers abroad now constitute by far Turkey's leading single source of foreign exchange earnings, and in 1972 were equivalent to 84 percent of all export earnings.

A related theme—namely, the transfer of skills alongside capital—which is of secondary concern in the context of chapter six is developed full-scale by Monson in chapter five. Drawing upon data derived from a unique sample of Turkish workers both in Turkey and Germany, Monson observes that industrial learning by Turks in Germany is five to six times more rapid than in Turkey and the productivity loss during learning therefore correspondingly smaller. Since the development of an industrial labor force is essential to the success of Turkey's industrialization efforts and for her joining the Common Market as an industrial competitor rather than solely as a supplier of primary products, Monson views the exportation of labor as an opportunity for Turkey to develop at least part of an industrial labor force more efficiently and less expensively than if workers were trained at home.

Each of the chapters two, three and four develops a social theme with respect to the migration movement. In chapter two Franz studies the legal status of alien workers and their dependents in the Federal Republic under currently existing legislation. Legal provisions affecting residence and work permits, naturalization and possible expulsion are analyzed. After noting the inadequacies of the present legislation for dealing with a migration movement which has assumed current dimensions, Franz discusses alternative proposals which have recently come to the fore. In view of the fact that the German labor market will in all likelihood continue to be heavily dependent upon the availability of foreign manpower in the future, Franz sees integration as the only appropriate road to pursue under prevailing circumstances.

Taking residential patterns of Turkish migrant workers in the city of Cologne as his field for empirical analysis, Clark explores in detail in chapter three the integration/segregation theme. His research discloses that the spatial and social segregation of the German and alien populations are, as it were, mutually reinforcing phenomena. While there is no section of the city which has developed as a Turkish "ghetto" in the usual sense of the term, nevertheless certain factory dormitories and densely inhabited apartment structures have assumed this role instead. Since a positive correlation was found to exist between perceived skill improvements and quality and type of housing, Clark interprets the lack of integration between the Turkish and German communities as a lost opportunity for Turkish development efforts to benefit from the migrants' potential in-depth exposure to European industrial society in its multiple aspects.

Based on case studies completed in West Berlin, chapter four constitutes what is basically a social anthropological analysis of the tensions, deviations and modifications which ensue when the family roles and cohabitation norms of Turkish society are subjected to circumstances peculiar to a non-integrated migrant community resident in an alien culture. Through the case studies which Miss Kudat discusses, the reader can see depicted in vivid form certain of the legal problems outlined by Franz and the types of segregation studied by Clark. Lest the inexperienced observer interpret certain residential patterns of the Turkish community abroad as customary in the country of origin, Miss Kudat points out that what is normatively proscribed and practically unobservable in Turkey is often normatively prescribed and readily apparent in Germany.

As Miller, Çetin, Monson and Miss Kolan indicate, systematic study of all phases in the migration cycle—pre-departure, residence abroad, and the period after permanent return to the country of origin—are equally essential if the dynamics and effects of the movement are to be fully understood. The unique contribution of chapter eight is that it does just this. The field study in Turkey upon which the chapter is based was designed in such a manner as to collect data from returned migrants, and from the industrial management employing them, pertaining to all three stages in the migration cycle. This data, therefore, allowed the author to both measure occupational mobility trends among the returned migrant population and to study certain variables which are thought to reflect the types of acculturation which occur as a result of exposure to West European society. Variables which in certain other chapters are treated only hypothetically, are in this chapter empirically measured and documented. Moreover, the same field study at one and the same time sought to measure the impact of emigration upon three Turkish labor markets in particular so as to determine what effects the loss of skilled manpower was actually producing among Turkey's leading industrial firms.

Just as the research of other authors represented here documents the exceptionally high loss of industrial skills through blue collar migration, so the work of Oğuzkan in chapter nine pinpoints the other side of the issue—namely, Turkey's loss of high-level professional manpower to the industrial nations of the West. In contradistinction to the average five to six years of formal education attained by the migrant population studied in the previous eight chapters, Oğuzkan's population was by definition restricted to those migrants who had attained the doctorate. His research disclosed that in comparison to the annual production and existing stock of doctorates in Turkey, the loss attributable to migration is very substantial and that by far the heaviest outflow occurs in the physical sciences and engineering—that is, in those fields deemed most crucial from the point of view of economic development.

The present volume reflects several convictions long harbored by this editor. The first of these is that in seeking to understand numerous social phenomena of the contemporary world, the single disciplinary approach is often found lacking, and the interdisciplinary orientation more often than not proves the more relevant and fruitful. A second conviction is that the late twentieth century is a time when parochial frames of reference have outlived their often presumed adequacy for coping with phenomena which have become essentially trans-national in scope. It seems reasonable to assume that phenomena of this nature are likely to be most perceptively analyzed by the investigator committed to the extraordinary discipline which empirical cross-cultural research in particular ordinarily imposes.

Finally, it is believed that as the demographic transition is achieved in more and more areas of the world and as further breakthroughs in death control technology are realized, increasing attention will come to be focused on migration studies both domestic and international. At the time of this writing it would seem entirely plausible that the migration phenomenon herein examined represents in microcosm developments which will likely evolve on a much grander scale not only in Europe but elsewhere as well as man orients his thinking and lifestyles toward the twenty-first century.

Los Angeles, California   R.E.K.
17 September, 1973

I

LABOR MIGRATION : AID TO THE WEST GERMAN ECONOMY?

G.E. Völker

ABSTRACT

This chapter aims to discuss some opposing views regarding the impact of labor migration on the West Germany economy. To this end, the phenomenon is analyzed from both micro- and macro-economic points of view.

As far as the micro-economic level is concerned, it would appear that mismanagement in a significant number of business firms constitutes a major reason for the heavy influx of foreign labor. Even though full employment exists in Germany, industry still continues to open new plants. Ostensibly, this practice would appear inconsistent with the given situation of full employment. Since the German Government does not assess these firms with the full cost of importing foreign labor, government policy would seem to favor this practice.

With respect to macro-economic considerations, the following hypothesis is tested : namely, that it is advantageous for the German economy to employ foreign manpower because such employment (a) increases income, (b) increases wealth, (c) keeps wages and prices relatively stable, (d) helps maintain full employment, (e) aids the balance of payments, and (f) improves infrastructure.

Over all, the hypothesis cannot be fully substantiated. Even though the in-migration of foreign manpower may possibly increase Germany's gross national product, it seems questionable whether *per capita* gross national product will increase. While material wealth will grow due to foreign labor, favorable consequences for human capital seem doubtful. The hoped-for effect that labor migration might stabilize wages and prices and help to maintain full employment cannot be validated.

As for the balance of payments, foreign workers may be considered advantageous as long as their remittances can be used as a counterweight to Germany's highly positive balance of trade. However, in light of the new dollar devaluation, the picture may soon change and foreign workers' remittances become a heavy burden. Finally, investments in infrastructure, necessitated by foreign workers, may be regarded as advantageous to the extent that these investments have the effect of increasing wealth. Nevertheless, such advantages can be realized only if foreign workers eventually return to their countries of origin.

In conclusion, it would appear that in the long run the disadvantages of labor migration may ultimately outweigh the advantages. This may be particularly true in the event an increasingly large number of workers should permanently remain in Germany.

1.1 *Introduction*

In September, 1972, some 2.35 million foreign workers were employed in West Germany, accounting for 10.8 percent of the total working population. Of the total foreign labor force, 511,600, or 21.7 percent, migrated from Turkey. Turks thus constitute the largest group of foreign workers in Germany.

The rapidly growing number of foreign workers in that country has attracted considerable attention from scholars. A glance at earlier discussions shows that writers' attitudes to the problems of foreign worker migration are closely related to Germany's business cycles. In the early 1960's, during the period of fast economic growth, most authors emphasized the advantages of labor migration. However, this was not the case during the recession of 1966-67 when Carl Föhl (1967 : 119 ff.) for example, stressed that the continued employment of foreign labor might well have reduced average productivity. Yet, with the recovery that followed warnings like Föhl's were once again muted, and most authors on the subject returned to the earlier views. Opposing positions were reconsidered during the recession of 1971-72 (Bundesministerium für Arbeit und Sozialforschung, 1972).

A survey by the weekly magazine "Der Spiegel" (1972) showed that 71 percent of the persons interviewed favoured a reduction in the number of foreign workers employed in Germany. Both the Chancellor, Willy Brandt, and the Secretary of the Interior, Hans Dietrich Genscher, appeared to be in sympathy with these findings. As a first step towards the solution of the growing problems created by the employment of foreign workers, they suggested putting a ceiling on the number of "guest workers" to be admitted in the near future. In contrast to this view, the Federal Bureau of Labor (Bundesanstalt für Arbeit 1972 : 4) stated in a report that foreign workers have become an integrated part of the German economy whose absence could hardly be imagined. At the conference, "Europe's Human Resources" in the spring of 1972, Walter Arendt, Germany's Secretary of Labor and Social Affairs (Arbeit und Sozialordnung) emphasized six major points to be borne in mind with regard to foreign workers in the Federal Republic :

(1) Employment of foreign workers is an important part of Germany's labor market policy. Up till now, this employment has had a positive impact on the development of the Federal Republic.
(2) Continuous growth in the number of foreign workers may reach a point where the high cost of integration and infra-structure will consume the advantages to growth.

(3) Extensive emigration of workers can produce long-run problems for the "sending" countries.
(4) A reduction in inequalities, the reason for unilateral labor migration, is necessary among European nations.
(5) To achieve greater equality, an active labor policy is necessary.
(6) Such a policy must include aid so that both foreign workers and their home countries might benefit from employment in Germany (Bundesanstalt für Arbeit, 1972:5).

Neither government officials nor scholars have a solution to the migration problem. It is too complex and multi-faceted for a single answer to be given. Depending upon whether the point of view is sociological, political, religious or economic, suggested "solutions" will differ. The discussion in this chapter is restricted to the economic impact of labor migration in general, and of Turkish labor migration in particular, on the German economy.

An extensive review of recently published works on labor migration shows that from a purely economic perspective nearly all discussions are based on two highly questionable propositions :

(1) The unfounded, or at least empirically untested assumptions, that employment of foreign workers slows down investment activity for rationalization and automation of production processes and that this employment depresses wages.
(2) The use of economic models so far removed from reality that conclusions based upon them almost invariably turn out to be erroneous.

The inadequacy of these propositions will be shown in the following discussion and alternative propositions suggested.

1.2 The Market for Foreign Workers

1.2.1 Foreign Workers in Germany : An Historical Review

The employment of foreign labor in Germany is not a new phenomenon. In 1895 already some 315 thousand aliens were at work in the *Deutsche Reich*. The number increased to about 500 thousand in 1900 and reached a peak of approximately 950 thousand in 1907. Most were seasonal workers. The figure for 1907 represented 4.5 percent of the total employed population (Wander, 1960).

Eva Seeber (1964) points out that in the late 1930's a new trend began in the employment of foreign workers—namely, the Nazi regime declared them an integrated part of the German economy. Most of these "integrated" workers were of Polish origin and worked in Silesia. Often the importance of these *Fremdarbeiter* for the economy during World War II has not been fully recognized.

After the war, Germany once again attracted foreign labor. The vigorous economic growth achieved in the fifties quickly absorbed the unemployment post-war conditions had created. Up to 1961 skilled workers from East Germany filled the gaps in the labor market. With the construction of the "Berlin Wall", however, the influx of migrants from the East stopped almost completely. Yet, German industry had become accustomed to the "easy" labor market of the 1950's and to the possibilities of rapid expansion without committing much capital to labor saving investments. It was in 1961 that the employment of foreign workers again began to assume importance in the Federal Republic.

Table I shows that in July, 1960, only about 279 thousand alien workers were employed. The number rose steeply in subsequent years and reached the unprecedented level of over 1.3 million by September, 1966, when the recession began. During the recession the number had declined to about 900 thousand by January, 1968, but in the economic boom which followed, the figure again rose sharply. By the middle of 1968 the one million mark was exceeded once more, and by September, 1972, the 2.3 million mark had been surpassed. While an increase in absolute numbers continues, the rate of increase is now diminishing. At present approximately eleven percent of the labor force is composed of foreigners.

Some 83 percent of the foreign workers employed migrate from countries with which the Federal Republic has concluded recruitment agreements (OECD, 1972). Two basic types of bilateral agreements have been signed (Deutscher Städtetag, 1971). In the first type, which deals with *Gastarbeitnehmern*, the respective countries agree on an exchange of trainees for the educational benefit of these trainees. Bilateral agreements of this type were signed with Austria, Belgium, Denmark, France, Greece, Holland, Ireland, Italy, Japan, Luxembourg, Spain, Sweden and Switzerland.

In the second type, which pertains to *Arbeitskräfte*, the signatories agree to jointly select workers in the sending countries for employment in Germany. On the dates indicated, Germany signed this second type of agreement with the following countries :

Japan (for miners only)   (November 21, 1956)
Greece   (March 30, 1960)

Table 1

Foreign Workers Employed in Germany

Date	Foreign Workers		Foreign Workers originating from				
	Total (× 1000)	Percent of Total Working Population	Turkey	Italy	Yugoslavia	Greece	Spain
31.7.1960	279.4	1.3	2,495	121,685	8,826	13,005	9,454
30.9.1961	548.9	2.5	—	224,579	—	32,284	61,819
30.9.1962	711.5	3.2	18,558	276,761	23,608 [a]	80,719	94,049
30.9.1963	828.7	3.7	32,962	286,968	44,428 [a]	116,855	119,559
30.9.1964	985.6	4.4	85,172	296,104	53,057 [a]	154,832	151,073
30.9.1965	1,216.8	5.7	132,777	372,297	64,060 [a]	187,160	182,754
30.9.1966	1,313.5	6.3	160,950	391,291	96,675 [a]	194,615	178,154
30.9.1967	991.3	4.7	131,309	266,801	95,730	140,306	118,028
30.9.1968	1,089.9	5.2	152,905	303,966	119,144	144,740	115,864
30.9.1969	1,501.4	7.0	244,335	348,977	265,036	191,210	143,058
30.9.1970	1,949.0	9.0	353,898	381,840	423,228	242,184	171,671
30.9.1971	2,240.8	10.3	453,145	408,015	478,321	268,653	186,585
30.9.1972 [b]	2,352.2	10.8	511,600	426,400	474,900	270,200	184,200

Source : Bundesanstalt für Arbeit. Ausländische Arbeitnehmer 1971 (Nürnberg, September, 1972), 54.
[a] Figures for 30. June.
[b] "Jahresbericht der Bundesvereinigung der Deutschen Arbeitgeberverbände" (Cologne, 1972), 86.

Turkey	(October 30, 1961;
	revised September 30, 1964)
Morocco	(May 21, 1963)
Portugal	(March 17, 1964)
Italy	(February 23, 1965)
Tunisia	(October 18, 1965)
Yugoslavia	(October 12, 1968)
Korea (for miners only)	(February 2, 1970)

Graph I shows that up to 1969 Italy was Germany's major labor-supplying country. After the 1966-67 recession, increasingly more workers migrated from Yugoslavia and Turkey. In the years 1970 and 1971, Yugoslavs took the lead followed by Italians and Turks. At the beginning of 1972, the Turkish contingent was the largest. With Yugoslavia's promulgation of a new law in 1972 to restrict the emigration of highly trained labor, the already dominant role of Turkish workers in the German economy was augmented.

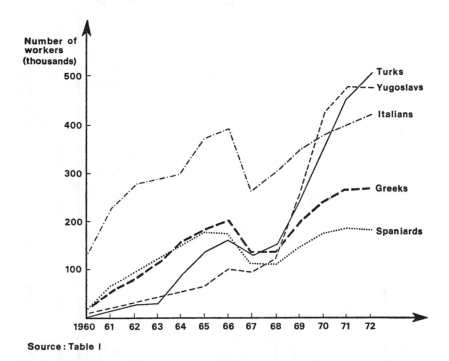

Graph 1
Demand for Foreign Workers in Germany
1960-1972

1.2.2   *The Demand for Turkish Workers*

As indicated above, on October 30, 1961, Turkey and Germany signed a bilateral agreement for the employment of Turkish workers in Germany. This agreement was revised in September, 1964, which revision took effect in January, 1968.[1] Once the revised agreement was operative, the number of Turkish workers increased rapidly from 123,386 in January, 1968, to 511,600 in September, 1972. This represents an average annual increase of 97,053 or approximately 42 percent.

Opinions differ on the reliability of these figures. It is generally assumed that the actual number of foreign workers is well above the number of those officially registered. The estimated number of unregistered foreign workers varies widely from place to place. The Ministries of Internal Affairs at the provincial level of government put it at about one percent of the total, but one may reasonably assume that the actual number of foreign workers is larger than that shown in the official statistics (OECD, 1972). For Turkish workers, it is estimated by Turkish authorities that 40-100 thousand are working in Germany without permits (Economic News Digest, 1971 a). German authorities estimate this figure to be not more than 30-40 thousand (UPI-News, 1971).

Between 1960 and 1970 the economically active population of German nationals decreased from 26.2 to 25.4 million. During the same period the total labor force in Germany increased from 26.5 to 27.2 million. This increase resulted from the migration of foreign workers (Monatsberichte, 1972 c). The Council of Experts points out in the annual Federal Report that since World War II there was never such a disproportion between the demand and supply of labor (Sachverständigenrat, 1970).

This growing demand from German industry for foreign workers in general, and Turkish workers in particular, can be attributed to the following observations.

Foreign workers are needed :

(1) to compensate for the loss in labor brought about by the desire of an increasing number of young Germans for university level education;
(2) to compensate for labor shortages arising from the growing tendency of German workers to seek more specialized jobs;
(3) to compensate for the changing age distribution among the economically active German population (see Graph 2);

---

[1] The agreement was published in the "Bundesanzeiger", No. 22 (1968).

(4) to compensate for the fulfillment of labor unions' demands for shorter working hours, longer vacations, and earlier retirement;

(5) to satisfy the additional demand for goods and services created by foreign workers themselves and their accompanying families.

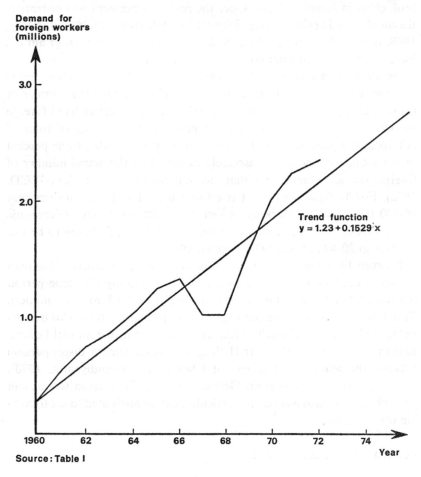

Graph 2

Total Demand for Foreign Workers
1960-1975

More Turkish workers are required :

(1) because of the rising demand from German industry for trained workers and Turkey's willingness to supply skilled labor while other sending countries have curtailed theirs;

(2) because of their greater flexibility in accepting available jobs;

(3) because Turkish workers are generally less prone than others to come with dependents and stay permanently, thereby reducing secondary costs to Germany;

(4) because of the abundant supply of labor in Turkey and the relative ease of recruiting the required type of worker.

To predict the future German demand for foreign workers in general, and Turkish workers in particular, is difficult. On the one hand, there is growing objection on the part of the German public to more foreign workers entering the country. The Bavarian Secretary of the Interior, Merk, recently declared in an official letter to the Federal Secretary of the Interior, Genscher, that the present government policy with regard to foreign workers needs to be changed. He further indicated that if the current rate of increase in alien workers continues, unsurmountable problems will be created in Germany's major industrial areas. There are already severe housing shortages together with problems of schooling and infra-structure. If an additional 600 thousand foreign workers arrive in 1973 as estimated by the Federal Bureau of Labor, a critical situation will be encountered.

Neither federal nor provincial government has the financial means to alter the situation in the short run (Hannoversche Allgemeine Zeitung, 1973). Nevertheless, it can be expected over the next five to ten years that industry will continue to demand more foreign workers mainly due to unfavorable developments in the ratio of economically active Germans to the general population (see Table 2). These demands from industry will also persist because German industry tends to favor short-run profit maximization (available by employing foreign labor) to long-run profit maximization (available by making labor-saving investments to modernize industry).

Several statistical methods can be used to predict the future demand for foreign workers. Graph 2 shows the demand for foreign workers between 1960 and 1972. If a linear trend function is used for making projections, 2.6 million workers may be expected by 1975 and 3.4 million by 1980.[2] As can readily be observed from the graph, the trend function

---

[2] The linear trend function was calculated from the total number of foreign workers, in Germany as given in Table 1. For simplicity a hypothetical zero point was set at 1966. Since $a = 13$ and $x = 0$, the normal equation can be written as : $y = na$

$$xy = b \Sigma x$$

The trend function is $y = 1.23 + 0.1529\ x$

in all likelihood under-estimates the actual demand for the next two to three years.

Table 2

Index of Total and Working Age Populations in the Federal Republic of Germany between 1965 and 1980
1965 = 100

Year	Working Age Population (%)	Total Population (%)
1965	100	100
1970	98.5	102
1975	98.2	104
1980	102	105

Source : *OECD Observer* (Paris, October, 1966), 21.

Table 3

Estimated Number of Turkish Workers in Germany, 1972-1980

Year	Estimated Number of Turkish Workers	
	A	B
1972 (Sept.)	511,600	511,600
1973	550,440	519,860
1974	585,396	526,881
1975	616,856	532,849
1976	645,171	537,922
1977	670,654	542,233
1978	693,588	545,898
1979	714,229	549,014
1980	723,807	551,662

Assumptions : In both cases "A" and "B" 100,000 new Turkish workers arrive in Germany each year.

Column A : assumes a return migration late of 10 percent per annum.

$$TW_n = 0.9 \, (TW_{n-1} + 100,000)$$

Column B : assumes a return migration rate of 15 percent per annum.

$$TW_n = 0.85 \, (TW_{n-1} + 100,000)$$

Of these additional foreign workers, a large number will undoubtedly come from Turkey since Turkey has a large reserve of unemployed workers who are willing to emigrate. Be this as it may, the future demand for Turkish manpower is often over-estimated. Table 3 projects estimated numbers of Turks at work in Germany from the present time through 1980. It is based on the assumption that each year for the next seven years there will be 100 thousand first-time departures from Turkey. Moreover, Column "A" assumes a return migration rate of ten percent of workers currently in Germany while Column "B" assumes a rate of 15 percent. Under the ten percent assumption, the total number of Turkish workers in Germany would increase about 183 thousand by 1980 while under the 15 percent assumption the increase would approximate only 32 thousand. This sizeable difference reflects why some Germans, who favor a reduction in the number of foreign workers, demand a higher recycling rate.

Table 4 shows the distribution of Turkish workers by industrial sectors in Germany. In January, 1972, about 41 per cent (184,713) were employed in iron and metal industries and 26 percent (116,467) in manufacturing. In both sectors Turks constituted the largest single group of foreign workers.

1.2.3   *The Supply of Turkish Workers*

At the end of 1971, Turkish manpower, inclusive of migrant labor abroad, stood at 15.62 million. Of this number, 13.84 million were employed full or part-time in Turkey and 600 thousand were at work abroad. The remaining 1.18 million unemployed make, in relation to the total available labor force, an unemployment rate of 7.5 percent (Economic News Digest, 1971 b).

It is not uncommon for critics of the official unemployment figures to point out that if underemployment, together with low productivity employment, were fully taken into account, the actual unemployment rate would approximate 18 percent in the non-agricultural sector and seasonally as high as 60 percent in the agricultural sector. However, this observation seems to be questionable. Y.S. Brenner (1965) pointed out that

Unemployment, or even partial unemployment, should never be confused with under-employment. The former describes a situation in which workers and other resources cannot find profitable utilization. The latter describes employ-

Table 4

Foreign Workers Employed in the Federal Republic of Germany
(Jan. 1972)

Sectors	Turkey	Yugoslavia	Italy	Greece	Spain	Other Countries	Total	Women (incl. in Total)
Agriculture	3 201	3 569	3 165	672	1 903	5 637	18 147	2 236
Mining	32 873	8 221	10 262	3 209	3 888	11 894	70 347	1 685
Iron and Metal Producing Industries	184 713	144 070	136 701	130 308	73 406	118 963	788 161	197 250
Manufacturing Industry	116 467	79 067	104 487	90 315	53 422	89 401	533 159	231 515
Construction Industry	62 480	119 693	67 148	11 046	12 348	63 406	336 121	4 041
Trade, Banking, Insurance	13 945	19 232	19 450	9 783	8 225	56 479	127 114	49 638
Services	11 312	30 073	21 097	7 850	6 944	37 033	114 309	68 118
Transportation	10 641	6 364	10 680	2 355	8 118	12 334	50 492	5 328
Public Sector	14 044	24 604	11 313	8 889	7 744	54 236	120 830	76 954
Total	449 676	434 893	384 303	264 427	175 998	449 383	2 158 680	636 765
Women (incl. in Total)	100 763	138 826	95 542	113 597	53 372	134 665		

Source : Der Bundesminister für Arbeit und Sozialordnung, Arbeits- und Sozialstatistische Mitteilungen, No. 4 (Bonn, April 1972).

ment with low productivity. The former is concerned with the number of people who are unemployed; the latter with the productivity of their labour.

While the unemployed can migrate abroad without any direct effect on the Turkish economy, the migration of underemployed workers will affect it.

In September, 1971, more than 1.2 million Turks were registered with the local Turkish labor bureaus for employment in Germany. Officials at the Istanbul recruitment office of the Federal Republic of Germany believe that workers with special skills wait an average of up to two years before they can expect to be considered for employment abroad. For workers without special skills the waiting period can be as long as seven years. In 1971, some 46 percent of all newly employed workers sent to Germany by the Istanbul recruitment office were by German standards skilled. No other country sent as high a percentage of skilled workers as did Turkey (Bundesanstalt für Arbeit, 1972:35).

Graph 3 shows that in 1971, 70.6 percent of all Turkish workers hired for employment in Germany came from Western Anatolia (15,938, or 25 percent), Ankara and Central Anatolia (14,793, or 23.2 percent), and Istanbul and Thrace (14,278, or 22.4 percent). From the Turkish point of view this development is problematic. While unemployment appears highest in eastern Turkey, the fact remains that the majority of workers emigrate from the most developed areas of Turkey where well-trained workers are required. At a recent United Nations Industrial Organization meeting, this paradoxical situation was discussed. Turkish industry officials requested development funds to train unskilled workers for skilled positions that become vacant through the emigration of job holders to Germany.

1.3 Labor Migration : Gain or Loss to the German Economy?

There is a large volume of literature on the effects of Turkish and other labor migration upon the German economy. Most authors regard these effects as positive (Bundesarbeitsblatt 1970, 1971) (Der Arbeitgeber, 1971). A possible explanation for this orientation might be the fact that foreign workers undoubtedly increase gross national product (GNP) or perhaps also the growth rate of GNP (Rüstow, 1966:35).

Joseph Stingl (1970), President of the Federal Bureau of Labor (*Bundesanstalt für Arbeit*), pointed out that with two million workers from foreign countries employed in Germany, the public is beginning to question their value for the economy. Stingl came to the conclusion that from an economic and social-political point of view migrant workers are a great asset for the Federal Republic and that without their help Germany's economic growth would have been slower. Helmut Jelden (1970) adds that without sufficient foreign labor a yearly increase in GNP greater than three percent would not be possible in the long run.

Number of workers hired:

▦ — 10,000 – 16,000

▥ — 5,000 – 9,999   Source:
                           Bundesanstalt für Arbeit
☐ — under 5,000

Graph 3

Areas of Origin of Turkish Workers Hired
in Germany during 1971

Andrés Dimitriu (1971) demonstrates in yet another manner the advantages of labor migration for Germany by employing Karl Marx's idea of surplus value (*Mehrwert*). This concept is defined as the difference between the value of production and the cost for variable and constant capital (Marx, 1885). In this system, surplus value can only be produced by the labor factor. Since foreign workers are primarily employed in the production of goods, Dimitriu concludes that they contribute more than proportionally to Germany's surplus value and that their employment is therefore an advantage for the German economy.

All these authors seem to see only one side of the problem. Foreign workers apparently have advantages for the German economy, but they also have disadvantages. For objective analysis, the problem needs to be divided into two parts. Firstly, it is necessary to determine whether foreign labor migration in general, and Turkish migration in particular, is advantageous for German industry in a micro-economic sense. Secondly, the macro-economic effects of migration need to be identified and evaluated.

1.3.1 *The Micro-economic Effects of Labor Migration*

Between September, 1971 and September, 1972, the total number of Turkish workers increased in Germany by 58,900. Assuming a yearly return rate of ten percent, altogether about 100 thousand new workers would have arrived during that period. A major problem for these newly arriving workers, and their employers, is that of adjustment to German industrial life styles. Fassbender (1966) pointed out that the costs of adjustment are directly proportional to differences in culture and to levels of formal and technical education. A harsh climate, the difficult German language, strict and confusing laws, together with rules and regulations at the new work place, all require a high degree of adjustment on the part of arriving workers.

For the employer the adjustment period is also difficult. A questionnaire filled out by the German recruitment office in Istanbul provides the employer with the only advanced information available about the new employee. No information is at hand regarding the quality of the worker, his previous training, health, ability to manage the job, or willingness to adjust.

Solving adjustment problems requires both time and money. Ernst Klee (1972) in his collection of articles shows that in many cases German personnel managers are not prepared to cope with these problems. This lack of preparation in cross-cultural human relations often inflicts lasting wounds. For personnel managers dealing with Turkish workers, a study of Turkish cultural history seems advisable. Both Turks and Germans tend to be extremely sensitive and proud people. With proper management, this pride can become an incentive for good work.

The initial costs of employing a Turkish worker are relatively high. Besides a recruitment fee of 300 DM per worker, the employer must pay the air or train fare from the German border to the new residence. In addition, there are initial costs for a medical examination, translation services and possible on-the-job training. These costs may be equivalent to two months salary. Furthermore, employers are partly responsible for foreign workers' housing. Present laws require at least six square meters of dormitory space per worker. It is estimated that the initial cost of providing this space approximates 10 thousand DM.

Despite high initial costs, increasingly more foreign workers are demanded by industry. Since the labor surplus in Greece, Italy, Spain, and Yugoslavia is diminishing, growing numbers of Turkish, Portugese, Moroccan, and Tunisian workers are being hired. In the future, this could have the effect of inflating initial adjustment costs because workers from most of the latter countries tend to have greater cultural and educational differences than those from the former countries. These rising adjustment costs might well become a regulating factor in the future demand for foreign workers.

Regional German newspapers serve as indicators of current labor demand. In week-end issues, 20 to 50 pages of job advertisements is normal. Statistics show that in an average year 400 thousand jobs cannot be filled in Germany. In April, 1971, 206 thousand persons, or 0.77 percent of the labor force, were unemployed in Germany. This figure reflects a situation of what economists call full employment. Industry claims that foreign workers alone can fill these vacancies. However, a paradox appears. Except during the 1966-67 recession, the number of foreign workers has increased yearly while the number of unfilled positions has remained constant. This might justify the conclusion that not objective circumstances but mismanagement has created the labor shortage.

Year after year, industry has justified the growing demand for foreign labor by pointing to large amounts of real capital lying idle because of an inadequate labor supply. For certain years this argument might have been valid. However, if the same argument is used repeatedly year after year, it seems more appropriate to assume that business, voluntarily or involuntarily, mismanages. Investments are made in machines for which labor is unavailable.

Three possibilities exist for "solving" this apparent problem of mismanagement. First, firms may try to hire German workers even though the unemployment rate in Germany is exceedingly low. Therefore, firms must compete for one another's employees by offering higher wages, better working conditions, and other fringe benefits. As long as these costs are lower than the cost of hiring foreign workers, the company will obviously prefer the former alternative. One might suppose from the multitude of advertisements that this is the alternative which most companies regard as their first choice.

Second, firms may hire foreign workers. Despite the additional cost and adjustment problems involved, management's argument in favor of hiring foreign labor often runs as follows : Since the investment has been made, orders have been taken, and promises made to supply products by a certain date, and because no domestic labor is available, foreign workers must be hired at all costs.

Third, a drastic way to solve the problem would be to admit the mistake and write-off the investment as soon as possible. In the long run, this might be the optimal solution from the point of view of the company's productivity and competitiveness in world markets.

Some scholars question the feasibility of the third alternative. They point out that in 1950 industry required 207 hours to produce goods valued at 1,000 DM whereas in 1966 just 83 hours were needed. The increase in productivity had a labor-saving effect. Yet, there is a limit to the possibility of substituting capital for labor, and in some industries such as construction, this limit has already been reached (Dröge, 1968). There are undoubtedly technical and economic limits to factor substitution. However, the construction industry serves as a good example for demonstrating the retarding effects produced by reliance upon foreign labor.

In January, 1972, some 336,121 foreign workers were employed in construction. If the value of stocks is taken as an indicator, most construction companies appear to be prospering. International comparisons, however, cast doubts upon their future profitability. In Germany, construction work is still extremely labor intensive in nature. Production methods in many sections of this industry remain the same as in 1930. Consequently, the cost of a well-equipped single family house, excluding the price of land, is nearly twice as high as in a comparable location in the United States in spite of the fact that labor costs in that country are much higher.

In this industry, the availability of foreign labor appears to have had a retarding influence. Werner Steinjan (1972) points out that despite increasing mechanization, labor productivity has actually descreased in the construction industry. This decrease he attributes to heavy reliance upon foreign labor.

Economic theory offers an elegant solution to the question whether or not a firm should hire foreign workers. In a competitive factor price system, firms aim for a situation in which every factor is hired until marginal productivity is equal to cost. In addition to defining and calculating marginal productivity and cost, the firm's aim must be profit maximization. This theoretical assumption is, however, unrealistic. In practice, most firms work for satisfactory returns simply by a rule of thumb. Hence, German industry seems to be satisfied to employ foreign labor as a substitute for German labor at the cost of failing to invest as much as possible in labor-saving equipment. In the long run, therefore, labor migration could have the effect of retarding the development of German industry in world markets. If the recruitment of Turkish labor becomes more costly than recruitment from western countries, in the future German industry may opt in favor of labor-saving investments.

1.3.2   *The Macro-economic Effects of Labor Migration*

To demonstrate the macro-economic effects of labor migration in general, and Turkish migration in particular, the following hypothesis will be used :

The employment of Turkish and other foreign labor is advantageous for the German economy because : (1) it raises income, (2) it increases wealth, (3) it keeps wages and prices relatively stable, (4) it helps maintain full employment, (5) it has positive effects on the balance of payments, and (6) it helps improve the general infrastructure.

1.3.2.1   *Income*

The effect of labor migration on income may be viewed in terms of effect on gross national product (GNP). Undoubtedly, an influx of foreign workers will increase total production and thereby raise GNP. However, an increase in GNP cannot *ipso facto* be regarded as an advantage for the German economy. If a precise indicator is desired, the term "income" must be defined as per capita income measured as per capita GNP (Rüstow, 1966:35). Very important for per capita GNP is labor productivity.

Carl Föhl (1967:127 ff.) showed that labor productivity with a purely German labor force would be higher than productivity with a mixed German-foreign one. He argued that without foreign workers new private investments would result in older companies being abandoned by their employees. Attracted by higher wages, they would move to new companies where higher wages become feasible if it is assumed that labor productivity is greater in the new industries than in the old. However, if the possibility of employing foreign workers exists, old industries will hire them to continue operating even though total labor productivity will then decline. Föhl estimates that with approximately ten percent of the German labor force being composed of foreign workers, labor productivity has been depressed by 9.09 percent.

These findings are, of course, only valid under the given assumptions in which two specific economic situations are compared—the one with, and the other without, foreign workers. Given foreign workers, it is assumed that there is a tendency for older industries, operating with low labor productivities, to continue producing. However, the results must be modified to include the following possibilities : (1) that labor productivity is equal in both old and new industries, (2) that technological disadvantages in the older industries are offset by good working attitudes of foreign workers, and (3) that new investment is not for replacement of old industrial capital, but rather for expansion leading to economies of scale.

Marios Nikolinakos (1973:10) believes that Föhl's reasoning is based on a general mistake in bourgeois economic thinking. Nikolinakos, who follows Karl Marx's ideas, asserts that labor is the only source for capital accumulation and that without an additional labor force no investments are feasible. He concludes, therefore, that foreign workers are an advantage for the German economy. Christoph Rosenmöller (1970) also questions Föhl's findings. Rosenmöller, who feels the problem must be seen from a global perspective, argues that foreign workers have a positive impact on income since they increase labor mobility.

Most scholars agree that labor mobility is beneficial to the economy and may result in higher labor productivity. Labor mobility may be increased in two ways. First, if foreign workers are employed, Germans, will then be able to move more freely to optimal positions. Secondly, since foreign workers accept jobs where labor is most needed, they contribute to overall labor mobility.

While in theory the first point above appears to augment labor mobility, in practice its effects seem questionable. Germans have strong ties both to their places of origin and work. Moving from job to job, as is not uncommon in the United States, is virtually unknown in Germany. One reason for this may be that the German social security system is more heavily dependent upon private employers' pension plans than is the case in the United States. Termination of employment prior to retirement age often results in complete loss of private benefits. As to the second point above, it may be said that foreign workers increase labor mobility for the most part only with respect to their first place of employment. As soon as they are settled in a job the advantages of rapid mobility are gone, for their contract compels them to remain with the same company for not less than one year.

Still another argument against Föhl's reasoning might be that without foreign workers, Germans would move to new high productivity industries, thus improving overall average productivity per German worker. However, according to the marginal productivity theory, workers are hired up to a point where the value of the marginal product is equal to the wage rate. If workers accept lower wages, the operation of older firms will continue, even though investible surplus from these firms might actually pay for the building of new plants. The fact remains, however, that the absence of foreign workers would increase the real wages of Germans, force a substitution of capital for labor, and increase both capital-labor ratios and labor productivity of German workers along with their wage rates.

It may further be argued that foreign workers will promote a redistribution of income in that they will accept less skilled jobs, allowing Germans to move into more highly skilled, better paid ones. To assume that per capita income is declining is therefore spurious, for under these circumstances the Germans' (not the foreign workers') per capita income will in fact rise. Looking to the future, however, when higher levels of integration between the German and alien populations may well be achieved through longer periods of employment and modified naturalization laws, it may be more accurate to revise this restricted definition of per capita income to include foreign workers. If the German and alien populations are combined for purposes of computing per capita GNP, it would appear that while foreign workers have helped to increase *total* GNP, their presence has not brought about an increase in *per capita* GNP.

In the event Turkish workers were treated as a separate group, this conclusion should perhaps be altered. If it is assumed that foreign workers as a whole have a neutral or negative impact on Germany's per capita income, Turkish workers would be the least responsible for this result due to their high working morale and the fact that approximately 46 percent of all workers now being sent by Turkey possess certain technical skills required by German industry. This percentage is the highest of any sending country (Bundesanstalt für Arbeit, 1972:40).

1.3.2.2 *Wealth*

Income and wealth are concepts very closely related, yet distinctly different. Wallace C. Peterson (1967) defines wealth as "all material things which possess economic value", consisting of "goods that can command other goods and services in exchange." It is most important to note here that while wealth is a stock concept, income is a flow concept. Missing from this definition of wealth is investment in human skills and knowledge. In contrast, Theodore W. Schultz (1961) points out that the wealth concept should be based on both material and human capital, since both require investment for their attainment. Furthermore, he believes that the growth of human capital may be the most distinctive feature of the modern economy, contributing in the long run more to the growth of output than conventional forms of wealth. In this chapter

wealth is defined as the sum of all goods together with the level of education and training of a nation at a particular point in time.

Foreign labor migration might affect German wealth in two ways :
First, the nation's stock of goods might be increased, and secondly, the
level of education and training might be elevated.

1.3.2.2.1 *Impact of Foreign Workers on the Stock of Goods*

Foreign workers increase total income in Germany, and the portion
of this income that is not consumed during a certain income period adds
to the wealth of the economy. Basically, abstention from consumption,
i.e., saving, occurs in two ways—through forced and voluntary non-
consumption. With regard to the former, if it is assumed that the value
of foreign workers' production exceeds their pay, then the difference is,
for the worker, forced non-consumption. The amount of this difference
will add to the country's wealth if the receiver, the company owner, does
not consume but invests this amount.

H.J. Rüstow (1966:35) found that the employment of additional foreign
workers demands investments which require a sacrifice in consumption
for the German economy lasting over a time span of about six years. As
long as more foreign workers enter the country each year, the ultimate
end of this sacrifice will be progressively postponed into the future.
Rüstow concludes that the advantage derived from the employment of
foreign workers—namely, an increase in per capita consumption—has not
yet been realized.

Werner Steinjan (1970) reaches a similar conclusion. He used a simpli-
fied input-output analysis to show the impact of labor migration on the
wealth of the economy. In this analysis he assumed that the foreign
worker's share in the GNP is equal to that of the German worker's—
namely, 20 thousand DM per year. To find the former's contribution to
the increase in wealth (*Beitrag zur Wohlstandssteigerung*), he substracted
from this amount their expenditures for consumption, costs of social
security, and transfer payments to their home countries. The residual
amount of approximately seven thousand DM was considered to be the
foreign worker's contribution to wealth. This contribution, however, is
obtained at a cost. If it is assumed that the average capital investments
are about 50 thousand DM per worker (a very conservative estimate
considering that the investment may be as high as one million DM per
worker in the chemical industry) and that the investments for schooling,
housing, and transportation total approximately 100 thousand DM per

worker, it will take a number of years before foreign workers actually bring full advantages to the German economy.

With regard to the latter concept, voluntary non-consumption, it may be said that German wealth will increase if foreign workers do not spend all their income on consumption goods during any one specified income period. In general, the marginal propensity to save may be taken as an indicator for non-consumption and consequent contribution to wealth. Since foreign workers have a high marginal propensity to save, it might be mistakenly assumed that their impact on wealth is disproportionately high. However, this reasoning may hold true only for that limited period of time their savings remain in Germany before being repatriated to the home countries from where a certain portion return to Germany as additional export demand.

Without question, the employment of foreign workers results in an increase in wealth. This might be an advantage for the economy to the extent that growing material wealth increases production possibilities. However, the advantages derived from increased wealth cannot be fully attributed to foreign workers since the initial sacrifice in consumption is made by the German economy and not by the foreign workers themselves. Moreover, it may be argued that the very conditions which create employment opportunities for foreign workers lead to a situation wherein investments are not allocated in an optimum way.

1.3.2.2.2 Impact of Foreign Workers on Human Capital

Since the educational level of foreign workers is comparatively low, most scholars reject the possibility that their presence might elevate the general training level of the nation at large. In the case of Switzerland, A. Nydegger (1963) found that the presence of foreign workers resulted in a lower average quality of the economic factor labor. This he sees as a negative impact on human capital and wealth which may lead to retarded economic growth in the future (Nydegger, 1964). On the other hand, Heinz Salowsky (1972:20) feels that such a negative impact will not arise in Germany primarily because the percentage of foreign workers in the total labor force is much lower in Germany than in Switzerland.

The actual advantage the employment of foreign labor has for human capital formation in Germany is a residual one. Unless foreign workers are available and willing to accept lesser skilled jobs, Germans previously employed in these positions would not be free to take additional training and thereby elevate the nations' human capital reserves. Furthermore, the integrated classroom instruction of foreign workers' children and German children may, on the one hand, be disadvantageous for the former due to language problems and different educational backgrounds, but on the other widen the educational horizons of both groups. While integrated instruction does not necessarily increase human capital, it might never-theless be desirable from certain other points of view such as quality of life.

1.3.2.3 *Wage and Price Stabilization*

The impact of Turkish labor migration on Germany's wage-price stability is manifested in two ways : (1) A growing labor supply holds wages down and increases price stability. (2) Increasing numbers of workers inflates the demand for goods and services. This would tend to raise prices which, in turn, would encourage labor unions to demand higher wages.

Table 5 shows indices for wages, foreign workers, and the cost of living between 1962 and 1971. As a growing number of foreign workers entered the country between 1962 and 1966, wages and prices rose steadily. During the 1966-67 recession this trend abated, but beginning again in 1968 it reappeared. To be sure, Table 5 offers no evidence to support the idea that an increasing number of foreign workers between 1962 and 1971 depressed wages. Whether wages were in fact depressed by this additional labor force, has yet to be investigated.

Because competition is the major factor in holding wages down, logic would dictate that if foreign labor competed with German labor for the same positions, wages would be depressed. However, since foreign workers primarily fill gaps created by skilled Germans seeking higher paid positions, wage depressing competition does not actually exist.[3] Moreover, a high degree of unionism in Germany tends to equalize possible wage depressing effects of the influx of foreign labor. It may therefore be concluded that the growing labor supply does not seem to have a clear wage-depressing function.

Two interesting parallels may be drawn. Firstly, between 1945 and 1959, nominal wages rose in Switzerland between 0.6 and 4.5 percent per year.

---

[3] In 1971, for example, 71.8 percent of all foreign workers entering the German labor market for the first time were unskilled and therefore competed only with untrained German workers. Bundesanstalt für Arbeit, (1972: 40).

After 1960, the growth rates increased to between 5.2. and 8.2 percent. Because foreign workers entered Switzerland after 1960, it would seem that the influx did not depress wages considerably (Gnehm, 1966). Secondly, as J. Isaac (1952) points out in the case of the United States, migration of workers from Europe had practically no depressing effect on real wages there.

Table 5

Wages, Foreign Workers, and Cost of Living Developments 1962 to 1971

Year	I Wages[a]		II Foreign Workers[b]		III Cost of Living[c]	
	Index (%)	Change of Index	Index (%)	Change of Index	Index (%)	Change of Index
1962	100		100.0		100.0	
		+ 7		+ 16.4		+ 3.0
1963	107		116.4		103.0	
		+ 7		+ 22.1		+ 2.4
1964	114		138.5		105.4	
		+ 8		+ 32.5		+ 3.6
1965	122		171.0		109.0	
		+ 9		+ 13.6		+ 3.8
1966	131		184.6		112.8	
		+ 7		— 45.3		+ 1.6
1967	138		139.3		114.4	
		+ 6		+ 13.8		+ 1.7
1968	144		153.1		116.1	
		+ 9		+ 57.9		+ 3.2
1969	153		211.0		119.3	
		+ 19		+ 63.0		+ 4.4
1970	172		274.0		123.7	
		+ 24		+ 40.8		+ 6.7
1971	196		314.8		130.4	

[a] OECD, *Main Economic Indicators* : *Germany* (March, 1972), 78; *Ibid.* (June, 1968), 76. (All figures changed to the base 1962 = 100).
[b] Calculated from Table 1 using September 30, 1962 as the base.
[c] Statistisches Bundesamt, *Statistisches Jahrbuch für die Bundesrepublik Deutschland* (Wiesbaden, 1972).

Table 5 appears to provide stronger evidence in support of the second than the first alternative mentioned earlier. That is to say that an increasing number of workers inflates the demand for goods and services.

This in turn tends to raise prices and cause unions to demand higher wages. In Table 6 linear regression analysis, based on the figures of Table 5, is used to support this alternative. The change in the foreign worker index is taken as the independent variable (X) and the change in cost of living index as the dependent variable (Y). Since including it would introduce unjustified bias, the recession of 1966-67 has been excluded from the calculations. The resulting correlation coefficient (r) of 0.452 would at first glance appear to indicate a positive correlation between the number of foreign workers and the cost of living.

However, this result also indicates that a linear regression line may not adequately represent the relationship between the variables X and Y. A more precise result may be obtained by using R.A. Fisher's rules of judgement for correlation coefficients having a small number of data (Fisher, 1940). In the given case, a linear relationship between X and Y would be justified if "r" turned out to be 0.7067 (assuming a probability of 95 percent with n=8 and two degrees of freedom). Since in fact "r" is only 0.452, it seems reasonable to conclude that foreign workers do not have a significant influence on the cost of living in Germany. Be this as it may, there are many other factors which do influence it.

From this, it is difficult to reach a clear conclusion as to which of the two alternatives is the more probable. On the one hand, without foreign workers, wages in certain markets might have increased even more than they did; on the other, additional demand created by foreign workers might have "overheated" the economy and lead to price and wage increases. A point in support of the latter idea that additional foreign workers create a demand-pull effect is to be noted from a study of the specific character of their direct and indirect demand.

In 1967 Ursula Mehrländer (1969:123) calculated foreign workers' marginal propensity to save at 0.455. Based on her estimate, foreign workers produce more than they consume which should result in dampening price increases. Yet, this would only hold true in a closed economy where a high rate of saving will slow down, or even reverse price increases. In an open economy, however, savings decrease effective demand only if the amount saved is removed from the economic cycle. In the case of foreign workers' savings, remittances sent home are quite often immediately used by that country to satisfy import needs. It follows that with some time lag, remittances may reappear on the German Market as additional export demand.

Although a demand-pull effect exists, its strength should not be over-

Table 6

Calculation of the Coefficient of Correlation Between the Indices of Foreign Workers and Cost of Living
(Figures taken from Table 5)

Year	Change in the Index of Foreign Workers X	Change in the Index of Cost of Living Y	$X - A_x$	$(X - A_x)^2$	$Y - A_y$	$(Y - A_y)^2$	$(X \cdot Y)$
1962	16.4	3.0	− 16,1125	259,6127	− 0.6	0.36	49.2
1963	22.1	2.4	− 10,4125	108,4202	− 1.2	1.44	53.04
1964	32.5	3.6	− 0,0125	0,0002	0.0	0.0	117.0
1965	13.6	3.8	− 18,9125	357,6826	+ 0.2	0.04	51.68
1967	13.8	1.7	− 18,7125	350,1577	− 1.9	3.61	23.46
1968	57.9	3.2	+ 25,3875	644,5251	− 0.4	0.16	185.28
1969	63.0	4.4	+ 30,4875	929,4877	+ 0.8	0.64	277.20
1970	40.8	6.7	+ 8,2875	68,6826	+ 3.1	9.61	273.36
	Σ 260.1	Σ 28.8		Σ 2718,5688		Σ 15.86	Σ 1030.22

$N = 8$ $\sigma_x = 18,434$ $r = 0.45$
$A_x = 32.5$ $\sigma_y = 1,408$ $\sigma_r = 0.28$
$A_y = 3.6$

estimated. Neither should the possibility be ruled out that another variable such as aggregate demand may be responsible for the demand-pull effect. In any case, it is more probable that the presence of foreign workers causes price and wage increases than that it dampens wages.

These findings should perhaps be modified to some degree when applied to Turkish migrant workers. Because of the high percentage of trained workers sent from Turkey, competition between them and German workers might possibly have arisen. Any such competition might have helped to diminish price increases. However, their relatively great demand for consumer products might have a demand-pull effect on prices and indirectly on wages.

1.3.2.4 *The Labor Market*

It is sometimes argued that foreign workers are advantageous for the German economy because if need arises, they can be used as a "safety valve" in the labor market (Maier-Mannhardt, 1972). After World War II, Germany experienced five economic cycles. Using low points to mark the beginnings and ends of these cycles, they were as follows : 1949-1954, 1955-1958, 1959-1963, 1964-1967, and 1968-1971. W. Vogt (1968) sees export demand as the main reason of these cycles. Growing export demand creates an expansion of export industries which via the export accelerator influences investment goods industries.

Table 7 shows that the growth rate of the gross national product and industrial net production had some influence on employment. While the impact was least noticeable with respect to total employment, it was most noticeable with regard to the employment of foreign workers. This dependency is clearly shown in Graph 4 where up to 1966 the total number of foreign workers is seen to have increased constantly. Allowing for some time lag, growth rates followed the fluctuations in GNP and net industrial production. A decrease in the number of foreign workers occured for the first time during the 1966-67 recession. Whereas in September, 1966, there were 1.3 million present, in January, 1968, only 900 thousand remained. During this same period, unemployment in Germany rose from 0.7 percent in 1966 to 2.1 percent in 1967 (Monatsberichte der Deutschen Bundesbank, 1972 a).

Because of these fluctuations, H.J. Tauscher (1968) develops the idea that foreign workers serve a buffer function in the German labor market. The reason why this function did not become more obvious during the 1963 and 1971 low points in the economic cycles is that in those years GNP did not fall drastically. Continuing this line of thought, M. Nikolinakos (1973:65) interprets the role of foreign workers as that of a reserve army of laborers who are invited during boom periods and dispensed with during recessions. If foreign labor is used as a buffer, high employment can be maintained in the industrial nations while unemployment is exported to the sending countries. However, Nikolinakos overlooks the fact that during recession periods the "army of foreign workers" can not just be sent home.

Table 7

Growth Rates of Gross National Product, Net-Production in Industry, Total Employment, Industrial Employment, and Foreign Workers
1961-1971
(Growth Rates to Previous Year)

Year	GNP (1962 Prices) [a]	Net-Production in Industry [d]	Total Employment [a]	Employment (Industry) [d]	Foreign Workers [c]
1961	5.4	6.3	2.0	3.1	96.5
1962	4.0	4.3	1.6	0.3	29.6
1963	3.4	3.4	1.2	— 0.9	16.5
1964	6.7	8.6	1.1	0.3	18.9
1965	5.6	5.3	1.4	1.9	23.5
1966	2.9	1.8	0.1	— 0.7	7.9
1967	— 0.1	— 2.4	— 3.2	— 6.7	— 24.5
1968	7.2	11.8	0.7	0.3	9.9
1969	8.0	13.0	2.8	5.2	37.8
1970	5.3 [b]	6.1	2.3	3.7	29.8
1971	2.9 [b]	1.8	0.6	— 0.6	15.0

Sources :

[a] Statistisches Jahrbuch für die Bundesrepublik Deutschland. Statistisches Bundesamt (ed.) (Wiesbaden, 1970), 490.
[b] Der Fischer Welt-Almanach, *Zahlen, Daten, Fakten* (Hamburg, 1973), 56/57.
[c] Bundesanstalt für Arbeit, *Ausländische Arbeitnehmer 1971* (Nürnberg, 1972), 4.
[d] Monatsberichte der Deutschen Bundesbank, 24. Jg., No. 4 (April, 1972), 64-65 and 23 Jg., No. 1 (January, 1971), 62-63.

Wilhelm Weidenbörner (1970) points out that foreign workers must be treated as equals with German workers. Almost without exception Turks hired through the official German recruitment office in Istanbul are given one year contracts which cannot be cancelled at will. In general, it can be said that such contracts provide greater protection than the

notice period to which German workers are entitled by law.[4] The decrease
in the number of foreign workers during the 1966-67 recession resulted
from the hiring of fewer workers after current contracts expired as well
as from their own decisions to return home.

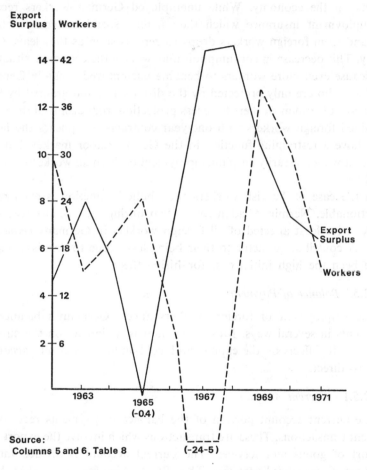

Graph 4

Percentage Change in Export Surplus and Foreign Workers Employed
1962-1971

[4] The period of notice granted by law is regulated in the *Kündigungsschutzgesetz*
of August 10, 1951. For *laborers* the period of notice is 14 days. For *employees* it is
six weeks starting from the end of a year's quarter. There are special regulations for
employees with one company for more than five years.

To what extent is the argument valid that a reduction in the foreign labor force during the recession helped Germany maintain domestic unemployment at a low level? If one ascribes to the idea developed above that additional foreign workers either directly or indirectly "overheat" demand, a decrease in their number may then be seen as having retarding effects on the economy. While unemployed German workers receive unemployment insurance which they mainly spend on consumption, demand from foreign workers drops to zero as soon as they leave Germany. This decrease in consumption may worsen the economic situation and cause even more workers to become unemployed—mainly German workers who are only protected by the dismissal period granted by law. Since most German workers have less protection from dismissal than that provided foreign workers with one-year contracts, it appears the latter may have a restraining function in the German labor market, but not one that will necessarily keep unemployment of German workers at a low level.

In the case of Turkish workers the "buffer" function is even more questionable. Nermin Abadan found that during the 1966-67 recession Turks were least affected of all foreign workers in Germany (Abadan, ms.). A contributing factor to their being less prone to dismissal might have been the high initial cost for hiring them.

1.3.2.5 Balance of Payments

The employment of foreign workers affects Germany's balance of payments in several ways. Most important is its impact on the current account. Its effects on the capital and gold-and-reserve-assets accounts are less direct.

1.3.2.5.1 Current Account

The current account portion of the balance of payments records all current transactions. These are transactions which involve the export and import of goods and services. The current account is divided into a number of specialized accounts. The effects which foreign workers have upon the economy can best be seen from two of these accounts—(1) the balance of trade and (2) the balance of private remittances and government transactions.

1.3.2.5.1.1 The Balance of Trade

Table 8 shows Germany's balance of trade between 1962 and 1971. In all years under consideration export values increased and except for

1965, were greater than import values. In other words, except for 1965, Germany has had a positive balance of trade. Since foreign workers were employed in export industries, Ursula Mehrländer (1969:131) assumes that they contributed to the growth of this industry. However, comparison of percentage change in export surplus to percentage change in number of foreign workers (Table 8, columns 5 and 6) seems to throw doubt upon this assumption. Statistical analysis shows, rather, that increases in demand for foreign workers have *followed* increases in export surplus after a time interval of two years.

Between 1962 and 1963, export surplus increased from 4.4 to 7.9 percent while percentages of foreign workers decreased from 29.6 to 16.5. Only after a two-year time lag did the growth rate of foreign workers increase from 18.9 percent in 1964 to 23.5 percent in 1965. Again, when export surplus decreased from 7.9 percent in 1963 to 5.3 in 1964, percentages of foreign workers decreased from 23.5 percent in 1965 to 7.9 in 1966. This trend holds true for all years under consideration except for the period between 1967 and 1968 when the export surplus growth rate remained nearly constant.

Table 8

Germany's Balance of Trade 1962-1971
(million DM)

Year	Total Export	Total Import	Export Surplus	Percentage Change in Export Surplus	Percentage Change in No. of Foreign Workers
1	2	3	4	5	6
1962	68,707	65,677	+ 3,030	+ 4.4	+ 29.6
1963	75,011	69,080	+ 5,931	+ 7.9	+ 16.5
1964	83,549	78,123	+ 4,426	+ 5.3	+ 18.9
1965	91,950	92,345	— 395	— 0.4	+ 23.5
1966	103,750	97,058	+ 6,692	+ 6.4	+ 7.9
1967	112,011	96,083	+ 15,928	+ 14.2	— 24.5
1968	126,761	108,543	+ 18,218	+ 14.4	+ 9.9
1969	144,466	129,790	+ 14,676	+ 10.1	+ 37.8
1970	161,747	150,015	+ 11,732	+ 7.2	+ 29.8
1971	177,162	166,190	+ 10,972	+ 6.2	+ 15.0
1972					+ 5.0

Source : Statistisches Jahrbuch der Bundesrepublik Deutschland (1966), 314; (1968), 510; (1972), 528.

Table 9
Foreign Workers' Remittances*
1964-1971
(million DM)

Home Country	1964	1965	1966	1967	1968	1969	1970	1971	1971 Remittance Per Worker DM
Italy	630	858	962	766	850	950	1,150	1,300	3,383
Yugoslavia	—	—	—	—	250	550	950	1,250	2,874
Turkey	150	280	360	339	350	550	900	1,200	2,669
Greece	253	347	385	314	300	400	500	600	2,269
Spain	325	440	463	373	300	350	450	500	2,841
Other Countries	203	268	359	385	100	200	350	450	—
Sum	1,561	2,193	2,529	2,177	2,150	3,000	4,300	5,300	
Change in Remittances (%)		+ 40.5	+ 15.3	— 14.0	— 1.3	+ 39.5	+ 43.3	+ 23.3	
Change in the Number of Foreign Workers (%)[a]	+ 18.9	+ 23.5	+ 7.9	— 24.5	+ 9.9	+ 37.8	+ 29.8	+ 15.0	
Change in Export Surplus (%)[b]	+ 5.3	— 0.4	+ 6.4	+ 14.2	+ 14.4	+ 10.1	+ 7.2	+ 6.2	

Source : Monatsberichte des Deutschen Bundesbank.

* All figures are estimates of the Federal Reserve Bank.
[a] From Table 7.
[b] From Table 8.

From this analysis it might be deduced that foreign workers do not seem to be a prerequisite for a boom in the export industry. Rather, they are demanded after an export boom has accelerated production in other industries. Therefore, the impact of foreign workers on the export industry seems more indirect than direct in the sense that they fill openings created by Germans who transfer to export-oriented industries, and the backflow of their remittances originally sent to the home countries influences German export demand. What effect foreign workers have upon imports cannot be ascertained from available statistics.

1.3.2.5.1.2   *Balance of Private Remittances and Government Transactions*

Private remittances are payments from individuals inside Germany to individuals outside Germany and are free of any obligations. In other words, they are private gifts or grants.

Table 9 shows that foreign workers' remittances increased in all years between 1964 and 1971 except for the two year period 1966-68. The growth in remittances is mainly caused by the increasing number of foreign workers and their rising per capita income (Monatsberichte der Deutschen Bundesbank, 1972 b). In 1971, Italian workers' remittances were largest (3,383 DM per worker) followed by those of Yugoslavs (2,874), Spaniards (2,841), Turks (2,669), and Greeks (2,269).

Table 10 indicates the increasing importance of these remittances in the balance of private remittances and government transactions. In 1971, Germany's deficit within this account was 10,551 million marks of which more than 50 percent was due to foreign workers' remittances. If it were not for other components of the balance of payments, by itself this huge deficit could be potentially dangerous for the German economy. However, when Germany's very positive balance of trade is taken into consideration, this deficit in the balance of private remittances and government transactions account may at present be a welcome counter-balance. As for the future, a comparison of growth rates of foreign worker remittances and those of export surplus seems to indicate that export surpluses from the balance of trade may no longer be adequate to cover deficits arising from balance of private remittances and transactions.

In actual practice, the transfer of foreign worker remittances affects the balance of payments primarily in two ways. First, workers may exchange their German marks for foreign currency within Germany in which case funds are drawn from the foreign reserves of the *Bundesbank* (Federal Bank). In this case, the total amount of German currency in

Table 10

Germany's Balance of Private Remittances and Government Transactions
1968-1971
(Million DM)

Items	From Foreign Countries				To Foreign Countries			
	1968	*1969*	*1970*	*1971*	*1968*	*1969*	*1970*	*1971*
Private Remittances :								
Foreign Workers	—	—	—	—	2,150	3,000	4,300	5,300
Others	271	584	639	627	1,292	1,633	1,671	1,845
Government Transactions	1,148	1,601	2,110	2,674	5,289	6,002	5,837	6,707
Total	1,419	2,185	2,749	3,301	8,731	10,635	11,808	13,852
Balance	—	—	—	—	— 7,312	— 8,450	— 9,059	—10,551

Source : Statistisches Jahrbuch für die Bundesrepublik Deutschland 1972.

circulation decreases as does the stock of foreign currency held by the *Bundesbank*. Assuming that the banking system does not increase its credit with the Federal Bank, the decrease of money in circulation will have a slow-down effect on the economy. If, on the other hand, the banking system equalizes the decrease in German currency by increasing its credit with the Federal Bank, an advantage may still arise from the Federal Bank's increased influence on the investment market via their credit policy. The decrease in the *Bundesbank*'s stock of foreign currency may also be advantageous as long as reserves are high.

Secondly, foreign workers may take German marks with them to their home countries. If through conversion the money is used to increase foreign reserves there or if the workers are permitted to save it without first converting it, this has the same effect as saving of income. The German market does not lose goods, and choices of consumer goods for Germans do not decrease. However, if the money is neither used to increase foreign reserves nor saved, the probability is high that at least part of it will affect demand for German export goods. Increased export demand, in turn, may adversely affect price stability.

1.3.2.5.2 *Capital Account and Net-Gold-and-Reserve-Assets Account*

Between 1969 and 1970 more capital was exported than imported by Germany. In 1971, due to heavy speculation against the exchange rate of the German mark, this situation was reversed. The employment of foreign workers in Germany has virtually no effect on the capital account. However, if in the future more German industries should choose to move production facilities to developing countries instead of importing foreign workers, effects upon the capital account would undoubtedly be substantial.

The effects of foreign workers' employment on the net-gold-and-reserve-assets account are negligible since in most cases workers prefer to transfer German marks to their home countries. For Turkey this has resulted in most of her foreign exchange reserves being in German marks. Only if workers were to demand large amounts of foreign exchange in Germany would the net-gold-and-reserve-assets account be affected in any significant way.

1.3.2.6 *Infrastructure*

Recently an increasing number of scholars have been emphasizing the growing cost of infrastructure attributable to the needs of foreign workers (Frey, 1971) (Salowsky, 1972:46) (Geiselschlager, 1972). Although Germany cannot be considered one of the classical countries of immigration, nevertheless human, social and economic factors now demand an integration of foreign minorities into German society. Some if not many analysts assume that this integration would increase the positive impact of foreign workers on the German economy (Bundesarbeitsblatt, 1970:281).

The prolonged periods an ever increasing number of workers have now resided in Germany make many wish to live there permanently and have their families join them. To make this possible, substantial investments in housing, schools, hospitals, transportation facilities, and other forms of infrastructure will be required.

Based on 1962 prices, Rüstow (1966:37) estimated the required investment for infrastructure (including housing) to be about 25 thousand DM per foreign worker. If the cost of living index from Table 5 is employed to determine the present value, a figure of 32,500 DM results. Multiplied by the number of workers employed in September, 1971, total investment requirements for infrastructure approximate 73 billion DM.

Only a small portion of this amount has thus far been invested. The more workers immigrating permanently, the more pressing will be the demand for investments in infrastructure. This leads to the question whether the German economy is able to make these investments. Some critics who denounce, for example, the housing situation of foreign workers in Germany demand action from the government. However, most of the time they seem to overlook the fact that even a government has limited resources.

By 1970, 78 billion marks had been spent by federal and state agencies for infrastructure and housing. In relation to the total population (inclusive of foreign workers), this amounts to about 1,240 DM per capita. If in the future investments in infrastructure are shared by foreigners and Germans, it is estimated that it will take about 20 years to make the required investment of 73 billion marks in order to adjust infrastructure to the present number of foreign workers. The time period may, of course, be shortened if both industry and foreign workers are willing to contribute to ease the burden.

There can be no question that investments in infrastructure are an integral part of the total cost of recruiting foreign labor. If it is assumed that the German economy is in fact able to carry this burden, then these investments may be considered as advantageous to the economy since they increase wealth. It is an entirely different question whether invest-

ment in infrastructure constitutes the optimal use of investment funds.
This question can only be answered by applying cost-benefit analysis
on a macroeconomic level.

In conclusion, the hypothesis that it is advantageous for the German
economy to employ Turkish and other foreign workers could not be
proved correct in all aspects. Although the migration of foreign workers
would seem to increase Germany's GNP, it seems open to debate whether
income, measured as per capita GNP, increases. While material wealth
is augmented by the presence of foreign workers, the effect of this
presence on human capital could not be fully determined. The hoped-for
effect that labor migration might stabilize wages and prices and help
maintain full employment could not be fully validated. Foreign workers'
impact on the balance of payments will only be advantageous to the
extent that the balance of private remittances and transactions is seen as
a counterweight to the positive balance of trade. However, the recent
devaluation of the American dollar and re-valuation of the German mark
may soon change this situation. Investments in infrastructure necessitated
by foreign workers are advantageous for the German economy since
they increase material wealth. The question remains whether these
investments will bring an optimum return or whether they could better
be used in other ways.

1.4 *Final Remarks*

This article has shown that the impact of foreign labor on the German
economy has many facets. A strictly positive or negative answer as to
whether migration is an aid to the German economy cannot be given.
However, it does seem that most of the reasons ordinarily given in support
of foreign labor are debatable from a purely German economic point
of view.

The problem of foreign labor in Germany becomes even more complex
when political and social issues are added to economic considerations.
In light of proposed European integration, approaching these issues from
what appears to be in the best interests of any one single nation alone may
soon prove an outmoded form of analysis. Beginning in 1976 there will
be free movement of labor within the Common Market. Some analysts
envision a mass migration of Turkish workers into Germany at that time.
While restrictions on immigration are a reliable means of curbing any
such flow, they undoubtedly would not function in the interest of a
"United Europe". An alternative may be to substitute capital export for

labor import. However, the threat of nationalization of capital, import-export restrictions imposed by foreign governments as well as lack of supplying industries may discourage German industry from investing in economically less developed nations. To eliminate the threat of nationalization, the governments of Common Market countries might take measures to guarantee foreign investments. In the long run, capital export from and restricted labor import into the highly industrialized nations of Europe might then lead to a truly "United Europe" with limited social differences.

REFERENCES

Abadan, N., (unpublished manuscript), La Recession de 1966/1967 et ses repercussions.
Der Arbeitgeber, 1971, Ausländische Arbeitnehmer, (9).
Brenner, Y.S., 1965, Problems of Under-employment in West Africa, *Africa Quarterly*, (2):106.
Bundesanstalt für Arbeit, 1972, *Ausländische Arbeitnehmer 1971*, Nürnberg:4.
Bundesarbeitsblatt, 1970, Ausländische Arbeitnehmer in der Bundesrepublik Deutschland and Grundsätze zur Eingliederung ausländischer Arbeitnehmer verabschiedet, (4); 1971, Zwei Millionen ausländische Arbeitnehmer, (7/8).
Bundesministerium für Arbeit- und Sozialforschung, 1972, *Ausländische Arbeitnehmer in der Bundesrepublik Deutschland*, Ausgewählte Veröffentlichungen als Hinweise, Bonn.
Deutscher Städtetag, 1971, Hinweise zur Hilfe für ausländische Arbeitnehmer, Köln : 21-30.
Dimitriu, Andrés, 1971, Die Umwelt der ausgewanderten Arbeiter (paper for discussion no. 1). (Ulm).
Dröge, Friedrich Wilhelm, (ed.), 1968, Gastarbeiter-Europäisches Proletariat?, *Gegenwartskunde : Zeitschrift für Gesellschaft, Wirtschaft, Politik und Bildung*, Opladen, 17:290.
Economic News Digest, 1971 a, Union of Chambers of Commerce, (18). (Ankara).
Economic News Digest, 1971 b, Undersecretary of the Ministry of Labor, (28). (Ankara).
Fassbender, 1966, in Unternehmerische und betriebliche Probleme, *Probleme der ausländischen Arbeitskräfte in des Bundesrepublik Deutschland*, Beihefte zur Konjunkturpolitik, Berlin, 13:50-55.
Fischer, R.A., 1930, Statistical Methods for Research Workers, *Biological Monographs and Manuals*, Edinburgh and London, (5):176.
Föhl, Carl, 1967, Stabilisierung und Wachstum bei Einsatz von Gastarbeitern, *Kyklos*, 20:119-146.
Frey, Rene L., 1971, Infrastruktur-Möglichkeiten und Grenzen, *Wirtschaft und Recht*, Zürich, 1:1 ff.
Geiselschlager, Siegmar, 1972, *Schwarzbuch : Ausländische Arbeiter*, Frankfurt : 96 ff.
Gnehm, A.H., 1966, Ausländische Arbeitskräfte : *Vor- und Nachteile für die Volkswirtschaft*, Bern and Stuttgart : 125.
Hannoversche Allgemeine Zeitung, "Bayern : Drei Millionen Gastarbeiter sind zuviel". 6 Jan., 1973:1.

Isaac, J., 1952, International Migration and European Population Trends, *International Labor Review*, 66:206.

Jelden, Helmut, 1970, Wenn die ausländischen Arbeitnehmer zurückkehren, *Auslandskurier*, (5):36.

Klee, Ernst, (ed.), 1972, *Gastarbeiter : Analysen und Berichte*, Frankfurt.

Maier-Mannhardt, Helmut, Gäste als Arbeitsventil, *Süddeutsche Zeitung*, 3 Jan., 1972:4.

Marx, Karl, 1885, *Das Kapital*, Kritik der politischen Ökonomie, Bd. II : Der Zirkulationsprozess des Kapitals, Abschnitt 3.

Mehrländer, Ursula, et al, 1969, *Beschäftigung ausländischer Arbeitnehmer in der Bundesrepublik Deutschland unter spezieller Berücksichtigung von Nordrhein-Westfalen*, Köln and Opladen : 123.

Monatsberichte der Deutschen Bundesbank, 1972 a, 24(4).

Monatsberichte der Deutschen Bundesbank, 1972 b, 24(7):8.

Monatsberichte der Deutschen Bundesbank, 1972 c, 24(8):65.

Nikolinakos, Marios, 1973, *Politische Ökonomie der Gastarbeiterfrage*, Hamburg : 10.

Nydegger, A., 1963, Das Problem der ausländischen Arbeitskräfte im Rahmen der schweizerischen Konjunkturpolitik, *Schweizerische Zeitschrift für Volkswirtschaft und Statistik*, 99:321 ff.

Nydegger, A., 1964, Das Problem der ausländischen Arbeitskräfte, *Wirtschaft und Recht*, Zürich, 16(3):207.

OECD, Manpower and Social Affairs Directorate, 1972, German Labour Market Policy Examiners' Report, 6:1.

Peterson, Wallace C., 1967, *Income, Employment and Economic Growth*. New York:32.

Rosenmöller, Christoph, 1970, Volkswirtschaftliche Aspeckte der Ausländerbeschäftigung, *Ausländische Arbeitnehmer in der Bundesrepublik Deutschland*, Sonderdruck aus *Bundesarbeitsblatt* (4):6.

Rüstow, H.J., 1966, Gastarbeiter : Gewinn oder Belastung für unsere Wirtschaft, *Probleme der ausländischen Arbeitskräfte in der Bundesrepublik Deutschland*, Beihefte zur Konjunkturpolitik, Berlin, 13:35 ff.

Sachverständigenrat, 1970, Konjunktur im Umbruch : Risiken und Chancen, *Jahresgutachen 1970/71*:15.

Salowsky, Heinz, 1972, *Ursachen und Auswirkungen der Ausländerbeschäftigung*, Köln.

Schulz, Theodore W., 1961 (March), Investment in Human Capital, *American Economic Review*.

Seeber, Eva, 1964, *Zwangsarbeit in der faschistischen Kriegswirtschaft*. Berlin.

Der Spiegel, 1972 (23 Oct.), 44:60.

Steinjan, Werner, 1972, Die Rechnung geht nicht mehr auf, *Deutsche Zeitung*, 52 (20 Dec.):12.

Stingl, Joseph, 1970, Das Problem der Gastarbeiter, *Auslandskurier*, 5 (Oct.):1.

Tauscher, H.J., 1968, Die ausländischen Arbeitnehmer in der Westdeutschen Wirtschaft, *DWI-Berichte*, 19:15 ff.

UPI-News, Illegale Türken müssen die Bundesrepublik verlassen. 2 Feb., 1971. (Bonn).

Vogt, W., 1968, *Die Wachstumzyklen der Westdeutschen Wirtschaft*. Tübingen:3-8.

Wander, H., 1960, Die Beschäftigung ausländischer Arbeitnehmer in der Bundesrepublik Deutschland, *Sozialer Fortschritt* 9(10):244.

Weidenborner, Wilhelm, 1970, Beschäftigung ausländischer Arbeitnehmer in der Bundesrepublik Deutschland, *Ausländische Arbeitnehmer in der Bundesrepublik Deutschland* (3):3.

II

THE LEGAL STATUS OF FOREIGN WORKERS IN THE FEDERAL REPUBLIC OF WEST GERMANY

Fritz Franz

ABSTRACT

This chapter examines the policy formulated by the West German Government to deal with the status of foreign workers in that country. It analyzes the provisions of relevant legal documents including international treaties and the German constitution. In particular, it studies the 1965 version of the *Ausländergesetz* (Aliens Act) as well as judicial interpretations of this Act handed down in specific cases.

Of primary concern is the impact of the *Ausländergesetz* upon the following : (a) ability of the worker to obtain and renew residence and work permits, (b) his vulnerability to expulsion from Germany, (c) residency and citizenship status of parties to mixed marriages, (d) naturalization rights and (e) status of accompanying dependents.

The discussion examines the ensuing debate on criticisms of the *Ausländergesetz* and cites alternative proposals which have been presented. It concludes by recognizing the difficult task lawmakers face in balancing domestic interests with those of foreign workers, but notes the urgency of dealing with the problem if serious social conflict is to be avoided.

The catastrophes of two world wars have produced immense population shifts. Cautious calculations show that about 70 million people in Europe alone were forced to leave their native countries as a consequence of events in the wars, of racial or national intolerance and of political repression.[1] Experts familiar with the subject speak of "the century of the refugees and stateless" and the "age of the mass exodus." [2]

---

[1] Martin Kornrumpf, *Das Weltflüchtlingsproblem*, Weggis Report 1960, Vol. 2, 11 of Schriftenreihe der Fürst Franz Josef von Liechtenstein Stiftung ; Paul Frings, *Das Internationale Flüchtlingsproblem 1919 bis 1950*, Frankfurt/Main, 1951; John Hope Simpson, *The Refugee Problem*, Oxford, 1939; Malcolm J. Proudfoot, *European Refugees : 1939-1952*, Evanston, 1956; Louise W. Holborn, *The International Refugee Organization*, London, 1956.

[2] Elfan Rees, *Jahrhundert der Heimatlosen*, Evangelisches Verlagswerk, Stuttgart, 1959; Otto Kirchheimer, *Gegenwartsprobleme der Asylgewährung*, Vol. 82 of Schriftenreihe der Arbeitsgemeinschaft für Forschung des Landes Nordrhein/Westfalen; Fred W. Riggs, *Das Welt-Flüchtlingsproblem*, Europa-Archiv 1951, 3807.

Apart from occasional upheavals that have led to collective movements of refugees,[3] taking flight for political reasons in Europe is now restricted to matters of individual fate.[4] These may be tragic, but are not without hope or help. The European countries (except for Spain, Malta and the eastern block, but including Yugoslavia) have ratified the Convention Relating to the Status of Refugees signed at Geneva on July 28, 1951,[5] with its protocol added on December 16, 1966.[6] This Convention, which grants foreign refugees an indispensable minimum of legal, financial and political security in host countries, constitutes the most significant international agreement that has come into being under the aegis of the United Nations Office of the High Commissioner for Refugees.[7] As a result of the protection provided by it, the legal status of refugees in Europe can now be regarded as guaranteed.

Present day European migration, incited by new forces at work, is predominantly from south to north. In the agricultural regions of the southern and south-eastern periphery there is a shortage of jobs; in the industrial regions of central and western Europe labor is needed. Instead of taking industry to people, the European countries have chosen to bring people to industry. While France, West Germany and Switzerland are the major labor-importing countries, Austria, Belgium, Luxemburg, the Netherlands and Sweden also supply their economies with substantial amounts of foreign labor. Even certain labor-exporting countries themselves employ foreigners from less developed regions. The pilgrimage has also spread to North Africa. Moroccans in Spain, Algerians in France and Tunisians in West Germany are today considered an essential part of the European labor market.

These workers do not migrate of their own free will, but rather under the compulsion of financial necessity. In following the call of the host country that offers them work they are in search of secure jobs which they cannot find at home. West Germany has made recruitment agreements with Greece, Italy, Portugal, Spain, Turkey and Yugoslavia which

---

[3] Hungarian uprising of October, 1956; Soviet occupation of Czechoslovakia, August, 1968.

[4] Yearly about 5000 persons apply for asylum to the German Bundesamt für die Anerkennung ausländischer Flüchtlinge in Zirndorf near Nürnberg.

[5] 189 United Nations Treaty Series (UNTS) 137 = Bundesgesetzblatt (BGBl.) 1953 II 559.

[6] 606 UNTS 267 = BGBl. 1969 II 1293; 1970 II 194.

[7] See Atle Grahl-Madsen, *The Status of Refugees in International Law*; Otto Kimminich, *Der Internationale Rechtsstatus des Flüchtling*, Köln, 1962

provide for the sending country to present suitable and willing workers
to a local commission, liaison office or delegation of the German Federal
Labor Bureau (Bundesanstalt für Arbeit).[8] The applicants are recruited
according to the numbers and qualifications required by German firms
and receive work contracts which tie them to their jobs for a period of
one year. Upon entering Germany the migrant worker is issued an
identity card which replaces the entry visa and is valid as a work permit
for a stipulated period of time. At the workplace living accommodations
must be provided which, according to guidelines laid down by the Federal
Minister of Labor and Social Affairs, must constitute an area, for a group
of up to four persons, of at least eigth square meters per person, of which
six square meters are for sleeping purposes.[9] Each worker must have his
own bedstead, mattress, pillow, blankets and sheets, and not more than
two bedsteads may be placed over one another. A clothes closet, chair
and food locker must also be provided on an individual basis whereas
the required table and kitchen are to be used communally. A wash basin
must be installed in the room when there are five occupants and a shower
with hot and cold water for 20. Men and women must be accommodated
separately.

At the workplace the law makes no distinction between aliens and German nationals. Stipulations of contracts on wages, paid holidays,
industrial safety standards, work hours, maternity leave and legal
protection through the industrial courts apply equally to foreign and
German employees alike. Neither is any distinction made in the law on
strikes, in the payment of overtime or in voluntary payments such as
pensions, bonuses and allowances. Both can invest in and draw on the
national savings plan. To the extent that it does not contravene standing
contractual agreements with individuals, the law on notice and dis-
missals is equally applicable to foreign employees who are also entitled to
participate in works council elections.[10] In health, accident, pension
and unemployment insurance benefits as well as in family dependents
allowances, foreigners enjoy in return for the same duties the same rights
as their German counterparts. Moreover, insurance periods in foreign
countries are credited.

---

[8] Bundesanzeiger (BAnz) No. 25/61 (Greece); 219/61 (Spain); 104/64 (Portugal);
63/54 (Italy); Gemeinsames Ministerialblatt (GMBl) 1962, 10; 1964, 507 (Turkey see
also BAnz No. 22/68); BGBl. 1969 II 1107 (Yugoslavia).

[9] Richtlinien für die Unterkünfte ausländischer Arbeitnehmer of 29 March 1971
BAnz No. 63/71.

[10] §§ 7, 8 Betriebsverfassungsgesetz of 15 January 1972, BGBl. I 13.

By giving equal treatment to foreigners in the fields of labor and social legislation, the Federal Republic fulfils obligations in international law that it assumed when becoming a signatory to certain international agreements—namely, the ILO Convention No. 97 Concerning Migration for Employment on July 1, 1949,[11] and the European Social Charter on October 18, 1961.[12] In other important areas there is an absence of internationally binding norms. It is especially in questions of entry, residence and expulsion that countries adhere to their rights of sovereignty with respect to admitting foreigners. Except where economic amalgamations such as the European Economic Community have made labor mobility across frontiers possible for nationals of the various countries and their families,[13] individual countries wish to remain "masters in their own house" as far as admitting foreigners is concerned and to be free to decide whether and which foreigners may be admitted, turned back or expelled.

The European Convention on Establishment of December 13, 1955,[14] bilateral friendship treaties and treaties on residence existing between the Federal Republic and a number of other countries have not altered this principle.[15] The obligations contained in them are vague. Although the member states grant each other's nationals certain occupational liberties and the enjoyment of civil rights, they reserve the right of judging the decisive question of lawful residence according to domestic law. Only certain declarations of good intent are to be found in the treaties, wherein the countries assure one another that they will facilitate the entry and residence of each other's nationals.

Under these circumstances the question of a country's domestic regulations on residence is of central importance for the foreigner's existence. What is common to all such regulations is that foreigners, with regard to residence, are subject to exceptional law. Whereas according to Article 13 of the Universal Declaration of Human Rights dated December 12, 1948 [16] and Article 3 of Additional Protocol No. 4 attached

---

[11] 120 UNTS 71 = BGBl. 1959 II 87.

[12] European Treaty Series No. 35 (35 ETS) = BGBl. 1964 II 1261.

[13] Rome Treaty establishing the European Economic Community on 25 March 1957, 298 UNTS 11.

[14] 19 ETS = BGBl. 1959 II 997.

[15] Such treaties exist *inter alia* with Greece (BGBl. 1962 II 1505); Iran (Reichsgesetzblatt-RGBl.-1930 II 1002; BGBl. 1955 II 829); Turkey (RGBl. 1927 II 76; BGBl. 1952 II 608); Thailand (RGBl. 1938 II 51); USA (BGBl. 1956 II 487); Dominican Republic (BGBl. 1959 II 1468).

[16] Annex to United Nations General Assembly Resolution 217 (111).

to the European Convention for the Protection of Human Rights and
Fundamental Freedoms [17] and dated September 16, 1963, a country's
own nationals are guaranteed the enjoyment of freedom of movement,
foreigners remain excluded from this.[18] The latter are selected according
to expediency criteria, and turned back or expelled if they become undesirable, troublesome or an inconvenience. The "sacro egoismo" of the
nation and the "priority of national interests" have been the criteria
governing admission of aliens since the time European principalities
formed themselves into nation-states which, in turn, accepted it as their
responsibility to assist nationals, but not foreigners, to acquire a maximum
of wordly goods. That such is in fact the case is not, of course, so frankly
admitted. Nations look for formulae that will create the appearance of
a "liberal and outward-looking aliens policy." [19] The cold calculation
of the use effect for the state is hidden behind agreeable catch-all phrases
which can readily be manipulated but whose end result in benefiting the
alien is nil.

Indeed, regulations of this kind are to be found in residence stipulations in most European countries. General provisos with flexible, indeter-
minate legal concepts form the framework for ostensibly normative
facts behind which a broad field of official discretion opens out. Whereas
in the German National Socialist state it was the foreigner's merit that
might allow him to be favored with a residence permit, the Federal
Republic places the protection of its interests before the official discretionary decision.[20] Other countries emphasize the priority of "public
order, security and the economy" (Belgium), or of "public peace, order
and national security" (Netherlands, Austria), or they simply put the
refusal of a residence permit at the discretion of the authorities which
in practice amounts to the same thing.[21] The same holds true with regard
to the law on expulsion irrespective of the fact that the withdrawal or

---

[17] 46 ETS = BGBl 1968 II 423.

[18] Cf. Article II Basic Law of the Federal Republic of Germany (Grundgesetz
für die Bundesrepublik Deutschland (GG) of 23 May 1949-BGBl-: "Alle Deutschen
genießen Freizügigkeit im ganzen Bundesgebiet".

[19] Official reason given for the draft of the German Ausländergesetz, Bundestags-
Drucksache IV/868 p. 10.

[20] § 1 Ausländerpolizeiverordnung -APVO- of 22 August 1938 versus § 2 Ausländergesetz -AuslG- of 28 April 1965.

[21] Cf. Gerard Lyon-Caen, Report 4.874/V/66 -D of the EEC-Commission, Direction of Migrant Workers; Ulrich Erdmann, *Das Ausländergesetz vom 1965 im Inter-
nationalen Vergleich*, Verwaltungsarchiv 1968, 311; Diemut Majer, *Der Standesbeamte*
1971, 38.

non-renewal of the residence permit results in police intervention comparable to sanctions in criminal law and which as a general rule leads to the loss of the basis for existence in the host country.

When viewed against this background the stipulations on residence in the current West German Aliens Act dated April 28, 1965, and found in *Bundesgesetzblatt* I, 353 do not seem unusual. They lay down that foreigners who wish to stay in the country for more than three months and/or wish to work there require a residence permit. Granting the permit is at the discretion of the authorities (§ 2). The permit can be granted for a definite or indefinite period, restricted to a given area, extended, endorsed with provisos, and also be further limited at a later date (§ 7). After at least five years residence the permit can be issued as an authorization of residence not restricted to a given area nor specified period of time but can still be endorsed with provisos (§ 8). If the foreigner should "prejudice important interests of the Federal Republic" he can be expelled. Besides criminal acts and endangering the security of the state, the law also includes as "important interests" begging and vagabondage, destitution and indecency, and the contravention of regulations concerning registration of domicile, customs matters, business matters and the like (§ 10). Those receiving an expulsion order must leave the Federal Republic without delay (§ 12). The same legal obligation to leave the country affects those who are not, or who are no longer in possession of a valid residence permit. If the foreigner does not depart voluntarily, he may be forcibly deported (§ 13). In preparation for the deportation and to ensure that it takes place, he may be put under detention by court order (§ 16) and also be sentenced (§ 47).

The subordination of the foreigner to the discretionary powers of the authorities prevails also at the workplace. According to the regulation on work permits (VO) dated March 2, 1971, and found in *Bundesgesetzblatt* I, 152, the required permit will be granted "depending on the situation in the labor market" for a maximum of two years and subsequently for a maximum of three. It can be tied to a specific occupation in a specific firm (§§ I, 4 VO). After five years of uninterrupted employment the work permit is granted independently of the occupation, firm and developments in the labor market, and after ten years it can be granted for an indefinite period (§§ 4 11, 2 1 No. 1 VO). A precondition, however, is the possession of a valid residence permit (§ 5 VO). If the residence permit has expired or been invalidated, the work permit automatically expires (§ 8 1 No. 1 VO). The law imposes no obligation upon the authorities to take into consideration the interests and needs of the individual.

The intellectual fathers of the act were bureaucrats who praised their concoction as being "far more generous than those of comparable western countries." [22] In many respects, they said, it is "liberal to excess" [23] and "has been praised both at home and abroad as thorough progress." [24] Its liberal spirit "has already received outspoken recognition abroad" and "it may well be said that it is the most liberal aliens act in the world." [25] A commentator on the act thanked the legislators for "having had the courage to forge a new path" and expressed the hope that "this would not remain an isolated achievement of the Federal Republic." [26]

Seldom have both legislators and the public been more deceived. In reality, the Aliens Act is much more severe and restrictive than its predecessor, the Aliens Police Decree of the Third Reich (APVO), dated August 22, 1938, and found in the *Reichsgesetzblatt* I, 1053. According to this former law, the authorities were obliged to grant a residence permit where the foreigner "merited" it. The new body of law rejects this obligation ("may be granted") and transfers the admission criterion from the subjective credentials of the foreigner, located in himself and governable by him, to the nebulous formula of the "interests of the Republic", over which the foreigner exercises no influence.

The same shift in emphasis is to be found in the law on expulsions.[27] The limit of sentences allowed by the Aliens Police Decree for unauthorized residence (imprisonment for up to six weeks and/or a fine of up to 150 RM, § 13 1 APVO) has been extended to imprisonment of up to one year and/or a fine of up to 10,000 DM (§ 47 1 No. 2, AuslG, § 27 of the criminal code-StGB). Six new categories of punishable offences have been added which make certain other acts subject to the same sentence. In addition, the law enumerates ten violations which are punished as illegal acts. Normal limits on fines stipulated under the Law on Illegal Acts (not less than five DM nor more than 1,000 DM) are extended to 5,000 DM for premeditation and 2,000 DM for negligence (§ 48 AuslG). Apart from this, deportation arrest of up to 58 weeks is admissible (§ 16 AuslG). No neighboring country of the Federal Republic, including the German

---

[22] Günter Weißmann, *Ausländergesetz* (Commentary, p. 34).

[23] Gerhard Heuer, *Publications of (German) World University Service*, Vol. 8, p. 26.

[24] Heuer, *Frankfurter Allgemeine Zeitung* (FAZ), 21 December 1965, p. 6.

[25] Arno Kloesel/Rudolf Christ, *Deutsches Ausländerrecht* (Commentary), foreword to the first edition.

[26] Werner Kanein, *Ausländergesetz* (Commentary), foreword p. 7.

[27] § 10 I No. 11 AuslG versus § 5 Ausländerpolizeiverordnung.

Democratic Republic, permits such periods of arrest. Where deportation arrest is allowed at all, its maximum duration is ordinarily limited to ten days or at the very most three months.

The Aliens Act has practically eliminated the foreigner's legal protection against the refusal of a residence permit or of its renewal. Whereas according to the former law recourse to legal action has essentially the effect of postponing deportation [§ 11 IV APVO, Art. 19 IV GG, § 80 1 of the Verwaltungsgerichtsordnung (VwGO)], the Aliens Act (§ 21, III 2) excludes this possibility. Consequently, the foreigner must now leave the territory of the Federal Republic even though he has logded an appeal against the government's refusal to renew his residence permit. He might evade the exit obligation by applying to a court for a postponement order pending appeal (§ 80 V VwGO), but he will not be informed of this possibility. Such an application is, moreover, only successful in the rarest of cases because the courts, not without cause, take the point of view that "the legislator has decided in principle not to grant a foreigner the opportunity of being authorized to await the decision about his appeal in the Federal Republic." [28] Should the application be granted in an exceptional case, the foreigner all the same remains without adequate protection because his work permit lapses when his residence permit expires. (§ 8 VO).

Occasionally it is erroneously inferred from the sheer quantity of the forcign labor force permitted in the Federal Republic that the Aliens Act is liberal. This card is no trump either. In the final analysis, hard-headed economic interests are the decisive factor for admitting foreigners. When the commodity of manpower is in demand, legal safeguards are of secondary concern. "Interests of the Federal Republic" and the assertion that the "Federal Republic is not an immigration country" are convenient catch-all phrases which can readily be called up to relieve the country from the social responsibilities which result from employing migrant labor.

Administrative regulations call on authorities "to limit the residence permit for a foreign worker to, as a rule, one year at the most." [29] Neither a reason for the limitation nor advice about the right of appeal are given him. Should the foreigner after five years residence apply for an unlimited residence permit, he will ordinarily be told—again without

---

[28] Bayerischer Verwaltungsgerichtshof (Bay VGH), in Erhard Schüler/Peter Wirtz, *Rechtsprechung zum Ausländerrecht*, AuslG § 21 No 3; Oberverwaltungsgericht (OVG) Bremen in Deutsches Verwaltungsblatt (DVBl) 1972, 519.

[29] Allgemeine Verwaltungsvorschrift zum AuslG, No. 4 to § 7, GMBl 1967, 299.

advice about his right of appeal—that "a certification, by which the unlimited and unrestricted residence in the Federal Republic is guaranteed, is under legal stipulations currently in effect neither provided for nor possible." [30]

If the foreigner refers expressly to the entitlement to residence accorded in paragraph eight of the Aliens Act, he is usually informed that this entitlement is subject to the qualification that the interests of the state not be jeopardized. Such jeopardy was deemed to exist when, for example, a Turk of good reputation after nine years residence gave it to be understood that, in order to complete the minimum social insurance contribution period, he wished to remain another six years.[31] Practice thus converts the spirit of the regulation into its opposite. Although approximately 1.5 million migrants have already been working in the Federal Republic for five years or more, only 7,000 authorizations of unrestricted residence have thus far been issued. A long period of residence is felt to be dangerous and is often used as an excuse to refuse further extensions because "the critical point has been reached at which permanent settlement is threatening." [32] Should the foreigner after eleven years of residence entertain the thought of naturalization, the culminating point is ordinarily thought to have been surpassed.[33] Not without cause, senior administrative officials see the spirit of the existing Aliens Act to be that of protecting the host country and its citizens from immigrants. At least this is the current practice endorsed quite overwhelmingly by the superior and federal administrative courts.[34]

Thus, in naturalization rights as well foreign workers have little if any chance. By law naturalization can occur if the foreigner is of good reputation and can support himself and his dependents in the Federal Republic.[35] According to previous legal precedents, however, this possibility exists only after a ten-year period of residence. Yet even after the expiration of this period it will not be the interests of the foreigner which

---

[30] Case of Angelique Marinopolous, published in Edition Suhrkamp, Vol. 539 p. 264 (Ernst Klee, *Gastarbeiter- Analysen und Berichte*).

[31] Bundesverwaltungsgericht (BVerwG), Case I B 51.72 (20 August 1972).

[32] BayVGH in *Neue Juristische Wochenschrift* (NJW) 1970, 1012.

[33] See Fritz Franz, Ausländer ohne rechtsstaatliche Garantien, *Recht und Gesellschaft* 1972, 361 (364 Fn. 10).

[34] There are only a few decisions in favor of the plaintiff. See Franz, *Jahrbuch für Internationales Recht*, Vol. 15 (1970) p. 328, Fn. 50.

[35] § 8 of Reichs—und Staatsangehörigkeitsgesetz of 22 July 1913—BGBl III No. 102-I.

are decisive but rather those of the state alone.[36] Thus naturalization is conceived as an act of grace which is ordinarily not a viable option for a foreign worker if he/she is not married to a German spouse.

Only foreigners who have already concluded their marriage with a German citizen are considered something of an exception. The problem of the German-foreign mixed marriage was dealt with in the fundamental decision handed down by the Federal Administrative Court on February 27, 1962 :

"As a rule one begins with the premise that marriage partners, if both do not possess domestic citizenship, must from the start come to terms with transferring the marital residence abroad, and that the transfer of the marital residence abroad does not at once lead to endangering the grounds of the marriage. In general it can be expected of a wife that she will follow her foreign husband abroad".

This decision, which has been followed by the lower courts, next calls attention to the fact that the duty or expectation to follow will be required only of the German wife and not of a German husband married to a foreign woman. Indeed foreign women married to German husbands have until now not been deported.[37] However, considering the equality of rights accorded husband and wife (Article 3, paragraph 2 GG), the absurdity of this ruling is brought into focus by the fact that the determination of the place of marital residence no longer belongs to the husband alone but to both spouses.[38] Thus it seems out of the question to speak of the German wife's duty to follow. Above all, it overlooks the fact that in the Federal Republic the German wife enjoys freedom of movement (Article II GG) and therefore can demand to be allowed to stay and live in the country. That she also has the right to live a married life in the Federal Republic by agreement with her foreign husband whom she can freely choose should follow automatically from the precept to protect marriage contained in Article 6 of the constitution.

In the law of the European Economic Community it is considered self-evident that the freedom of residence therein guaranteed is also to be

---

[36] Parts 2.2 and 4.2.1 of Einbürgerungs—richtlinien of 1 March 1971; on the decision see BVerwGE 4,298; 6,186; 7, 237.

[37] Heldmann in *Studentische Politik*, I, 1970, p. 34

[38] Oberlandesgericht (OLG) Celle, NJW 1954, p. 1526; Bundesgerichtshof in Zivilsachen, Entscheidungssammlung (BGHZ) II Appendix p. 62; OLG Schleswig, *Zeitschrift für das Gesamte Familienrecht* (Fam RZ) 1957, p. 420; also OLG Düsseldorf, Fam RZ 1969, p. 153.

accorded to dependents regardless of their nationality.[39] However, neither being born in the Federal Republic nor being born of a German mother *ipso facto* entitle a child to German citizenship. A child born in the Federal Republic of a German mother and an alien father, which child has never left Germany and knows no language but German, may for seemingly just cause be deported independently of his parents.[40]

Criticism of the Aliens Act and the ways it is implemented is growing. One hundred fifty well-known persons [41] sent a petition to the German Federal Parliament in which the replacement of the Aliens Act by the "1970 alternative draft" is demanded.[42] At the 1971 Ecumenical Whitsunday meeting in Augsburg representatives of both major churches took up the demand.[43] The Conference of German Municipalities in a comprehensive study pointed out the dangers of segregation and proposed systematic measures of integration.[44] The National Committee of the German Trade Union Confederation passed a resolution on February 9, 1973, for the reform of the Aliens Act in which it is stated :

The law on aliens currently in force is based, in its historical origin, on the principle of mere tolerance. What stands to the fore here is the discretionary power of the authorities. The spirit and application of the Aliens Act have led, particularly with regard to the residence permit, to marking restrictions onto the permit and to expulsion—to a real and legal insecurity of immigrant workers that is no longer bearable for them and also to considerable disadvantages even when German interests are taken into account.

In a period of increasing international, political and economic interdependence, cooperation and liberalization, the law on aliens, with its obsolete principles of an authoritarian state and its narrow-minded nationalistic prejudices, is an anachronism.

On May 18, 1973, the Diaconic Mission of the Protestant Church, the German Caritas Association, other organizations and private individuals presented the Federal Minister of the Interior and his counterpart officials in the provinces with concrete proposals for improving the legal position of migrants.[45]

---

[39] §§ 1 paragraph 2, 7 Aufenth G/EWG.

[40] BVerw G, Case I C 62.66 (16 July 1968); Baden-Württembergischer VGH, Entscheidungssammlung (ESVGH) 18, 104.

[41] The list of petitioners appears in Edition Suhrkamp, Vol. 539, p. 52, Fn. 79.

[42] Franz/Heldmann/Kasprzyk/Majer/Pätzold, Ausländergesetz '65-Alternativentwurf '70, Kritik und Reform, in *Studentische Politik* I, 1970.

[43] Oekumenisches Pfingsttreffen Augsburg 1971, Dokumente, Res.92, p. 365.

[44] Deutscher Städtetag, Hinweise zur Hilfe für ausländische Arbeitnehmer, No. 6, 1971 der Sozialpolitischen Schriften.

[45] Speaker : Georg Albrecht, Düsseldorf.

As a result of this criticism the first signs of a new orientation in the interpretation of the alien policy are now beginning to manifest themselves. On May 10, 1972, the General Administrative Regulation for the Implementation of the Aliens Act [46] was altered so that residence is basically to be permitted to the foreign marriage partner of a German. Adjudication is following the new course, even though to some extent hesitatingly and with reservations.[47] In the 38th sitting of the German Federal Parliament on June 6, 1973, the Federal Minister of Labor and Social Affairs announced an "Action Program" of the Federal Government in which the so-called rotation principle—the compulsory return to their native countries of migrants long in residence—was rejected :

From social and humanitarian considerations the Federal Government rejects the compulsory termination by official intervention of the residence of migrant workers after the expiry of a given period of time. On the contrary, a longer period of residence should lead to improved status as regards residence rights. Appropriate modifications will be inserted into the Administrative Regulations for the Implementation of the Aliens Act.[48]

The Rhineland-Palatinate provincial committee of the Christian Democratic Union has expressed itself in the same manner.[49] Likewise a verdict of the Federal Administrative Court should be emphasized by which a Spanish grandmother was successful in her application for a residence permit which she had made in order to be able to look after the children of a Spanish married couple who were migrant workers. The Federal Republic, said the Court, is a social and constitutional state which cannot evade certain welfare obligations towards migrant workers whom it has recruited.[50] Finally it deserves to be mentioned that the Council of Europe is preparing a convention relating to the legal status of migrant workers.[51]

---

[46] GMBl 1972, 331.

[47] BVerwG, Cases I C 20.70; 52.70; 33.70 (all of 3 May 1973): see also OVG Berlin, NJW 1972, 2196 (II. Senat) versus OVG Berlin, Case I B 44.72 of 18 April, 1973 (I. Senat).

[48] Bulletin der Bundesregierung No. 70, 1973; cf. Grundsätze zur Eingliederung ausländischer Arbeitnehmer und ihrer Familien, Bundesarbeitsblatt 1972, 379.

[49] Abgeordnetenhaus von Berlin, Drucksache 6/979 of 29 June 1973; Deutschland-Union-Dienst No. 7 of 16 February 1973.

[50] Case 1 C 35.72 (3 May 1973).

[51] Council of Europe, Doc. 2883 of 7 January 1971; cf. Grahl-Madsen, The Legal Position of the Alien in Council of Europe Member States, Bergen (Norway) 1973.

Though important, these recent developments should not be over-emphasized, for they represent no more than a gleam of hope on the horizon. As before, the government continues to cling to the illusion that the Federal Republic is not an immigration country. Yet it was not long ago that German expellees and refugees from eastern Europe were integrated into the west German community at an enormous infrastructural cost. Although the measures taken then by no means met with the approval of the majority of the taxpayers who had to bear these costs, today few doubt the correctness of the path followed. The expellees and refugees, once they had become integrated and settled, contributed decisively to the West German economic miracle. If the Berlin wall had not been built and the influx from the East had continued, it seems reasonable to assume that further infrastructural improvements would have been made. Why the same should not be possible with regard to foreigners who have been invited into the country remains unclear.

Multiple considerations dictate that the Aliens Act should be revised. Constitutional principles are violated if a person is evaluated solely or primarily by his use effect for the community. Human dignity, the basic right to the free development of the personality and the duty of the state to protect marriage and the family (Basic Law of the Federal Republic, Articles 1,2,6) cannot sanction prohibitions against migrant workers' settlement and being joined by their families. The blanket powers of the Aliens Act, which appear to accord the authorities full power to regulate the migrant's residence and occupation, do not satisfy the constitutional requirement of adequate precision. Because they fail to define the limits of the intermediate authority, the door is left open for arbitrary decisions.[52]

In Sweden foreign workers are called "immigrants." Numbering 420 thousand among eight million Swedes, their proportion in the total population closely corresponds to that of foreigners in West Germany. After three years of work, immigrants to Sweden receive an unlimited residence permit. They are entitled to 240 hours of language instruction during paid working hours. As soon as their children have completed the required years of schooling, they receive a letter, written in seven lan-

---

[52] Cf. Fritz Franz, *Zeitschrift für Rechtspolitik* (ZRP) 1970, 229; Diemut-Majer, ZRP 1972, 252; Helmut Rittstieg, JZ 1971, 113 and NJW 1972, 2153; Christian Tomuschat, *Zeitschrift für ausländisches Öffentliches Recht und Völkerrecht-* Vol. 33, 1973, 179 ff (201 ff.) versus Peter Wirtz, ZRP 70, 247 and Hans-Joachim Rose, Juristische Rundschau 1973, 221.

guages, from the highest educational authority, soliciting their participation in high school education as follows :

Have you and your children over the age of 16 thought about your further education? If not, now is the right time to do so... As an immigrant, do not hesitate to go to a school or to the labor exchange should you be interested in educating yourself further... Instruction is free as are educational materials and schools meals. High school pupils may apply for financial assistance...[53]

Educational grants are also available in West Germany, but not to children of migrant workers.[54] The same holds true with respect to graduate grants.[55] In West Berlin in 1973 2, 467 children transferred from primary to secondary school of whom only 46 were foreigners.[56] In contrast, the proportion of foreigners in the population of West Berlin stands at 7.5 percent.[57] Training for a trade or profession is likewise supported in the Federal Republic by government grants, but only for Germans, displaced persons, persons entitled to asylum and nationals of the European Economic Community.[58] Also barred to foreigners are social insurance aid for establishing and guaranteeing the basis of existence, for preventive health care, helping handicapped persons re-adjust, maintaining the household and helping the sick and aged.[59]

In the long run foreign labor seems indispensable. Each year because of the top-heavy age pyramid, approximately 100 thousand Germans withdraw from the economically active population without it being possible, especially since the birth rate is declining,[60] to replace them with young Germans.[61] If the economic boom continues, the demand for labor will rise. It can be satisfied neither from the Common Market nor by lengthening work hours. Even if market conditions were to slacken off, the economy would apparently remain dependent on migrants since the German worker would be reluctant to sacrifice the job mobility made possible for him by the presence of his foreign counterpart.

---

[53] *Die Zeit* No. 25, 15 June 1973.

[54] §§ 8 II, 68 II, III Bundesausbildungsförderungsgesetz of 26 August 1971-BGBl I, 1409.

[55] § 5 Graduiertenförderungsgesetz of 2 September 1971 -BGBl. I, 1965.

[56] *Der Tagesspiegel*, 21 June 1973.

[57] ibid., 24 June 1973.

[58] § 40, II Arbeitsförderungsgesetz of 25 June 1969—BGBl I, 582.

[59] § 120 Bundessozialhilfegesetz of 18 September 1969 -BGBl I, 1688.

[60] From 18 per 1000 population in 1960 to 12 per 1000 in 1972.

[61] Werner Steinjahn in "Kalte Schulter für Fremde", Düsseldorf Stadtakademie 1971.

Migrant workers contribute considerably to increasing national income. Nine out of ten are under age 45, the overwhelming majority are in Germany without their families, and they produce more than they consume. Moreover, they pay the same taxes and other social contributions as German workers without making comparable demands upon the full range of public services. Costs of their previous education and training are borne by the sending countries.

If the Federal Republic does not wish to exclude migrants from the domestic labor market, it will of necessity have to come to grips with integration. As history teaches, a lack of rights produces social tensions and conceals explosive dangers. The list of measures necessary to promote integration is headed by legal guarantees on residence presently missing in the Aliens Act. These guarantees constitute the key to integration. Without them, long-term planning is impossible.

III

RESIDENTIAL PATTERNS AND SOCIAL INTEGRATION OF TURKS IN COLOGNE

JOHN R. CLARK

ABSTRACT

While there is no distinct Turkish neighborhood in Cologne, there is nevertheless a high degree of residential segregation. Two-thirds of the city's Turkish population lives in buildings which are occupied largely or wholly by Turks and other foreign groups. Factory dormitories account for a large measure of this segregation. Not only are 40 per cent of Cologne's Turks concentrated in 40 dormitory buildings, but most of the larger dormitories are located in relatively remote corners of the city. Turks in private housing are often crowded into sub-standard buildings largely occupied by foreign workers who pay rents substantially higher than the city average.

Spatial segregation is coupled with social segregation. In general, Turkish-German social contacts are few. Turks in segregated and sub-standard housing feel they have learned fewer skills in Germany and hold a less positive view of Germans than those who are spatially integrated.

This chapter discusses the residential distribution of Turkish migrant workers in Cologne and the effects of this distribution both upon their integration into German society and upon the quality of their European experience. It deals with the extent of residential segregation in that city and with defining the socially meaningful criteria which determine what residential segregation is in the context of a German city.

The chapter has three parts. The first is a brief description of the data sources used, while the second is a discussion of spatial patterns of residence. Together these two parts constitute the bulk of the discussion. The third section deals with the effect of residence on the quality of the migrant worker's European experience.

3.1 *Data Sources*

The data were gathered from the files of the *Arbeitsamt* (Labor Office) of the Cologne labor district and from 180 interviews with Turkish workers who live in the city. The *Arbeitsamt* maintains a card for each worker currently residing in the city including his address, birthplace, occupation and place of employment. Although workers are required by law to report changes in address and place of employment to the *Arbeitsamt*, there is no penalty for not doing so.

Consequently, of the 18,728 Turks in the *Arbeitsamt* file at the time of the field research, 16,407 could be located with certainty. Of the remaining 2,321, half or 1,161 were listed as being in Ford dormitories (*heimen*) by the *Arbeitsamt* but not by the *Jugend Sozial Werk* which administers them. Presumably, these men had moved to private housing but had not given their new addresses to the *Arbeitsamt*. The remaining 1,160 gave either no address or an address that could not be located, lived outside the city, or were assigned to temporary company housing for which no address was given. Thus, while employed Turks composed 2.2 percent of Cologne's population of 862 thousand, the group used for quantitative treatment here constituted 1.9 percent.

Interviews covered several subject areas including the worker's housing situation, experiences with the local housing market, and adjustment to life in Germany. All data were gathered between February and November, 1971.

3.2 *Residential Patterns*

A discussion of patterns of residence and segregation requires a prior delineation of the appropriate scale of study. In studies of ghettoization, the degree of segregation observed is frequently a function of the scale of observation. Generally, the smaller the unit of observation, the greater the observed segregation. For example, if Cologne as a whole were taken as the unit of analysis, Turks would appear to be evenly spread throughout the city, for at that scale there is no information about their distribution within it. At the opposite end of the scale segregation is complete, for each individual constitutes a discrete entity. Since these extreme scales are absurd, intermediate scales need be considered.

In studies of ghettoization in the United States sociologists and geographers ordinarily use census neighborhoods or blocks as units of analysis. This seems an appropriate scale for the United States where single family dwelling units predominate and where residents are prone to emphasize the external appearance of their block together with the ethnic and racial identities of those persons living in and near it. For example, the practice of "blockbusting", or having a minority family move into a previously all Caucasian block, is supposed to make the block undesirable for further occupancy by Caucasians.

In the German case, on the other hand, the individual apartment building tends to assume the role of the American block. German apartment buildings are very often designed as five-story walk-ups with one to three apartments per floor, a locked door facing on the street and a small high-walled garden in the rear. In this context, not uncommon concerns are cleanliness of stairways and noise levels within the building.

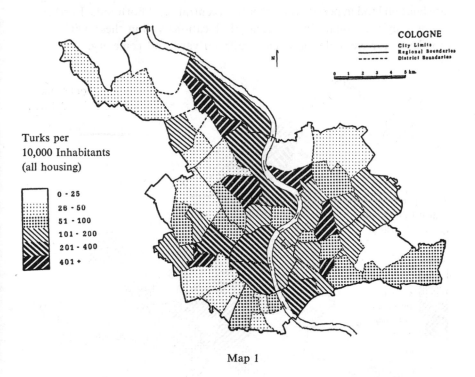

Map 1

As an example of large scale analysis, Map 1 depicts the distribution of Turks by neighborhood in Cologne. There is no Turkish ghetto in the sense that there is no region of the city where the bulk of the Turks are concentrated coupled with their exclusion from other areas. The greatest concentrations are in a discontinuous ring of neighborhoods about four to six kilometers from the city center. Conversely, there are relatively few Turks in the far reaches of the city and in the area to the south and west of the center.

The ring of heavy concentration exists because most of the large factory dormitories are located there. They are owned or leased by the employers and, in the case of the largest organizations—Ford, Klockner Humboldt Deutz (KHD), Deutsche Bundesbahn (DBB), and Felten & Guilleaume (F&G)—administered by the *Jugend Sozial Werk* (JSW). JSW is a social service organization originally set up to handle refugee problems during

and after World War II. The dormitories house three to four men to a
room for approximately 25 to 75 DM per man per month. They contain
anywhere from several dozen to over 1,300 men in a single complex
and provide common kitchen facilities. To keep costs at a minimum, they
are built on land in peripheral rather than central neighborhoods. Furthermore, they are usually in less desirable locations within these neighborhoods as, for example, between a railroad yard and cemetery.

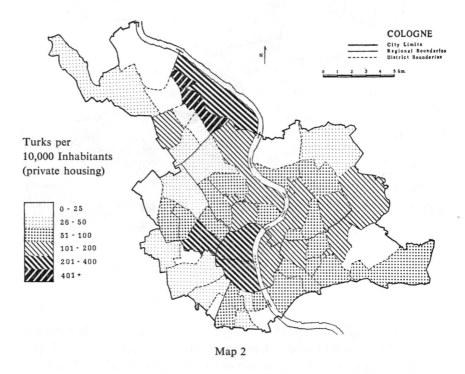

Map 2

The Taeubers' index of dissimilarity provides a useful measure for
comparing the degree of segregation in Cologne with that in certain
communities in the United States (Taeuber & Taeuber, 1965 : 28-31).
Table 1 shows that while Cologne is not as segregated as most American
cities, it is at least within the same range. When the Turks in private
housing only are considered (compare Map 2 to Map 1), the index of
dissimilarity in Table 1 drops from 72.9 to 56.2. In Map 2 the ring of
heavily Turkish neighborhoods which was apparent in Map 1 now dis-
appears, leaving the main concentrations of Turks in the central part of
the city and in the north. This indicates that the role of the dormitories
in determining the pattern of segregation is substantial.

Table 1

Segregation Indices of Negroes in Selected U.S. Cities (1960) and of Turks
in Cologne (1971)*

City	Segregation Index
Jacksonville, Fla.	96.9 (highest in U.S.)
Atlanta, Ga.	93.6
Chicago, Ill.	92.6
Kansas City, Mo.	90.8
Milwaukee, Wis.	88.1
Philadelphia, Pa.	87.1
Detroit, Mich.	84.5
Washington D.C.	79.9
New York, N.Y.	79.3
Elizabeth, N.J.	75.2
Oakland, Calif.	73.1
[Cologne (all Turks)	72.9]
Newark, N.J.	71.6
San Francisco, Calif.	69.3
Cambridge, Mass.	65.5
Sacramento, Calif.	63.9 (lowest in U.S.)
[Cologne (Turks in private housing only)	56.2]

* Source : Taeuber and Taeuber, *Negroes in Cities*, pp. 39-41.

The dormitories, although lacking any sign of blight, play a large part in the process of concentration described above. While 57.6 percent of the 16,407 Turks in Cologne considered by this study resided in private housing, the remainder, or 42.4 percent, lived in dormitories. Forty-two percent of them lived in 40 out of approximately 70,000 residential buildings in the city.

If the larger dormitories, complexes containing 250 Turks or more are analyzed alone, this concentration effect is even more striking. Not only is one-third of the city's Turkish population contained in the 17 buildings falling under this category, but the location of these buildings further isolates the inhabitants from the mainstream of the city's life. Some of the buildings are far from the centers of their neighborhoods and public transport service. Most are removed from predominantly residential areas and either border upon or are surrounded by railroads, cemeteries, industrial districts or gravel pits. Table 2 outlines the locations of the major dormitory complexes and the use of land surrounding them.

Table 2

Locations of ten major dormitories

Dormitory location	No. of resident Turks	No. of buildings	Distance to nearest tram stop (meters)	Surrounding land use	Percentage of surrounding area nonresidential *
Poll Poller Holzweg 10	350	1	700	railroad, gravel pit, auto dealer	100
Vingst Ostheimer Str. 135-137	480	2	50	residences, school	28
Buchheim Gronauer Str. 49-53	410	2	50	residences, open space, athletic field, highway	80
Stammheim Moses Hess Str. 58-60	663	2	100	residences, open space, highway	40
Altstadt Nord Bismarck Str. 52-54	310	1	50	residences	0
Braunsfeld Melaten Gurtel 21-23	901	1	50	industry, residences, cemetery	75
Mauenheim Neue Kempener Str. 203-205	430	2	150	railroad, highway athletic field, residences	75
Weidenpesch Etzel Str. 220-226	1312	4	900	railroad, cemetery, residences	90
Niehl Delmenhorster Str. 20	453	1	300	industry	100
Fühlingen Neusser-Landstr. 2	287	1	100	residences	0

* This statistic is computed on the basis of use of the land immediately adjoining that on which the dormitory stands. Streets are excluded. The type of land use directly across from the dormitory is included.

In sum, large dormitories, while housing many workers inexpensively, isolate them from the host population. Small dormitories are spatially better integrated. Table 3 shows the distribution of 23 small dormitories according to the percentage of nonresidential land use surrounding them and compares their surroundings to those of the large ones.

Small dormitories are very frequently five-story apartment buildings that have been converted to dormitories. They offer the same services as the large dormitories but often have the added convenience of being near German shopping and entertainment facilities. They are also closer to Turkish social centers and businesses. While in this case Turks still live in separate buildings from Germans, they nevertheless do live adjacent to the host population.

Unfortunately, for reasons of economy some companies are closing their small dormitories. For example, KHD has closed several small ones in the central city and moved their occupants out to new barracks in Poll. According to the JSW, Ford has plans to eliminate dormitories with fewer than 60 to 80 workers and is adding a fifth tower to its complex in Weidenpesch where already more than 1,300 Turks are housed.

Table 3

Comparison of Surroundings of Large and Small Dormitories

Percentage of nonresidential land use	Large Dormitories (Turkish population 250 and over per building)		Small Dormitories (Turkish population under 250 per building)	
	No. of dormitory buildings	Total No. of resident Turks	No. of dormitory buildings	Total No. of resident Turks
0- 20	2	537	12	750
20- 40	4	1143	5	223
40- 60			2	218
60- 80	5	1741	1	50
80-100	6	2175	3	127
Total	17	5596	23	1368

Housing in Cologne is in short supply. As of 1970, the number of people per residential room was rapidly approaching the 1939 density level (Statistiches Jahrbuch, 1971:76). Most Germans have difficulty finding suitable housing at reasonable cost, and due to multiple factors foreign workers have an even more difficult time. One important factor is the worker's desire to hold expenditures for rent to a minimum so as to increase his savings potential. Another factor is the German landlord's preference not to rent to transient minorities or force regular tenants, many of whom sign five or even ten year leases, to share a stairway with them.

As mentioned earlier, the public stairway is very important to German apartment dwellers. Behavior there is carefully regulated. Leases frequently stipulate how often each tenant is to clean his section of the stairs. Furthermore, occupants are expected to be quiet and not to have children running up and down during the day nor talkative guests on the stairs in the evening. Even with care it is difficult to move groups of people in and out of an apartment without making noise. Because of differential norms in observing these rules, landlords generally prefer German tenants to aliens and all-German buildings tend to remain that way.

As indicated above, the foreign worker's desire to accumulate savings also creates problems. The 300 to 400 DM that seems normal to the German family for monthly rent often appears exorbitant to the alien. Consequently, the latter frequently looks for a subdivided apartment where two small rooms can be obtained for approximately 200 DM per month. Usually it is older buildings without central heat or private lavatories which get subdivided. Frequently the heavily subdivided buildings are run by landlords who rent individual beds for 80 to 120 DM per month. Most often there are two or three beds in a room and the kitchen is also converted to a bedroom. Thus a two-room dwelling (two rooms plus kitchen) that would be rented to a German family for about 300 DM becomes a three-room dormitory with seven to nine beds. The total rent which the landlord then takes is from 700 to 1,100 DM. One respondent interviewed reported having once lived in a room which contained six beds. The landlord received 120 DM per month for each bed for a total rent of 720 DM for a single room.

Normally, landlords invest very little in maintaining these subdivided apartments which adds physical dilapidation to overcrowding. Responsibility for maintaining hallways, lavatories and bath, if any, is not assumed on a regularized basis which leads to deterioration of these common areas as well. Thus, single building ghettoes, more often than not, become single building slums. The dormitories, on the other hand, while having the same population density are generally clean and well maintained.

The rent paid by Turks indicates the relative difficulty foreign workers have in finding private housing. Among the 37 private dwelling households investigated in this study, the average monthly rent paid was 6.04 DM per square meter. By contrast, the city average for the most expensive category of housing (a dwelling containing up to 40 square meters of space built after 1967 with central heat, bath and lavatory in the apartment) was 3.33 DM per square meter. Most of the dwelling units occupied by the interview group were without central heat or bath and had a lavatory in the public hall. City averages for his type of housing ranged from 1.53 to 2.69 DM per square meter depending upon when the building was built and the size of the unit (Statistisches Jahrbuch, Anhang, 1971:15).

Detailed examination of the residential pattern of Turks shows how subdividing affects both where Turks can live and the place of the single building ghetto in the total housing situation. Usually a high proportion of Turks are concentrated in very few buildings.

Two areas have been selected for more detailed analysis at a small scale. The first shown in Map 3 and located in the northern part of the *Altstadt* (old city), is an area of the city where density of the Turkish population is comparatively high. The second, depicted in Map 4, is in Neu Ehrenfeld where there are relatively few Turks. While the pattern of ghettoization produced by subdividing is evident in the *Altstadt*, Neu Ehrenfeld typifies an area where subdividing has not occurred.

Three categories are used here to distinguish between segregated and non-segregated housing. Buildings with ten or more employed Turks as residents are considered to be segregated. It is likely that a building with ten working adults has either been subdivided into rooms or that at least three apartments in it are occupied by Turks. Frequently, other foreign workers live there also. Five to nine Turks per building is considered to be marginally segregated. While four adults could live in a single apartment by dividing it into two units, the addition of a fifth would generally mean that a second apartment within the same building would be occupied by Turks. Four or fewer Turks in one building assures a reasonable chance that they will have contact with German or at least non-Turkish neighbors.

Returning to the detailed maps, the area in the *Altstadt* shown in Map 3 covers 16 blocks which contain 377 Turks. Table 4 summarizes the residential pattern of Turks in this area. Here 71.9 percent of the Turks live in 2.9 percent of the residential buildings (total of lines 4, 5 and 6). If only the 76 buildings inhabited by Turks are considered, the same 71.9 percent live in 15.8 percent of the buildings where Turks have gained entry. This pattern of concentration is also evident in other older parts of the city.

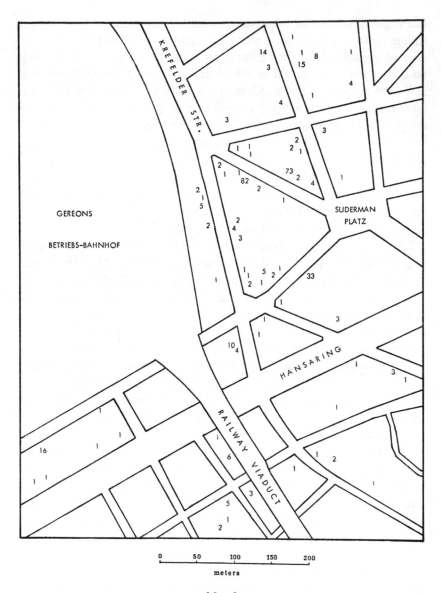

Map 3

Distribution of Turks in part of Altstadt-Nord. Numbers represent the number of Turks living in a single building at that location.

The second area selected for analysis, Neu Ehrenfeld, contains a barrier against Turkish penetration. The barrier exists because the apartments to the north of Nussbaumer Street are under a central administration and

Map 4

Distribution of Turks in part of Neu-Ehrenfeld. Numbers represent the number of Turks living in a single building at that location.

cannot be subdivided. Table 5 separates out the areas divided to the north and south by Nussbaumer Street in order to contrast the distribution of Turks in sections where apartments can and cannot be subdivided.

Table 4

*Distribution of Turks within that part of Altstadt Nord
shown in Map 3*

	No. of buildings	Percent	No. of Turks	Percent
Line				
1. Total no. of buildings	410	100	377	100
2. Total no. of buildings with Turks	76	18.5	377	100
Distribution				
3. 1-4 Turks	64	15.6	106	28.1
4. 5-9 Turks	5	1.2	29	7.7
5. 10+ Turks	5	1.2	87	23.0
6. Dormitories	2	0.5	155	41.2

As is apparent from the table, the northern section excludes Turks almost entirely. In the southern section, there are 6.4. times as many Turks per total number of buildings in the section as in the north. (Compare lines 1 and 3). While the overall proportion of Turks is small in the south, the area still exhibits the pattern of concentration that is characteristic of the more heavily subdivided areas of Cologne where the density of the Turkish population is relatively high. Lines 6 and 7 in Table 5 show that 51 percent of the Turks reside in one percent of the buildings in the southern section.

The pattern of concentration of Turks in relatively few buildings as shown in Maps 3 and 4 is repeated throughout Cologne. Table 6 outlines the situation for the city at large. As in the two smaller scale examples just discussed, two-thirds of all Turks reside in housing that is segregated to some degree, live in well under one percent of the buildings in the city and in 17 percent of the buildings that house any Turks at all (total of lines 1, 2 and 3).

3.3 Housing and the Quality of the Worker's Experience

Segregation in housing is coupled with low levels of social contact between Turks and Germans. Bingemer (1970:56), who surveyed the foreign worker population in Cologne, found that Turks come to

Germany with the highest expectations of any group of workers for establishing friendly relations with the host population but are the most unhappy about what they actually experience. It would appear to this author that the distance between Germans and Turks may be at least partly due to the distance between Germans and Germans who often tend to be reserved and prize quiet and privacy. Whatever the exact causes, the author observed only four contacts between Germans and Turks in Turkish living quarters during the course of ten months of constant contact with the Turkish community. This lack of social contact often results in negative feelings on the part of Turks toward Germans.

Table 5

DISTRIBUTION OF TURKS WITHIN THAT PART OF NEU EHRENFELD SHOWN IN MAP 4

North of Nussbaumer Street (subdividing not possible)

	No. of buildings	Percent	No. of Turks
Line			
1. Total no. of buildings	265	100	7
2. No. of buildings with Turks	4	1.5	7

South of Nussbaumer Street (subdividing possible)

	No. of buildings	Percent	No. of Turks	Percent
3. Total no. of buildings	290	100	49	100
4. Total no. of buildings with Turks	19	6.5	49	100
Distribution				
5. 1-4 Turks	16	5.5	24	49.0
6. 5-9 Turks	2	0.7	12	24.5
7. 10+ Turks	1	0.3	13	26.5

The effect of social isolation on development dividends anticipated by Turkish economic planners from the creation of a labor force experienced in Europe can hardly be positive. Much of the learning that could occur through exposure to European industrial life does not appear to take place. From among the respondents interviewed, 59.2 percent reported they had either learned no new skills or had lost some since coming to Germany. Only 16.4 percent had taken or planned to take vocational training courses.

Table 6

Numbers of Turks in Dormitories and Private Buildings
City-wide Totals

	No. of buildings with Turks	Percent of buildings with Turks	Percent of all residential buildings in city	No. of Turks	Percent of Turks
Line					
1. *Dormitories*	40	1.6	0.06	6964	42.5
Private buildings					
2. 10+ Turks	134	5.3	0.19	2329	14.2
3. 5-9 Turks	247	9.9	0.35	1589	9.7
4. 1-4 Turks	2096	83.2	2.99	5525	33.6
	2517	100.0	3.59	16407	100.0

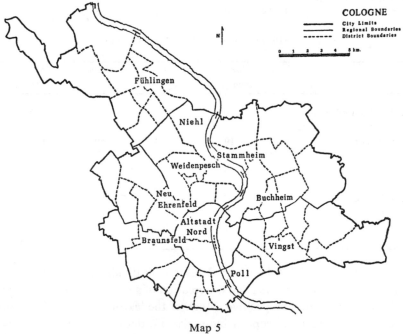

Map 5
Districts Mentioned in Text

A relationship appears to exist between a worker's perceived increase in skills and the quality and type of his housing. For testing this hypothesis, housing was ranked in four categories : (1) dispersed private (usually the best quality housing Turks have), (2) small dormitories, (3) large dormitories, and (4) private single building ghettoes (usually the lowest quality housing Turks have). Similarly, perceived skill changes were quantitatively scaled from one through five, with five representing the greatest improvement and one the greatest loss. As the average scores show in Table 7, the four groups line up in the order listed with workers in dispersed private housing perceiving the greatest improvement in skills while those in private ghettoes perceived either no change or some deterioration in skills.

Table 7

*Distribution of Respondents According to Skill Level
Change and Type of Housing Occupied*

Perceived Skill Change	Numerical Value	Dispersed Private	Small Dorms	Large Dorms	Private Ghettoes
Much improved	5	7	11	8	1
Improved	4	9	15	18	1
No change	3	13	21	14	4
Deteriorated	2	3	11	9	2
Much deteriorated	1	2	5	15	2
		—	—	—	—
Total Respondents		34	63	64	10
Average Score		3.47	3.26	2.92	2.70

In the interviews Turks were asked to choose from a list of personal attributes those which they thought best characterized Germans. Overall, positive terms were selected more often than were negative ones. As in the case of perceived skill improvement, the level of positive characterizations varied according to housing type with workers in dispersed private dwellings reporting the most positive stereotypes of Germans and those in private ghettoes the least positive. Differences were small but in the expected direction. To check for statistical interaction, the variable of perceived skill improvement was tabulated against that of stereotypes to determine whether the same respondents who felt their skills had improved also held positive stereotypes. No significant relationship was found to exist.

In conclusion, it may be observed that the variables of skill improvement and stereotype are in all probability independent of each other, but that type of housing is positively related to at least two different measurements of adjustment to life in Germany—namely, perceived change in skill level and perceived stereotypes of the German population. While there is a substantial amount of residential segregation of Turks in Cologne, there is no large scale Turkish ghetto or neighborhood as such. Dormitories play a major role in segregating Turks from Germans, and the trend of the year 1972 was to increase this segregation as workers were moved from smaller to larger dormitories. It may be deduced in other terms that this segregation represents missed opportunities for Turkish migrant workers, and hence industrialization efforts in Turkey, to benefit from exposure to European industrial experience.

REFERENCES

Bingemer, Karl, et al, 1970, *Leben als Gastarbeiter*. Köln, Westdeutscher Verlag.
Statistisches Jahrbuch der Stadt Köln, 1971. Köln, Lang'sche Druckerei.
Taeuber, Karl E. and Alma I., 1965, *Negroes in Cities*. Chicago, Aldine.

IV

STRUCTURAL CHANGE IN THE MIGRANT
TURKISH FAMILY

Ayşe Kudat

ABSTRACT

By using case study data collected in West Berlin, this chapter examines changes
that occur in the structure of the Turkish family as a result of labor migration to
Europe. It studies the deleterious effects which current laws, regulations and employment practices may often have upon the unity of the migrant family.

The discussion also analyzes changes which come about in household composition
and shows how patrilocal norms disappear among migrant families. Modifications
in division of labor, budget control and family roles are also examined. Particular
attention is given to the status of children and to the alienation of children from their
parents in migratory situations.

4.1 Introduction

Although the institution of the family manifests distinct differences
among various socio-economic groups and socio-geographical regions
in Turkey, certain basic structural elements are common to the family
wherever it is found. Two types of family—the peasant and urban lower
income—have been selected to illustrate the structural and normative
changes that Turkish families are experiencing as a result of mass migration to Western Europe. After outlining the general characteristics of these
family types, the discussion delineates how and in what specific respects
change is occurring in these basic features. In particular, it treats the
the effects of migration on household composition, division of labor,
budget control, extra-marital relationships and on children and young
adults.

The objective of this chapter is to familiarize the reader with some of
the changes and problems that Turkish migrants face abroad and to sti-
mulate further research in this area. Because the empirical data used
for analysis consist of random interviews, participant observations and
250 problem cases obtained in West Berlin, the study does not purport to
be statistically representative of the entire Turkish migrant population
either in West Germany or West Berlin. Even though the incidence of

the phenomena examined is believed to be sufficiently widespread as to merit systematic investigation by scholars and appropriate official agencies, all statements made should be viewed, therefore, only as preliminary observations.

4.2 Structure of the Turkish Family

The institution of the family manifests structural variations among different socio-economic groups and socio-geographical areas of Turkey. It would, therefore, be misleading to conceive of any one single entity as *the* Turkish family. Usage of the concept in the present context implies not the existence of one such entity but rather common structural elements generalized from a multiplicity of different entities. It is with the changes in these central structural and normative elements that the chapter is concerned. Because Turkish migrants in West Germany originate to a high degree from among peasants and low-income urban groups, characteristics of these two types of families in particular will receive special attention.

In Turkey the peasant family is characterized by a certain economic and authority structure. Processes of socio-economic evolution that have shaped peasant society have operated in favor of men, furnishing them with more privileged rights of property ownership. The specialization of labor that has also evolved is not, as sometimes stated, one between the household and the farm, but rather one between the household economy and the market. Although her cultivation efforts are, to some extent, periodic and not as intensive as that of the man, a peasant woman not only undertakes her household work but also helps in the cultivation of the family land. She ordinarily does not, however, participate in market interactions be they in the form of bartering or cash transaction. Self-subsistency in a peasant economy should not be taken to mean independence or isolation from markets, for peasants, especially today, are in constant interaction with them. The women, however, are excluded from these transactions and, therefore, from the control of cash receipts and expenditures. It is particularly her exclusion from this aspect of the household economic activity and her disadvantageous stand vis-a-vis property rights that place her lower in social status and inferior in decision-making to the man. Further characteristics of the peasant family are discussed as the need arises in various sections following.

Among urban low income groups the aforementioned differential social status is maintained by women's continuing low level of participation in economic activities outside the household. Yet, the urban culture counteracts the possible consequences to some extent and offers a more emancipatory socialization to both sexes. Moreover, the possible presence of the husband's relatives in the household which reinforces male control in rural areas, is much less frequently observed among urban families. Thus, despite minimal economic participation, urban women take a greater part in decision making and are somewhat more emancipated than their peasant counterparts. The foregoing observations are especially applicable in the metropolitan centers of Istanbul, Ankara and Izmir where greater opportunities for employment outside the home prevail. They are much less applicable to other provincial cities and towns where contacts with relatives are more intensely maintained, relaxation of social pressures on women does not come about, and men's unquestioned authority remains unshaken. As in the case of peasant families, control of money, property and decision-making authority are concentrated in the hands of men.

4.3   Household Composition

Massive labor migration to Europe results in important changes in the residential composition of Turkish households both in Europe and the homeland. Traditionally, and especially in rural areas, the residence pattern was patrilocal where married sons continued living with their parents after marriage. In practice, this pattern has proven economically unfeasible for the majority of peasants, workers and other lower and middle income groups. Today only the wealthy land-holding rural households manifest some tendency to conform to this pattern, and even among them the actualization of this traditional norm is of infrequent occurrence. In these cases, families are often able to provide their sons the necessary educational and material means to move from an agriculturally oriented occupation to an urban one. Thus, patrilocal residence is observable primarily among wealthy families in areas where tribal traditions are still alive and where professional specialization among younger generations is not yet visible.

Traditionally, children remain with their parents until marriage, and upon marrying women normally join the husband's family. Married daughters, with or without children, may return to live with their own parents if their husbands need to leave their communities for military service or work. More frequent, however, is the selection of the husband's parental household for such temporary stays. Similarly, when both spouses need to depart temporarily, a close relative of the husband, most frequently his parents, cares for the children.

In practice married sons tend to establish their own households even when they remain in their parents' community. With regional variations, traditional norms require either the eldest or the youngest son to remain with parents; in very fact, the son last to marry, regardless of birth order, shares his parents' household. Sons awaiting military service may also reside with their parents, leave their wives and children behind while in the service, and establish a separate household only subsequent to return.

It is not uncommon, therefore, for peasant households to manifest an extended-family character. In addition to paternal grandparents, other needy paternal relatives and widowed maternal grandmothers whose sons are unable to care for them are frequently present. Such a widow may also join one of her brothers' households and circumstances may give rise to the co-residence of unmarried sisters with the family of their married brothers. Affinal and maternal extensions are rarely found, and families of two or more brothers, after the death of their father, seldom co-reside.

Important changes take place in the composition of Turkish households as a result of migration to and settlement in urban areas. In contrast to the relative stability of the peasant household, the make-up of the migrant urban household tends to be more temporal in nature. Certain traditional bonds of affinity now come to be operationalized in the urban context. Peasants in search of jobs in the city often need to exercise not only paternal bonds but also those of kinship (*akrabalık*), neighborhood (*komşuluk*), fellow townsmanship (*hemşerilik*), friendship (*arkadaşlık*) and affinity (*hısımlık*). Any given migrant household, likely to have already utilized the same hospitality in the past, keeps its doors open to persons from any of these categories for temporary residency.

The migrant comes to the city not with a promise of a job but with its expectation. Until he finds a steady, satisfactory one, he ordinarily neither brings his family nor establishes a household of his own. For him this is a period of transition and adjustment during which he needs help both to reduce the economic pressures of a potentially lengthy period of unemployment and to learn from those with personal experience the appropriate search methods. Through the aforementioned types of personal bonds he not only gathers information but also obtains means of infiltration into certain work environments. Although circumstances under which a village family hosts distant relatives and acquaintances are few and the duration of temporary stays (other than those outlined above) are short, such is not the case for urban migrants who host for several months or longer distant relatives, friends, neighbors or even previously unknown friends of relatives or friends. Moreover, established migrant families in cities frequently house children of close relatives to help them overcome educational barriers confronted in the village or smaller towns.

Temporary members of migrant households in Turkish cities are almost always related, in one way or another, to the male household head. A friend, acquaintance or distant relative of the wife, lacking an equally close relationship with the husband, cannot expect hospitality in a migrant household. This is especially apparent when the spouses are from different communities. The wife's brothers constitute the main exception to this rule.

Another important observation to be made about the composition of these urban homes has to do with the rarity of female guests, be they married or single. This is a major point of contrast between migrant households in the homeland and those in Germany. In Turkey, a wife's migration to an urban area prior to her husband's occurs only under exceptional circumstances. It follows that an established migrant household would rarely be approached for temporary co-residency by a woman. Although migration of middle-aged women of deprived families would be tolerable, such instances are very limited. When sufficiently strong push factors exist for women's migration to cities, close paternal relatives would ordinarily be the only acceptable choice for co-residency. A final point to be noted about migrant households in Turkey is the non-acceptability of co-residency of men and women unless married to each other or related through ties of parenthood or as siblings. The unlikelihood of this type of co-residency is augmented by the small numbers of single men or women who would have established separate households for themselves.

Turkish culture has traditionally placed high value upon hospitality. Strangers in villages are welcomed whole-heartedly and migrant families in cities host relatives, acquaintances and friends without consideration of return. But in a foreign land the common bond of Turkish nationality leads to types of co-residency which would rarely find a parallel in Turkey. Co-residence norms operant among migrant families in the homeland partially lose their economic base and social utility abroad. Here new exigencies reshape these norms and, as a result, hospitality comes to be extended to a national group regardless of the sex of the needy person. This does not imply, of course, that close relatives, previous acquaintances and friends are not given priority over strangers and that the frequency of co-residence of the former is not higher than the latter. It simply means that what is normatively proscribed and practically unobservable in Turkey is normatively prescribed and readily apparent among Turkish migrants in Germany. One such example is illustrated by the following case study :

Case 1 : Female worker—age 33

Fatma had worked in various parts of West Germany for three years. An older Turkish man whom she met expressed concern about her having to work late hours. He suggested that she go with him to his town to look for another job and promised to make the necessary arrangements for her. He and his wife hosted her at their home for weeks in a generous manner. Because the job she found there was very fatiguing, upon receiving a letter from her husband informing her of the whereabouts of her brother-in-law, Fatma went to his home where she was roomed for another three months. Finally a job was arranged for her in West Berlin.

This author met her while she was cleaning the office building where the author is employed. Because she told of making little money, a weekend housecleaning job was offered her and accepted. After several months, however, she disappeared. Sometime later an unknown Turkish worker came to the residence and said he had taken to his home on the same street a woman who had the author's address. Upon going with him, the author found Fatma who explained she had returned to Turkey only to discover that her husband was living with another woman. He had spent all the money Fatma had remitted and, moreover, lost his job. Since there was no money to support their children she returned to West Berlin but had no job or place to stay. As the author was about to offer her hospitality, the worker entered the discussion and assured her that it would be best if she were to stay at his house to keep his wife company. In a matter of days, he arranged a job for her at the firm where he worked. Fatma remained at his house for almost two months during which time he accepted neither rent nor food contributions from her.

On the whole, the average duration of co-residency abroad is noticeably shorter than that observed both among peasants and rural-to-urban migrants in Turkey. Enduring co-residency appears to be based either on relations of parenthood or marriage or on a cost-sharing basis.

Having analyzed the norms which govern household composition in Turkey, the discussion will now systematically explore modifications which occur in the Turkish migrant community in Germany. First to be noted is the disappearance of patrilocal norms. Households are built or re-assembled in small increments, a process in which a patrilocal model is not necessarily followed. Increments to the original migrant as the nucleus are composed either of members of the nuclear family or persons related to him/her in a variety of ways. Paternal links no longer dominate the network of household relations, and norms favoring such links lose strength.

Unlike the households in the homeland the increments referred to here are not ordinarily built upon a nucleus composed of a man, his wife and children. Rather, they are usually more random in character, being built upon a single individual, a partially fragmented nuclear family or a new unit composed of individuals related to each other by ties of kinship or friendship. Thus, neither patrilocal families nor extended families based upon paternal additions to a nuclear family are observable.

Nuclear families tend to be fragmented differently according to successive phases of the migrant's stay abroad. When married workers, men or women, first come to Germany, only about one-fifth of the men and one-half of the women are accompanied by their spouses. Reunion is obtained in several ways : (1) A worker upon successful completion of the first year abroad may if housing is available invite his (her) spouse with or without their children. By law such an invitation precludes the spouse's employment prior to the expiration of a twelve-month stay. (2) Alternatively, the spouse may apply for employment in Germany while still in Turkey and receive priority consideration accorded to geographically separated married couples. (3) The spouse may visit in Germany as a tourist for three months after which he/she may either return to Turkey or remain illegally in Germany. While the first two alternatives permit accompanying children, the third ordinarily makes their presence difficult or undesirable. In any case, family integration seems to be the exception while fragmentation is the rule. Separation of the migrant from his family for at least the first year abroad is almost inevitable. Subsequent reunions are usually partial, excluding either one or all of the children. Thus, in only a small portion of migrant households abroad can one locate a complete nucleus composed of both spouses and all their children.

A migrant worker either lives in a *heim* with many others like himself without their families or in a private apartment ordinarily either with a portion of his family or with other workers previously unrelated to him. The following is a list of not uncommonly observed household configurations some of which would be normatively non-permissible and practically unworkable among corresponding groups in Turkey :

(a) male ego + wife (children in Turkey)
(b) (a) above + one or two children (remainder of the children in Turkey)
(c) (b) above + paternal or maternal grandmother
(d) (a) above + sister or sister-in-law

(e) (a) above + brother(s) or brothers-in-law
(f) (d or e above) + spouse of sister or others
(g) male or female ego + sibling
(h) (g) above + spouse of the sibling
(i) male or female ego + male or female distant or close relative
(j) single males (related as kin, friends, neighbors, acquaintances or colleagues)
(k) two previously unrelated couples, several singles
(l) (k) above + single Germans
(m) (a) above + ego's parents and siblings
(n) (m) above + ego's brother or sister-in-law (with or without a spouse)

Any given household throughout its existence abroad may assume multiple configurations as each arrival and departure affects the network of relationships. Its temporary nature is attributable to the overall high turn-over rate among the migrant population.

The section following will discuss women's role in the division of family labor. Here the effect of women's participation in the labor force upon household composition will be analyzed. Alien women working in Germany may, with or without their husbands' permission, complete the legal requirements for extending an invitation to their parents or siblings (as well as to their spouses and children) either for a three-month period as tourists or for longer. Proof of employment is sufficient for such invitations, and spouses need not be consulted. These arrangements can give rise to acute disputes between spouses not only because husbands feel their authority is being challenged by maternal dominance in the household but also because of stress resulting from space limitations.

Case 2 : Married male—age 30

My wife and I came here one after the other several years ago and left our children with my mother. We were saving well until the day my two sisters-in-law arrived unexpectedly. Then my wife told me she had invited them through the consulate and they were here to stay. I was extremely angered by this disrespectful, inconsiderate behavior. We live in a single-room apartment. Who are we to have guests? Because I go to work at 4:00 in the morning and must get up at 3:30, I have to retire early. My wife works in the later hours of the day, and each time I want to sleep those three women are chatting, planning to bring their mother along. We had no family life left. Then they started shopping. Let alone saving, we were in debt. I asked her to send the sisters away, but she refused. Meanwhile, one of them found a job and it became clear that she wasn't about to move out. I have now found a place to move to and will soon get a divorce.

When invitations are issued by men to their relatives similar tensions often arise. However, acquisition of household membership through affiliations with the husband is a continuation of norms observable in the homeland. The situation described above is a new development attributable to changes in the economic basis of the family and in mentalities and motivations of migrants in Europe. Extensions of membership to maternal relatives and independent legal actions taken by women prerequisite to such extensions are phenomena unique to international migrants.

The last observation to be made about membership in migrant households abroad has to do with cost and work sharing. Within the structural and legal limitations already specified, migrants may bring along persons of their choice. Apart from temporary hospitality extended to different categories of people, workers' choices generally favor the admission of those persons who would either, through employment abroad, share rental and other costs of the household or perform housework and child care tasks. The objective is to hold the number of complete dependents at a minimum so that savings may be maximized in as short a period as possible.

4.4 Division of Labor in the Family

An important change attributable to mass international migration is observed in the family division of labor at home and abroad. Woman's active economic participation manifested by her migration to Europe for employment purposes is a principal contributor to this change which is more visible among divided families at home than among working families in Europe. Although children are trusted with grandparents, other relatives, neighbors or acquaintances during mothers' employment in Europe, there are a considerable number of cases in which fathers try to assume the responsibilities of child care on the assumption that the mother's employment will only be for a short period of time. Since these cases manifest a clear-cut role reversal in which the wife is the principal bread-winner and the husband the primary child-carer, the discussion will focus upon them.

In these divided nuclear families the father ordinarily discovers the difficulty of caring for the children soon after the migration of the mother to Europe. He often approaches relatives with hints or explicit remarks to determine whether they would be willing to take the children. When negative responses result, they are often due to lack of promises of payment for the required care. A further step is to press his wife to hasten the request process so that he can join her promptly. The wife, on the other hand, either because she enjoys her new life style in Europe or because she does not have enough contacts and knowledge, cannot always put through a request for her husband in so short a time. The husband may also be refused employment in Europe on the basis of his health, age or job qualifications.

His final recourse if these steps fail is to request his wife to return, and if she refuses, to appeal to the Turkish Foreign Ministry, consulates, work attaches and friends abroad to bring pressure upon her. If the wife does not return and he remains unable to join her abroad, common alternatives which result are children being given up for adoption, the taking of a second wife illegally or divorce. Below is one among numerous case studies which exemplify these developments :

Case 3 : Female worker—age 26

Güllü came to West Berlin from a family of landless peasants in a small village in Anatolia. She had been married for eight years and had three small children. Her husband was a day laborer in agriculture, and in summers she also had worked on other people's land. Employment in Europe was their major hope for advancement, and though both had wanted to migrate, she was the first to be accepted. She left soon thereafter, assuming her parents and parents-in-law would help her husband in caring for the children. He moved in with her parents so that he could work while his mother-in-law looked after the daily needs of the children. Güllü remitted sufficient money for them all. When Güllü's mother became ill and later hospitalized, Güllü's husband and father cared for the household and children with the neighbors' help. However, when the mother died after two months of hospitalization, it became clear that the two men were no longer faced with a temporary problem. They repeatedly requested Güllü to return, but she declined since her first year's contract was not yet fulfilled and since she was saving to buy a house in the city and provide better education for her children. The villagers began to deride Güllü's husband for doing a woman's work. His final decision was to take another wife. Himself burdened by housework, her own father approved of his son-in-law's decision. When informed of the decision, Güllü ignored it rather than return as requested. Applying traditional religious norms now illegal, her husband took a middle-aged widow as a second wife.

This role reversal engendered by the woman's migration abroad has particularly strong repercussions in a tradition-oriented setting. Not only are those women who have actively participated in this new movement freed from inferior status in their households, but also those whose migration possibilities constitute a hope for the family are viewed differently. Given current trends, the effects of this fundamental change in the economic bases of role differentiation will no doubt spread into Turkish society much more widely.

Cases where men are left with the task of performing housework and child care mark a drastic change in a society where even a minimum amount of men's participation in housework is socially disapproved. Even among urban families in which both men and women work such participation is rare and its occurrence ordinarily disguised from those outside the household.

The change observed among working Turkish families in Europe, however, is usually less extreme and marked by a slow shift toward increasing participation of the husband in household chores. With minor changes, social norms governing the traditional division of labor still continue among a large portion of employed migrant couples. Even in households where the husband is unemployed, adherence to traditional norms is still observed. Often this is a cause of friction which in extreme cases can lead to divorce.

An employed wife may bring her husband to Germany either as a tourist or dependent. In either case, however, prior to the expiration of twelve months he has no legal right to take employment without first returning to Turkey. If a German employer requests him by name through the appropriate official channels in Turkey, he may assume the position by re-entering Germany from Turkey. Illegal employment along with its many risks is the only alternative.

4.5 Budget Control

The family authority structure and decision making procedures are also subject to change among families which migrate abroad. As already indicated, among the urban lower income groups in Turkey husbands are the principal bread-winners. Although wives are expected to participate in the production process in rural areas, the husband is the sole middle-man between the household and the market. Not only does he control cash earnings and disbursements in the family, but his control over property and income shapes the authority structure of the family as well. He becomes the principal decision maker both in economic affairs and in other power relationships. Social norms that have evolved on the basis of these economic realities preclude women's participation in decision making, especially in matters concerning property acquisition or disposition and income allocation. Even in those cases where both spouses contribute cash earnings, husbands tend to maintain their authoritative role.

A rather different situation emerges abroad. Interviews with voluntary organizations in charge of social problems of foreign workers as well as the case study data reveal that one of the major sources of dispute among working spouses is the allocation of household income.

Men frequently approach social service officials with complaints concerning the separation of bank accounts. When wives request employers to deposit their earnings to a separate account, the husband's authority is shaken. Not only does he lose control of spending but also of savings and investments. For any major investment he plans to make, he needs his wife's consent and support. The adjustment of both men and women to this change in balance of powers does not come easy.

Disputes also arise over the use of joint savings. Following the traditional pattern, husbands often arrange for the purchase of property in Turkey which they register in their own name rather than jointly even though joint remittances are used to pay for it. Precautions taken by wives to prevent such occurrences are frequently a source of irritation to husbands.

Because the institution of the family in Turkish society is built upon a very different economic structure, it experiences difficulties in adjusting its norms to this change. In some cases it is broken, in others it is shaken and in yet others it is reorganized around new principles. When reorganization occurs, a type of family is created in which rights and duties are much more widely shared. If a joint effort for the necessary adjustment is not made, an eventual breakdown of the union often proves inevitable. At present the permeation of these new norms is only beginning. If the migration phenomenon continues to become increasingly widespread and more prolonged, the incidence of these adjustment problems may be expected to proliferate.

4.6 *Extra-marital Relationships*

Of the 250 problem cases analyzed during the research, approximately one in seven involved adultery. With few exceptions both parties were Turkish. In no case was a Turkish woman known to have entered into extra-marital relationships with non-Turks. Although both married and unmarried men are known to form intimate friendships with women of other ethnic groups, Turkish women, in general, refrain from such friendships.

Once adultery is proven by a spouse, two alternative paths to recourse are open—criminal action or divorce. If the former is pursued on grounds of adultery, given sufficient proof, Turkish government authorities in

Europe may be asked to arrange for the deportation of the guilty party. Following a successful criminal case against his wife, a husband may obtain an easy divorce. Most often however, due to numerous difficulties involved, this route to recourse is not chosen. More commonly the spouse pursues a divorce case, hoping to obtain a financially profitable decision in his/her favor such as could not be obtained through criminal action. In yet other cases the continuation of a deteriorated marriage relationship may be preferred as long as the migrant spouse remits regularly. When the flow of remittances ceases, sometimes sufficient social pressure can be exerted to reinstate it.

In passing it need only be noted that in view of workers' extended separation from their families, the distorted sex ratios among the Turkish migrant population, and the disappearance of traditional social control mechanisms, the rate of adultery manifest among migrants abroad is by no means unpredictable. Even at such future time as the incidence of separation may be reduced and the sex composition of the population adjusted, the shift to a more liberal social environment and the changing economic status of women will undoubtedly perpetuate a higher rate of adultery among migrants than among non-migrants of similar socio - economic status in Turkey.

4.7 *Effects of Migration Upon Children and Young Adults*

As noted earlier, married migrants are seldom accompanied by their families during the first year of employment in Europe. Due to an acute shortage of housing and high rents, many spend months in search of a private apartment which must be found in order to obtain a residence permit for the family. Family reunion even after the first year is difficult for many to achieve. Because of the housing shortage and other demands made upon infrastructure, the police are often reluctant to initially grant or subsequently extend a residence permit for families with children. Reasons for the denial are frequently not made explicit, and few aliens seek legal advice to ensure the unity of their families.

Case 4 : Male worker—age 37

I am a carpenter and as such earn more than enough to support my wife and children. A year after I came, I made the necessary arrangements to bring them here. All four of my children were registered on my wife's passport. When they arrived the police gave them a one-year residence permit. Through official channels we later arranged a job for my wife which she was ready and legally entitled to start after one year of residence. Her work papers were in order but an extension of her residence permit was still needed. Although we went to the police numerous times with her passport, they kept delaying a definitive answer. Finally, without supplying a reason they informed us of their inability to extend my family's residence permit. I have the means to keep my family here. Why should I send them away? I will take the matter to court.

In many instances the worker himself prefers to leave his family in the homeland. Since saving is the principal objective in migrating, he finds it more feasible to have children remain at home with the spouse or other relatives so as to shorten the period within which the desired funds can be accumulated. Thus, most families remain fragmented minimally for the whole period of their stay. The discussion following will examine the various forms and consequences of family fragmentation.

Alienation is an almost inevitable consequence of young children being separated from one or both parents for an extended period of time. Not infrequently, normal parent-child emotional bonds come to be replaced by conceptualization of the absent parent(s) chiefly as the supplier of otherwise unavailable foreign consumer goods. This image of the parent tends to be reinforced by those in charge of caring for the children or others in the home community environment. The following case study illustrates these phenomena :

Case 5. Male worker—age 29

My wife and I have been working abroad for four years. Our two boys are staying in the village with their grandmother. When we left, the youngest was about three. At the end of our second and third years abroad we went back for a month to see the children. Television, pull-overs and shirts were among the orders with which we filled the car. Finally when we arrived home, the neighbors told us that the children were in the movies with their grandmother. I found them there sitting with other children. My younger son was nearer, so I went and touched him on the shoulder. He turned around and looked at me with no sign of recognition. When I said "Hello, Kadri, I'm your father from Germany", he politely replied "I'm sorry, sir, I did not recognize you at first". Then my older son came and reassured his brother by saying, "He's our father, he came from Germany and brought us many presents". We all went to the car, but they seemed more eager to see their presents than their mother. Upon finding that the trunk lock was broken, they became extremely angry, yet there was nothing to do but wait until the next morning. They eventually got their presents but meanwhile expressed disappointment at my not having a red car as expected but an old green one instead. I want to find a two-room apartment and bring my children here before they forget us completely. Not only can I not find a place, but also my wife objects to the idea. Perhaps we can at least bring them for the duration of their summer vacation.

Alienation from siblings also develops as a result of children's distribution among multiple households in the parents' absence. Unless migrants with more than two children have relatively well-to-do parents or in-laws in rural areas, they must almost invariably entrust them to relatives or friends who may be located in separate parts of the country. Alternatively, some children may accompany their parents while others are left in the home country. As a result, siblings see one another seldomly and in time may come to feel estranged and alienated.

Case 6 : Turkish Child in West Berlin

I was living with my grandmother in Bursa when my parents sent for me. Grandmother said it would be better if I were to go to Germany and that my two brothers and sister were also going. My brothers were then in the village with my other grandmother and my sister with my aunt in Istanbul. I remembered my sister well, but didn't know whether I would enjoy playing with my brothers whom I had only seen once in many years. My sister is older than I and had visited our parents in Germany one summer. She told me about it, but none of the things she mentioned made me want to go. Because my parents are seldom at home, my sister and I must help with shopping and cooking. My grandmother would never have asked such things of me. Although they buy things for me here, I am not very happy. I'm hoping they will send my brothers and me back to Turkey.

Just as children are alienated from their parents and siblings as a result of long-lasting separations, parents are alienated from their children. Of the 250 problem cases studied, nearly half involved child neglect. Numerous complaints are filed through official channels by persons responsible for child care—some legitimate, others obvious attempts at extracting higher rates of remittance above actual requirements.

To be sure, actual cases of neglect or even disappearance of the parent(s) abroad are not unusual. These cases are more frequent when only one parent migrates alone. The prolonged absence of reinforcing family relationships together with gradually strengthening extra-family ties and financial considerations tend to pull some migrants away from their families. While government agencies can ordinarily exert sufficient pressure to ensure the financial well-being of children, their emotional security and eventual reunion in normal family relations cannot be guaranteed.

Two further phenomena related to the separation of parents and children are child labor and the commercialization of child care in Turkey. Child labor results particularly when the mother takes employment abroad or when the migrant father ceases to remit. If the father chooses to preserve the unity of the household after the mother's departure, girls over age twelve are often expected to assume many of the home duties previously performed by the mother. Whereas adolescent daughters might normally be asked to assist the mother with housework, full-scale assumption of such responsibility, together with caring for the father and younger siblings, results only from the total absence of the mother. Similarly, in cases of the migrant father's neglect and the mother's unemployment young children must often find remunerative employment outside the household.

Counterpart situations sometimes arise in migrant families resident abroad. Working couples with pre-school-age children must sometimes ask older siblings to care for younger ones despite the illegality of keeping school-age children away from school. In still other cases, parents with high motivations to save try to arrange employment for their able-bodied children over age 14. Occasionally such employment is full-time and an illegal substitute for schooling whereas other times it is part-time in addition to schooling. Attempts at using children to bolster the financial resources of the family are not uncommon among Turkish workers. Many prefer to do so, but only some overcome the legal barriers.

Another important development in this respect is the increased demand in the German labor market for young women. Consequently, the number of females between the ages of 17 and 21 migrating from Turkey in recent years has risen significantly. The practice of allowing unmarried women to leave the parental household for employment outside the residence community is one which runs counter to firmly established traditional social norms in Turkey. The single exception is the institution of *evlatlık* in which in return for a small monthly wage payable directly to her father, a young girl goes to live in the household of an employing family for the purpose of performing household chores.

Thus, even though mobility for purposes of work outside the household is severely restricted for unmarried girls within Turkey, the incidence of their being permitted to migrate abroad is becoming increasingly more common. Since the money they remit is by no means negligible, the family stands to gain appreciably from allowing daughters to migrate.

Their migration tends to effect the authority structure of the family. Whether they come from peasant or urban working class families, their earnings abroad often far exceed the combined income of family members at home. Among these families there are those whose major and only steady source of income is that remitted by a young daughter in Europe. Consequently, these *de facto* breadwinners begin to enjoy elevated status and respect in the family. Rather than being ordered around, their opinions are now asked in many matters. For them the decision regarding a partner in marriage is usually made independently of the father. Suffice it to say that the actual or potential migration of daughters abroad in the role of breadwinner may make important contributions to changes in the structure of the Turkish family.

As for the commercialization of child care, the second point mentioned above, it should be stated as background information that in the social milieu from which the Turkish migrant comes, only under very special circumstances are children left with relatives for more than a few days or weeks. Trusting them to friends or neighbors for extended periods is indeed a rarity. Whereas traditionally grandparents would expect no remuneration for performing child-care functions, under present conditions circumstances are changing. Because the amount of children's allowance (*kindergeld*) received by workers abroad is generally known, remittances below this level are frequently met by protests even from grandparents.

Perhaps more important than the desire of close relatives to receive reimbursement for child care expenses is the development of a new household occupation along these lines. Many working couples, prior to their departure for Europe, now make arrangements not only with relatives but also with friends, neighbors and acquaintances for paid child care. Thus, children are entrusted to persons having little or no previously established emotional bonds with them. A letter dictated to this author by an illiterate female worker exemplifies such a case :

Case 7 : Letter from a migrant worker to her landlord in Turkey

I have no one else to turn to. My husband wants to come here. Both his parents and mine refuse to take our children. I beg of you to take my boy. I will send you 400 lira every month. In addition, I will send money for his clothing and books. If this money is not enough, let me know. You can rent our apartment with or without our furniture so that I will not have to pay you rent for an unoccupied apartment. Please read this letter to neighbor Ayla and ask her to take my daughter. I will also pay her, and my daughter is grown enough to help with the housework. I am counting on you. Tell my husband to come soon and not worry about the children.

Advertisements now appear in Turkish newspapers for kindergartens which board migrants' children. This represents a new market development designed to satisfy an acute need. If non-migrants also begin to patronize day-care centers, nurseries and kindergartens, the effect upon household composition, authority structure and role specialization in the Turkish family could be significant. Thus, by those eager to accept employment abroad, children may be viewed more as a financial burden than a social and economic asset. Consequently, social norms which have traditionally supported high birth rates are likely to change and fertility among the migrant population to decline.

V

DIFFERENCES IN INDUSTRIAL LEARNING BEHAVIOR OF TURKISH WORKERS AT HOME AND ABROAD : CAUSES AND CONSEQUENCES

TERRY D. MONSON

ABSTRACT

For industrialization to succeed, Turkey needs to develop an industrial labor force from a population largely rural and, for the most part, minimally educated and unaccustomed to industrial mores. This chapter analyzes the problems associated with converting this predominantly rural population into an industrial labor force.

A simple model of the conversion process is presented and applied to a unique set of data on Turkish workers employed at home and in West Germany. From the analysis, factors essential to this process are first isolated. An estimate is then obtained of the constraint placed upon Turkey's joining the European Common Market as an industrial competitor by the lack of an existing industrial labor force. The analysis shows that a potential exists for Turkey to use returned migrants as a basis for an industrial labor force and thus by-pass a large portion of the costs of generating industrial labor domestically.

5.1 Introduction

Turkey desires to enter the European Common Market within the next decade. The country would prefer to join as an industrial competitor rather than in the role of supplier of primary products to its more industrialized West European neighbors. To avoid this latter role, it faces the major task of transforming a basically agricultural economy into one capable of efficiently producing a range of industrial products. As of now, the characteristics of its economy resemble those of most developing nations—relatively low per capita income, a predominantly rural population combined with a rather small industrial sector operating behind high trade barriers, and an evolving social infrastructure system. A partial listing of requirements necessary for any economy to overcome these constraints and to compete effectively among industrialized nations would include modern technology, adequate plant and equipment, efficient management, and a skilled and industrially acclimated labor force.

It is the latter problem of labor force development with which this chapter is concerned. The development of an industrial labor force is essential to the success of Turkey's industrialization efforts. Technology, plant and equipment can be borrowed or imported, training requirements for management are fairly standard and well known, but industrial employees must be generated from a population largely rural, lacking basic industrial skills, and unaccustomed to the mores and patterns of industrial work.[1] This process can be time-consuming and costly. It could place Turkey at a disadvantage that would be difficult to overcome in the decade prior to entering the Common Market.

After analyzing the problems of converting agricultural into industrial labor, the discussion isolates out the essential elements of this conversion process in a model of industrial learning behavior. Finally in an effort to identify and approximate the constraint placed upon Turkey's industrial development, a comparison is made of this conversion process for a sample of Turkish workers employed in Turkey and West Germany. As a preview to some of the results of the following analysis, here it might be stated that in the sample those who were employed in Germany completed their industrial learning (conversion) in one-fifth to one-sixth of the time required for those employed in Turkey. As a consequence, the productivity loss during the learning period was also one-fifth to one-sixth of the loss associated with a worker in Turkey.[2] These results suggest that in addition to migration providing the major source of foreign exchange in Turkey, it provides an opportunity to develop at least part of an industrial labor force more efficiently and less expensively than if workers were trained at home. Others have recognized this possibility, references to it are made in the Second Five-Year Development Plan, and there are at present efforts to coordinate training in Germany with industrial labor needs in Turkey. However, there have been no known attempts as yet to determine the quantitative importance of this particular bonus which migration yields. The present study attempts to provide some preliminary rough estimates as to its importance.

---

[1] It is not meant to imply here that these problems are insignificant, but rather that they may be easier to attack than the problems of labor force development.

[2] Productivity losses are defined as the difference between the productivity level of a fully converted industrial worker and the productivity level of the worker who is learning, summed over the learning period. A more rigorous definition is given in footnote 10 below.

5.2 *Industrial Labor Force Development in Turkey*

A cursory glance through the data of the 1965 Census of Population and the 1964 Census of Manufacturing Industries provides an indication of the range and severity of the problems facing industrial labor force development. Ten years ago approximately 70 percent of Turkey's population was rural, 80 percent of the male population was relatively uneducated having primary school training or less, and 73 percent of the active population was employed in the agricultural and primary producing sectors of the economy. At that time, the industrial labor force was small. Including those workers employed in public or private sector large enterprises, it consisted of 300 thousand workers or about two percent of an economically active population of roughly 13.5 million. Undoubtedly these figures have changed somewhat since they were collected, but probably not enough to alter what appears to be an immense shortage. For industry to expand, agricultural workers must be recruited and converted into labor for all levels of the industrial occupational hierarchy.

The process of developing an industrial labor force is much the same in Turkey as in most developing countries—namely, agricultural workers must be converted into both highly skilled and lesser skilled industrial workers. Two elements are present in the conversion : (1) acclimation to industrial conditions, discipline, and work habits, and (2) learning a skill, process or operation associated with an occupation (Kerr *et al.*, 1960; Slotkin, 1969). Acclimation to industrial conditions is defined as the process whereby workers become committed to industrial employment as a way of life, consequently severing major connections with the agricultural sector and becoming dependent upon industry as a source of income. Common examples might include becoming accustomed to working eight to ten hour shifts for five or six days a week, adjusting to industrial working speeds and noise levels, and taking orders from supervisors. The skill learning element consists of training efforts undertaken by the firm or by the government to teach the worker a particular skill required for an occupation or by efforts of the worker himself to learn job-related operations or to familiarize himself with the operation of mechanical devices in general. Thus, by definition, a "trained worker" is acclimated to industrial conditions and has learned an occupational skill.

There are two different methods by which a worker becomes "trained." Training can be acquired by formal or informal means. Formal methods are government or industry-sponsored vocational education, apprenticeships, or other in-plant training programs. The key point in a formal training method is that it is systematized and emphasizes the acquisition of industrial skills. On the other hand, informal methods are implemented *ad hoc* by the worker himself as he learns through on-the-job experience. One can think of this method as almost being one of "osmosis", in which the worker absorbs the essential elements of working in industry as well as learning rudimentary industrial skills simply by exposure to industry. In spite of the absence of systematized methods of instruction, the worker nonetheless becomes "trained" as defined above. This informal method will be referred to as "experience-generated" learning throughout the remainder of the study.[3]

Turkish manpower programs are designed to augment the supply of skilled labor through government sponsored vocational education programs. Former agricultural laborers who enter industry in *skilled* positions have generally received formal skill training prior to or in conjunction with employment. They are therefore "trained"—acclimated to industrial conditions and possess a skill associated with their occupation.

On the other hand, this conversion process can be more difficult and time consuming for workers moving into *lesser skilled* industrial positions. Unlike the case of their more skilled counterparts, the needs of lesser skilled workers have often been overlooked by both government and industry. Formal training is rare. For example, it is easy to imagine the bewilderment of a worker formerly employed in the agricultural sector when he is placed in an industrial working environment. Being unaccustomed to the discipline and regularity of production speeds, and having little if any knowledge of industrial equipment, he faces the problems of acclimating to industrial conditions and learning basic industrial skills. Since little if any formal training is available, he must by default, overcome these problems through experience-generated learning (informal training).

Whether the agricultural worker becomes a skilled or a lesser skilled industrial employee, the costs of his conversion can nevertheless be substantial. In order to clarify these costs, it is first necessary to refer to the "investment in man" discussions of the economics literature.[4] This

---

[3] This concept is a more specifically defined component of Kenneth J. Arrow's "Learning-By-Doing" (Arrow, 1962).

[4] The terminology used in the following discussion is found in Gary Becker's classic discussion of "human capital" (Becker, 1964).

discussion will simultaneously allow for an analysis of present conversion techniques in Turkish industry.

Introduced here is a new nomenclature found in the analysis of costs and benefits of training. Training is defined as either "general" or "specific". Under ideal conditions, these definitions are designed to determine who receives the benefits of training and thus who should be willing to bear its costs.

"General" training provides a skill usable to many firms. It thus is a marketable characteristic carried by the worker from firm to firm. Under this heading fall the qualities of acclimation to industrial conditions in general but more importantly, a large portion of transferable industrial skills such as machine operation and welding. Since the worker benefits by higher future wages as he markets his saleable "general" training, he should bear its costs of acquisition up to the point where a marginal unit of extra training provides an equal benefit in his future income stream. Costs of general training include tuition and loss of earning power while the worker is engaged in formal training programs together with costs of subnormal productivity while he learns through an experience-generated learning process.

"Specific" training generates a skill usable only to the firm in which the training is provided. For example, the learning of an industrial operation particular to a firm as well as workers' adaptation to firm-specific work rules and conditions fit this classification. The worker cannot market his "specific" training since other firms place no value upon it. Accordingly, it provides no benefit to the worker. Its firm-specific nature allows the benefits to accrue only to the firm providing the training. Thus, the firm should bear its costs to the point where the value of a marginal unit of training equals its costs.

For Turkey, the training system is relatively successful for skilled labor categories only. Management recognizes the benefits of skilled labor training as being "general" in nature. Wage differentials between skilled and unskilled occupations reflect this recognition. With skilled workers commonly receiving twice the unskilled wage, there clearly are incentives for workers to forego several years of earning power to attend vocational schools. Furthermore, the Turkish government is aware of the nation's skilled labor shortage and has emphasized the formation and improvement of vocational training programs designed for skilled labor qualifications.[5]

---

[5] See, for example, the Republic of Turkey, State Planning Organization, *Second*

The training system for lesser skilled workers on the other hand has been only minimally successful in meeting the ideal conditions needed for the adequate provision of training. In the absence of formal training to provide either "general" or "specific" skills, the lower skilled worker learns by experience—a time consuming and potentially costly process. Management ordinarily takes the view that in the learning process of lesser skilled workers the benefits derived from the formal provision of "specific" training do not compensate for its costs and that experience-generated learning provides a "specific" form of labor skill. These attitudes manifest themselves in a lack of formal training programs and in industry's commonly recognizing educational differentials as important factors in determining wage levels but of attributing little value to differential experience levels.

The lack of formal "specific" training programs is in large part due to a high labor turnover rate. A figure of 20 percent change in personnel per year was the average figure quoted by Turkish firms during the process of data gathering for this study. With this high propensity of Turkish workers to change jobs in response to small wage differentials, management genuinely feels it will be unable to recoup the costs of any formal methods of "specific" training for its lesser skilled workers. Management's not recognizing that experience-generated learning provides "general" skills is inexplicable. It is highly likely that at least a minimum level of industrial acclimation as well as rudimentary industrial skills are absorbed as a worker becomes experienced. Nevertheless, in establishing wages, management persists in attributing little if any value to these "general" skills. This lack of recognition of the "general" benefits of experience is evident not only across firms but within each firm itself where frequently only small premiums are paid to workers as they acquire experience. In addition, placement practices do not adequately account for a worker's prior experience with another firm. For example, it is not uncommon to find a worker who had been employed as a welder at his last place of employment being presently employed as an assembly worker.[6]

Five-Year Development Plan, pp. 161-207. It must be noted here that in spite of the emphasis on government-provided vocational training, few programs have actually been implemented due to indecision as to which Ministry (Education, Labor, or Technology and Industry) should provide the training.

[6] This paragraph must be qualified due to the high levels of urban unemployment found in Turkey. Prior experience may actually be accounted for in management hiring practices. Management may prefer and be able to hire experienced over inex-

One thus finds a far from ideal situation with respect to training of lesser skilled industrial workers in Turkey. This situation seems to result from a misconception of the role of experience in generating skills required in the conversion of agricultural workers to usable industrial labor. If experience does in fact generate "general" skills, this misconception would appear to present a major problem in the Turkish labor market.

It is then possible that in Turkey there is a prevailing inappreciation of the problems of semi-skilled labor force development. To this issue, one further factor need be added. Turkey presently has a small industrial base and its corollary, a small industrial labor force. The question can then be asked to what extent does lack of a large industrial labor force impede a country's industrialization efforts. A small industrial labor force is likely to slow the growth of industry in two ways. For industry to expand, the industrial labor force must increase. This increase requires time for agricultural workers to be converted into the industrial employees needed for industrial expansion. Secondly, this conversion process is likely to be retarded by an insufficient existing industrial work force necessary to train the new entrants to industry Whether training is provided through formal means or through experience-generated learning, it is probable that the availability of industrially acclimated and skilled workers will be a key determinant in the rate at which new industrial workers can be supplied to industry. Thus, because it must start from the position of having a small industrial base, Turkey may be further disadvantaged as it seeks to compete with its economically more advanced European neighbors. Lacking an existing large industrial labor force, it may have to be very selective in its industrialization efforts due to an inability to expand its supply of industrial workers at a rapid pace.

Several problems of labor force development in Turkey have been briefly outlined. Since Turkey presently has a relatively effective system for augmenting skilled labor supply, the remainder of the chapter will concentrate on the problems of semi-skilled labor force development. The following three general areas will be investigated : (1) Because semi-

---

perienced labor while not giving a wage premium for experience. The fact that the worker is hired may be adequate compensation for his experience given the unemployment rate. Unfortunately, no information is available to support this contention. It was observed that prior experience was not important in the placement process (as opposed to the hiring process). Frequently an experienced worker's present occupation was in no way related to his previous employment. This factor would lead one to believe that experience is not recognized as being important or not recognized as providing a directly applicable industrial skill.

skilled labor is largely provided through experience-generated learning in Turkey, this particular learning process will be more carefully detailed. Such considerations as length of the learning period, learning speed, and factors influencing learning behavior will be addressed. (2) A corollary consideration is a determination of the costs of the conversion process. Insights into this concern may influence management and government to place greater emphasis upon training needs of semi-skilled labor, or at least, to more adequately compensate and utilize those workers who already qualify as experienced semi-skilled labor. (3) Finally, the discussion will investigate the extent to which lack of a pre-existing industrial base affects the development of labor necessary for successful industrialization efforts—i.e., the extent to which an existing labor force influences the conversion process of new entrants to the labor force.

For several reasons, these considerations are closely associated with the phenomenon of Turkish migration. Most importantly, for purposes of comparing relative learning behavior, a sample of Turkish workers employed in Turkey and in West Germany can be studied. Based on such a study, the present analysis discloses some rather striking differences in how experience affects the conversion process in two different industrial environments. Moreover, it suggests that for Turkey industrial experience obtained by migrant workers in Europe can, if transferred back, provide a low cost alternative to generating an industrial labor force in the homeland.

5.3 A Model of "Experience-Generated" Learning

As previously mentioned, the process of converting workers from agricultural into industrial labor consists of two elements : (1) acclimation to industrial working conditions and (2) learning an occupational skill. For skilled labor, the conversion process is systematized through the use of formal training methods with the emphasis being upon the skill learning aspect. But for semiskilled and unskilled labor, the focus of this study, a worker's productivity should rise over time as the conversion process occurs—even in the absence of formal training. For any given worker, this process is expected to depend upon time itself and such other factors as the firm's physical capital stock, the quality of the firm's labor force, and the socio-economic characteristics of the worker.

An inexperienced worker's productivity should be affected by time and on-the-job experience in a manner similar to suggestions of learning theory—i.e., increase at a decreasing rate (Blackburn, 1936; Hilgard, 1956). In addition to the direct effect of time itself, other factors are expected to influence learning behavior. A firm's capital stock can have a direct bearing in that capital-intensive firms may require more sophisticated skills and may be more alien to a worker displaced from the agricultural sector than firms which depend upon labor-intensive techniques of production. The worker's socio-economic background will also influence learning behavior. His level of education, place of birth and prior working experience will determine his exposure to and familiarity with industrial techniques and working conditions.

Finally, learning behavior will depend upon the quality of his coworkers. Quality here refers to the skill and/or experience level of the firm's labor force. For example, if two workers recently removed from the agricultural sector and employed in two firms identical in all respects except for labor force quality are considered, the worker employed in the more highly experienced and/or skilled labor force should adjust to the firm's work rules, accept industrial working conditions, and learn job-related skills more quickly than the other worker employed in the less experienced and/or skilled labor force. The mere presence of a higher quality labor force is evidence of the availability of more "trainers" to be used in an informal training process, or at least, is an indication of an "atmosphere" more conducive to better learning habits and more effective informal training.

This latter influence upon learning behavior is important in that it adds the other forementioned consideration to labor development— namely, that of who trains the labor force. In the absence of a high quality labor force, it can be expected that initial entrants to a firm's labor force will tend to learn slowly. Over time as these workers become experienced, productive, semi-skilled laborers, they not only raise their own productivity but simultaneously form the nucleus of a labor force capable of expediting the conversion process of workers who subsequently enter. These later entrants must undergo the same informal learning process as the initial group. However, the fact that they are now employed with better quality workers should positively influence their initial levels of productivity and rates of learning. In the following discussion this second aspect of experience acquisition will be referred to as the "indirect effect". If this aspect is included when analyzing Turkey's labor force development, it can be seen that in starting without an existing large industrial labor force, the nation faces a double constraint. Workers must learn through acquisition of on-the-job experience and their learning is likely to be slow.

These concepts are formalized in Equation (1) and Figure (1) :

Equation (*1*) $X(t) = f[k(t), h_1(t), h_2(t), e(t), s(t)]$

Equation (1) represents a worker's productivity path over time. If this worker is a new entrant to the labor force, he must undergo the conversion process through the informal means of experience acquisition. $X(t)$ refers to his productivity in time t which is considered to be his marginal productivity in a given time period. The notations on the right side of the equation represent those factors influencing a worker's learning behavior. Thus, $k(t)$ is the physical capital combined with the inexperienced worker in time t while $h_1(t)$ and $h_2(t)$ refer to the quality of the labor force with which the new entrant is associated. In economic terminology, the experience and skill levels of a worker are considered to represent his level of human capital. If this concept is expanded to encompass the firm's labor force at large, $h_1(t)$ then represents the number of skilled workers with whom the inexperienced worker is employed while $h_2(t)$, represents the experience content of the semi-skilled labor force with which he is in contact. The existence of a large number of skilled workers, $h_1(t)$, is expected to have its greatest effect upon the skill learning element of the transformation process and the experience content, $h_2(t)$, to have its greatest effect upon the process of acclimation to industrial working conditions.

The worker's experience level is denoted by $e(t)$, the partial derivative of Equation (1) with respect to e being the worker's rate of learning (the contribution of a marginal unit of experience to his productivity). Finally $s(t)$ is a description of the worker's socio-economic background incorporated here mainly for comparing learning behavior of workers with differing socio-economic backgrounds at a later point in the study. The signs of the partial derivatives of $X(t)$ with respect to k, h_1, h_2, and e are assumed to follow conventional micro-economic theory in that an additional unit of k, h_1, h_2, or e will increase the worker's productivity at a decreasing rate. Nothing can be assumed about varying levels of s.

In Figure 1, possible forms of the inexperienced worker's productivity trend over time are shown. In this diagram, it is assumed that (1) the worker is completely inexperienced upon commencing industrial employment; thus, his productivity depends upon human and physical capital and time beginning with $t = 1$; (2) experience generates productivity improvements similar to suggestions of learning theory (increasing at a decreasing rate); and (3) the skill mix and physical capital contents are held constant at the same level for all curves while the experience content of the firm's semi-skilled labor force changes from curve to curve but is constant along each curve. (h_2^1 represents the lowest experience mix).

The learning curves f_2, f_3, and f_4 suggest alternative effects of experience acquisition. In f_2 the change derives largely from an increase in the initial productivity level, while in f_3 the effect results primarily from an increase in the rate of leaning. If X^* is defined as the productivity level where learning is completed $(dX/dt \rightarrow O)$, then both f_2 and f_3 allow a shorter learning period. In f_4 the effect is a parallel shift in the learning curve allowing a higher productivity level to be eventually approached.

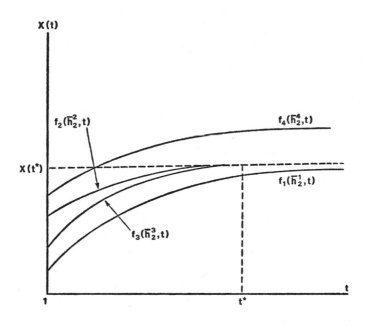

Figure 1

Representative Learning Patterns

It is unknown exactly how changes in the experience mix influence learning behavior of new entrants to the labor force. *A priori*, it is likely that an increase will improve both the rate of learning as well as increase the initial productivity level (as in f_3). This simple model will be used to ascertain the exact nature of this effect and thus approximate the extent that lack of an experienced labor force constrains Turkey's industrial development.

5.4 *Statistical Design*

5.4.1 *The Data*

The phenomenon of Turkish migration to West Germany offers a unique opportunity to test the model presented above and also to approximate the constraint that the lack of a large pre-existing industrial labor force imposes upon Turkey's goal of industrial development. In addition, this phenomenon permits an assessment to be made of the potential benefits migration can provide as an inexpensive means for Turkey to develop an industrial labor force. In the long run, it may very well be that this aspect of migration will be equal in value to the large amounts of foreign exchange presently being remitted by the migrant population. The results of this study possibly indicate that a much more intensified effort at recruiting and channeling migrants back into the Turkish industrial sector is warranted.

In December, 1971, there were at least 500 thousand Turks employed in the West German economy. Being from the agricultural sector, many of these workers were new to industrial work, were unskilled,[7] usually had no more than the basic five years of primary education offered in Turkey, and were employed in the lower echelons of the industrial labor force. While in Germany, those workers employed in semi-skilled or unskilled occupations usually were not provided with significant amounts of formal training. As a result, most of their productivity increases could be attributed to acquisition of on-the-job experience. For comparative purposes, it was thus possible to select Turkish workers in Germany and Turkey who had similar backgrounds, were employed in similar occupations, and had received minimal formal training. Finally, since each country has an industrial environment with distinctly different human and physical capital levels, a sample composed of similar workers employed in each country provides the data for comparing the costs of experience-generated learning.

With such a test in mind, the author collected data in Turkey and West Germany over the winter of 1970-71. Because of the problems of collecting and utilizing the data, the actual sample was small. The firms—five in

---

[7] There appears to be a dichotomy in the skill characteristics of migrant Turks. Roughly 70 percent are thought to be unskilled with the remaining 30 percent being highly skilled. See *Bundesanstalt für Arbeit*, 1961-71, for results of periodic surveys of Germany's migrant population. G. E. Völker's study in this volume suggests that the proportion of skilled to unskilled migrants is increasing. The 30-70 percent ratio thus may be somewhat erroneous or at least outdated.

Germany and five in Turkey—from a total of thirty firms contacted were willing and able to provide information. A total of 135 workers and eleven groups of workers comprised the sample which had two to eight workers per group. Because a large portion of the migrants worked in the metal industry and because individual productivity measures were difficult to find in the construction and manufacturing sectors where others were employed, the private sector metal industry was chosen as the industrial data source.[8] The four semi-skilled occupations studied were machine operators (shearers, turners, borers, and press operators), welders, die casters, and assemblers. Although the occupations varied in their degree of complexity, each required some training through experience before the sample member reached his full productivity level.

The actual data were classified in two categories. For each worker or group of workers data were necessary to estimate learning curves. These data were based upon piece work (incentive) wages in Germany and physical productivity normalized by the use of time standards in Turkey. In addition, data were collected on sample members' socio-economic backgrounds (age, sex, education, place of birth, prior industrial experience) and on firms' human and physical capital levels. Appendix Tables 1-3 provide summaries of the information collected.

In the process of obtaining data, several practical problems and restrictions limited the sample size, the variety of occupations, and the number of observations for each sample member. Included in these problems were (1) lack of detailed individual productivity records over time, (2) changes in industrial equipment and production processes over the period in which data were available, (3) productivity measures available for large groups only and (4) paced production techniques placing an upper limit on learning behavior.[9]

---

[8] The German industrial classification scheme is used here. This system incorporates all processes which work with metal into a broad sector entitled "the metal industry". In actual fact, some of the firms included in the sample could be classified as manufacturing firms—e.g., one firm assembled electrical components, another manufactured automobiles, and another manufactured refrigerators. Thus, this classification system is clearly arbitrary as to definition of boundaries. The major problem in using data on assembly operations was that individual productivity records over time necessary for this study often were non-existent because of the team nature of the production process. Whenever assemblers were included in the sample, data were available on individual or small group productivity. The metal industry offered a greater probability for finding these data than the manufacturing sector.

[9] See Monson, 1972, for further details of data collection problems.

Finally, it must be noted that the nature of the sample selection process was biased in the sense that workers who did not adapt to industrial conditions, did not learn their occupation, or for other reasons left the firm were excluded. Thus nearly all sample members had acclimated to industrial conditions, having been employed in industry for a minimum of three months. In addition there may be differences in psychological motivation between Turks employed in Germany and Turkey. Because of the migrants' interest in accumulating a large savings reserve for use upon return to Turkey, they may have been inclined to work harder than if employed in Turkey. Therefore, the sample is small and perhaps somewhat biased. Accordingly, although the sample members had relatively homogeneous socio-economic backgrounds, conclusions must be drawn cautiously.

5.4.2 Statistical Procedure

The data were processed in two distinct steps. In Step 1, the effect of experience upon productivity was isolated by estimating a learning curve for each worker from Equation (2) below. Sample data on each worker's productivity trend over time were used in this procedure.

Equation (2) $X(t) = X(1)t^E$ or $ln\ X(t) = ln\ X(1) + E\ ln\ t$

In the equation $X(t)$ is the worker's productivity in time t; $X(1)$ is his productivity on his first day of work; t is time units of experience (days); and E is the worker's "elasticity of learning" $(dX/dt \cdot t/X)$, a weighted measure of the slope of the learning curve (rate of learning).

Additional parameters were computed from the results derived from fitting Equation (2) to the sample data. For each worker, these parameters give (1) the time period in which further increments to productivity attributable to experience-generated learning approach zero (t*), (2) the absolute productivity change due to experience accumulation (ΔX^*), and (3) the productivity loss during the learning period (L*). For computational purposes, t* was defined as the time period (day) in which further increments to productivity were .001 or .1 %. In this time period, experience-generated learning was assumed to be completed. ΔX^* was computed as an alternative measure of productivity gains because of the dependence of E upon actual productivity levels (due to the weighting factor t/X). ΔX^* is defined as the productivity level associated with t* minus the initial productivity level—*i.e.*, $X(t^*)$—$X(1)$. L*, defined as the productivity loss in the learning period, is the area between the learning curve and the productivity level X(t*) extending from t = 1 to t = t*.[10] This difference roughly represents the cost of experience-generated learning defined in terms of lost productivity. The cost would be divided between the worker and the firm depending upon the specific or general nature of skills provided during the learning process. The area given by L* will be important in the subsequent discussion of relative learning costs.

Step 2 of the statistical analysis was designed to isolate the effects of firms' physical and human capital contents and sample members' socio-economic backgrounds in explaining differences in learning behavior between countries and among occupations. The parameters of Step 1 estimated for each sample member in Equation (2) above become dependent variables to be regressed upon a series of four variables which hypothetically are thought to influence learning behavior.[11] These four are explained below.

5.4.2.1 *Sample Members' Educational and Industrial Experience Backgrounds*

Educational and experience variables [12] approximated the human capital content of each worker. These variables included (1) the worker's years of general education; (2) his years of vocational education; (3) his months of experience in a similar job and (4) his months of general industrial experience. Each component was expected to contribute to learning behavior in slightly different ways. Job-similar experience and vocational education should have provided the worker with some of the skills required for his present job. General education was expected to provide the worker with a greater "capability to learn". General experience was thought to imply the worker had at least partially adapted to industrial conditions but might not have had the exact set of skills required for his current job. In addition, the existence of higher physical and human capital levels in Germany forced the author to hypothesize, *a priori*, that a month of German experience will have a greater impact upon

---

[10] Expressed mathematically, it is the area defined by :

$$L* = X(t*) \cdot t* — \int_1^{t*} X(t) \, dt$$

[11] To use this procedure, the trend data from Step I must be strong enough so that there is little left for other variables to explain. Otherwise, a specification error results (Griliches, 1957).

[12] Experience variables were necessary since not all sample members were totally new to industrial work.

learning behavior than a month of Turkish experience. Accordingly, experience was classified by country of origin.

5.4.2.2 *Other Socio-Economic Variables*

In addition to education and experience variables, it was necessary to include in the analysis such items as age, sex, and rural or urban birthplace. Age and sex were thought to have little effect upon learning behavior and were included simply as a check. Rural-urban origin may represent a difference in familiarity with modern industrial life and as such was thought useful for inclusion in the analysis.

5.4.2.3 *Firm Variables*

Human capital contents of firms' work forces were represented by (1) the ratio of salaried plus skilled personnel to hourly personnel (the skill mix h_1) and (2) the average duration of in-plant experience of the semi-skilled labor force in the department where the sample member was employed (the experience mix h_2). Salaried and skilled personnel were incorporated into one variable for the skill mix because of the over-lapping functions of skilled and supervisory personnel in many of the firms providing data.

Firms' capital stocks were approximated by an index of average plant semi-skilled wages. It is an admittedly weak measure but does provide a crude approximation to capital stock and differences in technology. To a large extent, differences in time standards, upon which the data for estimating learning curves were based, account for a major portion of capital stock differences. Consequently, this variable may be of little value. In any case, it must be carefully interpreted due to its inadequacy.

5.4.2.4 *Occupational Differences and Wage Payment Systems*

Two additional sets of dummy variables were included in the analysis to isolate effects of occupational difficulty and wage payment system upon sample members' learning behavior. Because some occupations appeared to require more skills or involved more difficult operations, casual observation of the varying operations performed by sample members in each occupation indicated a need for occupational dummies. *A priori* reasoning suggested that differences in wage schemes should affect learning behavior. With piece work wages, a worker has a greater incentive to begin at a higher productivity level and learn more rapidly than under a straight hourly wage system.

Using the above variables, multiple regression analysis was first applied to data on all sample members and then to data on only those workers who learned as evidenced from the results of Step 1. In order to determine whether there were significant differences in the manner in which the independent variables affected only those workers who learned through experience acquisition, zero-learning workers were excluded. Also since the latter often had prior industrial experience, their exclusion directs the analysis toward those sample members considered to be inexperienced.

Data were also grouped by country of employment. This grouping was designed to determine whether the variables affected learning behavior differently *within* each country as opposed to *across* countries. Both logarithmic and linear estimates were tried for the various data groupings. The latter provided higher R^2's and more significant coefficients than the former, thus indicating a limited amount of substitutability among the variables. The linear form was chosen as best representing the relationship between the dependent and independent variables.

Two statistical problems may have biased the results somewhat. Multicollinearity (inter-dependence) among the variables, especially the ones representing firm characteristics, was common. This multicollinearity represents a certain degree of production complementarity between skill and experience mixes and physical capital. In addition, the use of estimated parameters as dependent variables in Step 2 is likely to compound biases from the estimation procedure of Step 1. In light of both these problems and the other problems of data utilization, the results reported below are reasonably good. Nonetheless, caution must be used in interpreting the results because of potential weakness in the procedures followed and in the data itself.

5.5   Results

Step 1 : Evidence of productivity increases which were attributable to experience-generated learning and which conformed to Equation (2) was noticeable in a large portion of the sample. Learning was systematically more evident among those sample members employed in Germany than among those employed in Turkey. Eighty-one percent of the former fit the logarithmic learning pattern as opposed to 43 percent of the latter. On the average, the sample in Germany had absolute productivity gains (ΔX^*) 60 percent higher than the sample in Turkey. On a relative basis, the sample members in Turkey who did learn had much larger productivity gains over their initial productivity levels than migrant counterparts (260 percent versus 27 percent).[13] However, partially due to the weighting factor t/x, migrant Turks were characterized by higher initial productivity levels $(X(1))$ and lower learning elasticities (E) than their counterparts in Turkey. Productivity losses during the learning period (L^*) and the period itself required for learning to be completed (t^*) were both on the order of five to six times larger in Turkey than in Germany.

From the results of Step I, it can be safely concluded that Equation (2) is a fairly accurate description of the experience-generated learning process and that productivity improvements due to experience-acquisition are large and significant. Furthermore, learning was more systematic and more pronounced in Germany and entailed much lower learning costs than in Turkey. Table 1 summarizes average learning parameters by country and occupation.

Step 2 : Only results of the more important variables are reported for Step 2. Because several variables such as age, sex and urban-rural origin did not act as significant influences upon learning behavior, they are omitted entirely.[14] Others such as wage system and occupational differences were not of specific interest to this study although they occasionally did wield a significant influence. No regression tables are given here. Because of weaknesses in the data and procedures of Step 2, more

---

[13] Computed from $[X^* - X(1)]/X(1)$, using the notation as defined earlier.

[14] The insignificance of the sex and urban-rural split variables is important to note. From the sex variable, one can conclude that women do not have a comparative disadvantage with respect to men in industrial work (at least in the assembly operations where all women in the sample were employed). From the insignificance of the urban-rural variable, it can be inferred that knowledge of simple mechanical devices in general has permeated to the Turkish villages. It thus makes no difference upon industrial learning behavior if the worker comes from a rural or urban background. The process of converting inexperienced into experienced industrial workers depends upon other factors. That is to say, the classification rural or urban is of no relevance to a discussion of labor training in Turkey since workers from both areas learn equally as well under the same conditions. The problem is then solely one of converting inexperienced into experienced labor, not one of converting agricultural into industrial labor.

This latter interpretation may be erroneous since the variable measures only place of birth. It is possible that rural-born sample members had migrated to cities in Turkey before going to Germany or prior to assuming industrial employment in Turkey. A better variable would have been a worker's last place of residence (rural or urban). These data were not available.

Table 1

Average Estimated Learning Parameters by Country and Occupation

Category	Sample Size	Number of Sample Who Learned	X (1) (DM)	I (1) (%)	E	t* (days)	ΔX* (DM)	L* (DM)
Germany	64	56	5.0115	75.09	.060997	59	1.3635	25.2855
Machinists	22	21	4.6023	69.99	.064239	60	1.3321	25.5315
Die Casters	5	5	5.1236	87.30	.053016	59	1.0172	19.9310
Assemblers	25	21	5.0903	76.34	.062064	60	1.4568	28.2385
Welders	12	9	5.7225	77.29	.055381	52	1.4113	20.8341
Turkey	71 + 11 groups	30 + 5 groups	.3087	34.43	.246467	335	.8062	150.2002
Machinists	16 + 2 groups	11 + 1 group	36.24	36.24	.229434	313	.6288	129.2221
Die Casters	11	0	—	—	—	—	—	—
Assemblers	35 + 9 groups	19 + 4 groups	.3148	34.00	.254644	340	.8484	155.2218
Welders	9	0	—	—	—	—	—	—

(a) Average R^2's for the German sample members fitting the log learning curve was .871 with a range of .586 to .991. For the Turkish sample, the average R^2 was .670 with a range of .330 to .992.

(b) I is an alternative measure of productivity based upon the time standards system. When I = 1,000, the worker has achieved his time standard. E is the worker's learning elasticity; t* is the number of days for learning to be completed; ΔX* is the absolute productivity gain from learning; and L* is the productivity loss during the learning period.

emphasis is placed upon signs of the estimated coefficients than upon their absolute values.[15]

5.5.1 Sample Members' Educational and Experience Levels

Education variables, somewhat surprisingly, had a minimal effect upon learning behavior. When significant, more years of general education raised learning elasticities, implying that the more educated sample members did have a greater "capability to learn." Vocational education had no impact whatever on learning elasticities. Both types of education tended to lower initial productivity levels. This phenomenon is partially explained by hiring practices of employers in that more educated sample members were placed in machine operation—i.e., the occupation shown by regression analysis to be most difficult. Partial correlation coefficients between occupational and educational variables support this contention. Thus, it is likely these negative coefficients are not the result of detrimental effects of education upon productivity levels but rather of educational differences being used as a placement device.

Neither job-similar nor general experience obtained and utilized in Turkey affected learning behavior there. However, this same general experience significantly lowered learning elasticities and initial productivities when carried by migrants to Germany. The above-mentioned lack of significance for experience obtained and utilized in Turkey may be caused by its non-transferability (firm-specific nature) or by inadequate transfer due to Turkish hiring and supervisory practices. Both of these considerations were mentioned earlier in this chapter as problems of the training system for semi-skilled workers in Turkey. Unfortunately, it is impossible to identify the exact cause of this lack of significance and thus to comment on the empirical relevance of the earlier analysis. In all likelihood, it is a combination of non-transferability and hiring practices which accounts for this phenomenon.

The significant negative coefficients on Turkish industrial experience utilized in Germany may be interpreted in two manners. On the one hand they may reflect a large portion of experienced migrants being employed as machinists, an occupation shown to be difficult. On the other hand, if migrants with prior Turkish experience had to "unlearn" skills and working habits upon assuming employment in Germany, the experienced

---

[15] See Monson, 1972, for further information on the omitted variable and for detailed tables of the multiple regression results.

worker, accustomed to slower working speeds and less supervised working conditions in Turkey, might have encountered greater difficulty learning in Germany than did his completely inexperienced counterpart.

Both types of experience obtained and utilized in Germany had significant productivity effects. Job-similar experience raised productivities and lowered elasticities, thus indicating that the worker's learning behavior was a continuation of his learning curve from his last place of employment. General experience also tended to raise the intercept of the learning curve and lower elasticities. These results are a strong indication that German experience, whether general or similar, provided training which was transferable among firms in Germany.

5.5.2 Firm variables

Labor force skill and experience mixes and, to a lesser extent, the technology variable were usually significant in the regression analysis. The technology variable was highly significant in explaining variations across countries but virtually always insignificant in explaining variables within countries. The crudeness of the measure itself, as discussed earlier together with the nature of the firms' selection process minimized the effect of technological differences. Improved technology raised initial productivity levels and lowered elasticities. These results are not very conclusive, however, because sample members in Germany uniformly had higher initial productivities and lower learning elasticities. Thus it is possible to conclude either that technology makes learning more difficult or that learning in Germany was more difficult. Because of its ambiguity, it is best to disregard this variable.

The skill mix variable had a negative significant sign in regressions upon initial productivity levels, $X(1)$, and virtually no effect upon elasticities of learning. The existence of positive partial correlation coefficients between skill and technology variables on the order of .50 suggests a type of "automation" hypothesis—i.e., with advancing technology, more skilled workers are needed to service and maintain equipment while the operations performed by semi-skilled workers become more menial and have an associated lower productivity. In view of the fact that the term "semi-skilled" as used here is not very precise and represents workers in a continuum of skill levels, such an hypothesis is indeed possible. It implies that as technology advances, the occupational structure changes toward a preponderance of more skilled workers and workers in the lower ranges of this "semi-skilled" continuum. Thus new inexperienced workers entering a technologically advanced firm may actually be placed in a relatively lower skilled position, and consequently have a lower productivity than if they were employed in a firm with a lower level of technology.

The Turkish regressions produced different results. Here an improved skill mix raised initial productivity levels and had no effect upon elasticities. Noticeable here also was a negative partial correlation coefficient between the skill mix and technology variable (-.56). This result implies that technological change affects the occupational structure in Turkey by attempting to minimize the use of scarce skilled labor. Thus, in this sample the skill content of the labor force seemed to affect learning behavior through a changing occupational structure.

The regressions on the German data tended to corroborate the contention that experience contents of the semi-skilled labor force do have the indirect effect upon learning behavior of inexperienced workers as mentioned earlier. The effect of a higher experience content was that it raised initial productivity levels and tended also to raise rates of learning. These limited results indicate that parallel shifts in inexperienced workers' learning curves correspond to an improvement in the experience mix (as in f_4 in Figure 1). The analysis presented earlier is partially verified and the exact nature of the experience mix variations upon learning behavior is tentatively identified.

Negative coefficients, frequently significant, were found for the experience mix variable in regressions upon the intercept $X(1)$ in Turkey. The experience mix was never significant in other regressions. Also noticeable was a strong partial correlation coefficient on the order of .60 between the technology variable and the experience mix variable. This intercorrelation, combined with the strong negative one between the technology and skill mix variables, suggests another "automation" hypothesis. For Turkey, as technology develops, experienced semi-skilled workers may be substituted for scarce skilled workers. Thus, these negative coefficients reflect an occupational structure change in a manner opposite to that found in Germany. As technology improves in Turkey, the structure becomes more heavily weighted with experienced semi-skilled workers than with skilled labor. Consequently, new entrants to the labor force tend to be assigned lower skilled jobs than if they were employed in a less technologically advanced firm.

5.6   Conclusions and Policy Recommendations

This study of comparative learning behavior was constrained by a small sample size, imperfect data, and other miscellaneous statistical problems. Nonetheless, with caution the results can be generalized a bit further and their ramifications for Turkey's industrialization efforts indicated. Referring back to the three points discussed in conjunction with labor force development in Turkey, it has been shown that (1) inexperienced entrants to the semi-skilled labor force go through a conversion process of adapting to industrial working conditions and learning industrial skills, (2) this learning process can be long and relatively costly, and (3) experience levels of the semi-skilled labor force, but not necessarily the number of skilled workers with whom the inexperienced worker is employed, do have a significant influence upon learning behavior. The learning process is accurately described by Equation (2) and conforms to the usual conceptions of learning theory. The costs of this learning, in terms of lost productivity, can be substantial. In Turkey, the average learning costs were approximately equivalent to three or four weeks' wages (DM 150) and were thus quite large in relationship to average wage levels. Since most workers are paid straight hourly wages with little attention to premiums for accumulated in-plant experience, it can be assumed that by paying wages above a worker's productivity during the early stages of the learning process, the firm bears a major portion of the cost of this learning. Such a cost, multiplied over the thousands of workers required for industrialization, imposes a large burden on Turkey's limited resources. Finally, the quality of a firm's labor force as defined by its experience level did have an effect upon learning behavior and accounted, in part, for the more effective experience-generated learning evidenced in the German sample.

Precise comparison of learning patterns between the two countries was impossible because of data limitations. Nonetheless, as compared to the Turkish sample, one cannot fail to be impressed by the systematic nature of learning behavior in Germany as well as by its significant effects upon productivity. The evidence tentatively indicates that the already pronounced differences in human capital characteristics of the Turkish and German labor forces may be getting more, rather than less, unequal over time in spite of Turkey's intensified efforts to improve manpower programs. For this sample, experience in Germany (and utilized in German industry) had a greater effect upon productivity than experience obtained in Turkey (and utilized in either Turkey or Germany). German experience provided more systematic and larger productivity improvements, tended to be more transferable among firms, required a shorter learning period and was obtained at a much lower productivity loss that Turkish experience. In addition, increases in the experience mix had a pronounced positive effect upon learning behavior in Germany and if any effect, a negative one in Turkey. Thus, in spite of the observed higher elasticities, the experience-acquisition process occurs at a slower rate, is less systematic and more expensive in Turkey than in Germany. Human capital contents of the industrial labor forces can be expected to widen over time, further increasing the already large productivity differential existing between the two countries.

The results of this study indicate that lack of a large, experienced, semi-skilled labor force is a constraint upon Turkey's plans to enter the Common Market as an industrial competitor. Many questions have been left unanswered, especially those pertaining to the exact magnitude of this constraint. It was suggested that experience-generated learning costs are six times as expensive per worker in Turkey than in Germany. Strong measures are called for to overcome this constraint. Among them would be attempts at correcting structural problems in the Turkish labor market and utilizing the migrant population as a low-cost source of trained industrial labor.

In the former case, a balanced approach to the problem of labor force development in Turkey is necessary. Emphasis upon increasing the supply of skilled workers, improving technology or raising the capital stock is not in itself sufficient to ensure high levels of labor productivity. Efforts must be intensified to improve the efficiency of the experience-generated learning process of lesser skilled workers and to increase the transferability of the experience received from firm to firm. Efforts must also be made to define the training needs of semi-skilled labor and to develop effective alternatives to learning by experience. Formal training techniques may possibly prove to be a more efficient method of implementing the conversion process. It is likely that many of these problems can be corrected by greater sensitivity on the part of management to the training needs of semi-skilled labor so as to improve present hiring, placement, and training practices.

Although the exact value of using returned migrants in Turkish industry has not been specifically determined, the potential is nevertheless obvious. By recruiting the returned migrant population into industry, Turkey may be able to realize an additional bonus of developing at least part of an industrial labor force base at a relatively low cost. Efforts should be made to determine the effectiveness of returned migrants in Turkish industry and to expand and closely monitor programs designed to train migrants in Germany to fit Turkish occupational needs. As of now, there are many unresolved problems which may negate the potential benefits of such a program such as non-transferability of skills to Turkish industry, migrants' higher wage expectations, and cultural factors inhibiting desires for employment in Turkish industry upon return.[16] Assuming that these problems could be resolved, the Turkish government might be well advised to take a firm position in negotiations with West European nations. If Germany expects to continue receiving large quantities of skilled Turkish labor,[17] in return it should be willing to provide training either of an informal or formal nature which will in time directly benefit the Turkish economy. In this manner, the present drain in skilled labor would be eventually offset by a gain in trained industrial labor.

Appendix A : Data Collection

For purposes of isolating learning patterns as suggested in the text of this study, the question may be raised as to what type of experiment would produce an optimal set of data. The experiment should allow inexperienced workers with similar characteristics to be introduced into firms identical in all respects except the experience mix of their labor forces. These firms should be producing identical products with equivalent firm size, product volume, technology, capital equipment, management expertise, labor force skill contents, and wage systems. If all these factors were constant and if it were possible to isolate individual worker's productivities, then it would be possible to trace learning curves and impute differences among them to different experience mixes.

Obviously, the actual choice of firms and individuals from these firms for the sample could not possibly meet these severe restrictions. An effort thus was made to collect enough data on other factors which might influence industrial learning behavior, so that, in practice, the influences

---

[16] In informal discussions with migrants in Germany, few indicated a desire to return to industrial employment in Turkey. A rough estimate would be that approximately ten percent wished to utilize in Turkey their training acquired in Germany. Most others preferred to "go into business for themselves" meaning they were planning to buy a taxi, open a grocery store, bring back modern equipment for their farm, etc., upon returning to Turkey. This phenomenon is by no means restricted to Turkish migrant workers. See O.E.C.D., 1967, for discussion of motivations to migrate.

[17] In this volume Völker gives the figure of 46 percent of migrants placed through the Istanbul office of the German Employment Service in 1971 being skilled labor. With the slowing down of Yugoslav migration to Germany, one would expect an increasing German demand for skilled workers from other sending countries including Turkey. See footnote 7 above for complementary discussion.

of a variety of independent variables could be tested upon sample members' learning behavior.

Appendix Table 1

Distribution of Sample Members by Occupation and Firm

Firm Number	Assemblers	Machinists	Welders	Casters	Total
		GERMANY			
1	..	5	..	..	4
2	4	..	3	4	11
3	9	12	1	..	22
4	9	2	..	1	12
5	5	5	8	..	18
Total	27	23	12	5	67
		TURKEY			
6	38	..	9	11	58
7	..	10	..	..	10
		1 group			1 group
8	3 groups	..	..	..	3 groups
9	4	6	..	..	10
		1 group			1 group
10	6 groups	..	..	..	6 groups
Total	42	16	9	11	78
	9 groups	2 groups			11 groups
Total both	69	39	21	16	145
countries	9 groups	2 groups			11 groups

Note : 10 sample members could not be used in the statistical analysis because of incomplete data (in Germany 2 assemblers and 1 machinist, in Turkey 7 assemblers).

The data were collected over the winter of 1970-71. Thirty firms were contacted (14 in Turkey, 16 in Germany). Of these 30 firms, ten were able to provide usable data. From each firm, the following information on the quality of the labor force and supervisory personnel was obtained : (1) average semi-skilled wage in the plant, (2) average in-plant experience of the labor force and of the supervisory personnel, (3) average educational level of the supervisory personnel (not available for all firms), (4) supervisory hierarchy of the department and firm, (5) percentage of labor force by national origin, and (6) number of hourly and salaried employees for the department and firm. For each sample member, data were collected from company personnel offices, industrial engineering departments and manufacturing supervisors on the following items : 1) age, 2) education, 3) birthplace, 4) length of in-plant service, 5) length of total industrial experience, 6) present and beginning wage and wage changes while in the plant, 7) data tracing his productivity over time, 9) time standards for his occupation, and 9) a measure of job difficulty. In certain cases data were not available on every item.

Appendix Table 2

Summary of Sample Information by Firm

Firm Number	Average Age of Sample Members	Average Years Education of Sample	Percent of Sample Female	Avergae Prior Experience At Other Firms [a]	Percent of Sample with Prior Experience	Sample Size
1	34.5	7.0	0	7.5	25.0	4
2	32.4	5.0	0	10.9	18.1	11
3	29.2	7.7	0	23.2	47.8	22
4	31.6	5.9	0	24.0	33.3	12
5	31.9	5.1	0	16.7	27.7	18
6	24.0	5.5	24.1	5.5	8.6	58
7	24.6	5.0	0	N.A.	N.A.	10
						1 group
8 [b]	19.0	5.5	100.0	0	0	3 groups
	(18.5)	(5.75)	(100.0)	(8.75)	(25)	
9	27.2	5.1	40.0	26.4	40.0	10
						1 group
10	26.7	5.6	0	3.0	16.2	6 groups

[a] Months.

[b] Group enlarged to eight workers on January 15, 1971. Figures in parentheses refer to enlarged group.

All firms contacted in Turkey were from the private sector metal industry. Those firms not providing data did so because of lack of interest, unavailability of detailed records, lack of an occupational fit with the German sample, or non-comparable data over the period in which

Appendix Table 3

Summary of Sample Information by Occupation and Country

Occupation and Country	Sample Size	Average Age (years)	Average Education (years)	Average Prior Experience[a] (months)	Percent of Category with Prior Experience	Average Wage[b] (As of 12/30/70)	Percent Female
Machinists							
Turkey	16 2 groups	25.8	5.05	50.0	60.0	TL 3.702	0
Germany	23	32.1	7.00	41.2	50.9	DM 6.921	0
Welders							
Turkey	9	24.7	5.78	21.3	55.5	TL 4.303	0
Germany	12	31.8	5.58	17.0	33.3	DM 7.233	0
Assemblers							
Turkey	42 9 groups	24.2	5.21	8.0	14.2	TL 3.809	40.4
Germany	27	30.2	6.14	11.1	21.4	DM 6.688	0
Casters							
Turkey	11	23.4	5.53	10.4	27.2	TL 4.029	0
Germany	5	30.8	4.80	0	0	DM 6.782	0

a No experience information available for 12 machinists. Average experience and percentage with experience based on 6 workers only.

b Excludes TL 1.50 increase to workers in Firms 6 and 10 (given December 15, 1970).

observations were available (due to changes in industrial equipment or production processes).

All German firms contacted were also in branches of the metal industry. Those not offering information similarly did so because of lack of interest or major changes in production techniques or industrial equipment in the positions where Turks were employed. In addition, they frequently reported a small number of Turks in their employment or a lack of Turkish employees in positions where productivity was attributable to the individual.

In Appendix Tables 1, 2 and 3, the data are summarized. For a more detailed description of the procedures and the data itself, the reader is referred to Monson, 1972, pp. 28-46 and 113-139.

REFERENCES

Arrow, Kenneth J., 1962, The Economic Implications of Learning-by-Doing. *RESTUD*, 29:155-73.

Becker, Gary, 1964, *Human Capital*. National Bureau of Economic Research. New York.

Blackburn, J.M., 1936, *The Acquisition of Skill : An Analysis of Learning Curves*. Industrial Health Research Board, Report Number 73, London.

Griliches, H. Z, 1957, Hybrid Corn : An Exploration in the Economics of Technological Change. *Econometrica*, 25 : 501-22.

Hilgard, E. R., 1956, *Theories of Learning*. New York.

Kerr, Clark, John T. Dunlop, Frederick H. Harbison, and Charles Myers, 1960. *Industrialism and Industrial Management*. Harvard.

Monson, Terry D., 1972, Migration, Experience-Generated Learning and Infant Industries : A Case Study of Turkey. Ph.D. dissertation, University of Minnesota.

O.E.C.D., 1967, *Emigrant Workers Returning to Their Home Country*. Manpower and Social Affairs Directorate, Paris.

Republic of Turkey, State Planning Organization, 1969, *Second Five-Year Development Plan*, 1968-72. Ankara.

Slotkin, James S., 1969, *From Field to Factory—New Industrial Employees*. The Free Press, Glencoe, Illinois.

VI

MIGRANT WORKERS, WAGES AND LABOR MARKETS: AN ECONOMIC MODEL

Duncan R. Miller and İhsan Çetin

ABSTRACT

This chapter focuses on the individual emigrant Turkish worker and presents a model which attempts to explain why the average worker desires to migrate, the manner and timing in which he allocates his earnings abroad, and his aspirations upon return to Turkey. Workers' earnings abroad are disaggregated into a country and purpose matrix, namely (a) standard of living maintenance in Turkey and Germany and (b) asset accumulation in Turkey and Germany. Determinant social and economic factors are presented and analyzed.

Recent survey results are presented in an attempt to verify the major hypotheses of the model and ascertain major policy-oriented implications with special reference to (a) private rates of return, (b) employment impact, including skill acquisition and increased mobility, and (c) wealth effect in terms of utilization of savings. Because Turkey ranks as the primary supplier of emigrant labor to West Germany and workers' remittances represent the largest single source of foreign exchange earnings for Turkey, labor importation obviously has and will continue to have significant social and economic ramifications for both supplier and recipient economies.

6.1 Introduction [1]

Since its inception the recent international migration into and within the European community has given rise to socio-economic-political phenomena so large scale and multifaceted as to almost preclude comprehensive investigation. The dimensions of this labor movement yield implications far beyond simple employer demands and individual propensities to migrate. As a recent Council of Europe study indicates, labor force migration continues to have a momentous impact on both supplier and recipient economies. (Livi-Bacci, 1971). For example, between 1950

---

[1] The analysis in this article is restricted to Turkish workers, though obviously many of the observations and conclusions apply to other emigrant nationalities as well. For an overview of recent migration trends to Europe, see Livi-Bacci 1971 and McLin 1972. Detailed socio-economic data on emigrant Turkish workers as compared to 1) other foreign workers in Germany and 2) the domestic Turkish labor force are presented in Miller, 1971 b.

and 1965, total net emigration of the major Mediterranean labor supplying countries (Turkey, Portugal, Spain, Italy, Greece, and Yugoslavia),
Finland and Ireland represented a population movement equivalent to approximately one-quarter of their corresponding natural population
increase or, more importantly, in terms of economically active populations, an amount approaching one-half of their increase in labor force
new entrants. On the other hand, the scale of immigration into recipient
labor markets, as one impact indicator, can be gauged by the ratio of
increase in foreign workers to increase in the domestic work force. As
McLin reports, this ratio has averaged from about 22 percent for Belgium
to over 100 percent for West Germany. (McLin, 1972).

For present purposes, the West German experience is particularly
noteworthy since over 75 percent of Turkish emigrants reside there. The
macro impact of emigration on the Turkish economy is most evident in
two statistics, namely (1) the ratio of emigrants to the increase of the
economically active population, a measure of the impact on the Turkish
labor market, and (2) the relationship of workers' remittances to other
sources of foreign exchange, most notably exports. Although 1970 population census data are not yet available, calculations based on preliminary estimates indicate that between 1965 and 1970, emigration from
Turkey approached an amount equal to 50 percent of the increase in
total economically active population; furthermore, given historical labor
force participation ratios, emigration could easily represent amounts
exceeding 70 percent of the change in the active labor force.[2]

Remittances by emigrant workers have had an even more profound
impact on the Turkish economy, at least in terms of the balance of
payments. In fact, as Table 1 shows, workers' remittances have become
the largest single foreign exchange earner for Turkey. Consequently,
labor force migration into the European Community should be of
great concern to Turkish manpower and financial planners.

Although the Turkish Ministry of Labor recently established a special
directorate specifically oriented to emigrant workers, a comprehensive
emigrant worker policy has yet to be articulated. Unfortunately, even
though Turkish emigrant workers have been the subject of a number of

---

[2] Preliminary 15 percent sample results of the 1970 population census placed the
Turkish population at 35.7 million. Of this number, the economically active population (15 years of age and older) was 14.5 million, an increase of 976 thousand since
1965. Thus, gross emigration of some 485 thousand between 1965 and 1970 is equivalent to 49.3 percent of the increase in the economically active population.

scholarly investigations, a paucity of adequate data on all stages of this labor force transfer (before, during, and after migration) persists. Several surveys have been conducted to assess certain key socio-economic factors pertaining to workers either before or after migration, but except as reported elsewhere in this volume, no large scale investigation of extended duration has been undertaken throughout the whole time stream of the migration process. Indeed, no adequate data exist to indicate how many workers have returned. In fact, if Turkish manpower and financial planners are to integrate this labor migration phenomenon into the overall economic development planning for Turkey, a major effort in data collection and analysis is necessary. It is hoped that the analysis following will contribute to identifying the relevant variables and relationships to be investigated.

Table 1

Exports and Worker Remittances ($ Millions)

	1968	1969	1970	1971	1972
Major Exports					
Cotton	139.1	113.6	173.1	193.1	191.3
Tobacco	94.8	81.5	78.5	85.9	130.9
Nuts	84.0	115.2	95.6	92.3	125.3
Total Exports	496.4	536.8	588.5	676.6	885.0
Total Remittances	107.3	140.6	273.1	473.4	740.2
Export/Remittances (%)	21.6	26.2	46.4	70.0	83.6

The model presented in this chapter focuses on the individual emigrant Turkish worker and attempts to explain why the average worker desires to migrate, the manner and timing in which he allocates his earnings abroad, and his aspirations upon return to Turkey. It must be emphasized that, due to the lack of relevant data, the model remains hypothetical; however, existing evidence concerning possible determinant socio-economic factors is presented and some major policy issues are addressed.

6.2   *Emigrant Turkish Workers : A Framework for Analysis*

Among the major labor supplying nations, Turkey has experienced the most rapid increase in numbers in Germany as well as one of the most rapid increases in total workers' remittances. From January, 1963 to

January, 1973, Turkey's share of the foreign labor market in Germany increased from 4.0 to 22.4 percent respectively, or in absolute terms, from 32,962 to 528,239 workers over the same period. In fact, Turkey rose from the fifth largest supplier in 1963 to the largest supplier in 1972. Although total remittances for Turkey have grown fourfold since 1967, the average remittance per worker remains lowest of all the major labor supplying nations. This statistic may be misleading, however, since at least as far as the Turks are concerned, a stable pattern of asset accumulation and remittances seems to be occurring. Turks appear to allocate their earnings abroad for four major purposes, namely, (1) to maintain a certain standard of living for their dependents/family members remaining in Turkey, (2) to maintain a certain standard of living for the worker and his/her dependents residing in Germany, (3) to accumulate a certain level of assets (both liquid and durable) to bring back to Turkey upon return, and (4) to remit to Turkey for savings and investment purposes. Each of these purposes is described more fully below.

6.2.1 *Standard of Living Maintenance*

In Turkey : Since over 60 percent of the married emigrant workers do not take their spouses or children to Germany, earnings in the early period of employment in Germany are presumably devoted to maintaining a viable standard of living for their dependents at home. The same standard of living purpose may apply to other members of the extended family, especially elderly parents, and this process may therefore be applicable to unmarried emigrant workers as well. The amount of earnings devoted to standard of living maintenance is presumed to be a function of the size of the worker's family and the standard of living its members enjoy in Turkey.

In Germany : Analogous to the standard of living sought for family members in Turkey described above, emigrant workers seek for themselves a standard of living during their stay in Germany which ordinarily is presumed to be lower than that of their German counterparts. The amount of earning required for this purpose depends on the number of dependents residing in Germany, the length of stay the worker intends to spend in Germany, and, as will be articulated below, the amount of assets he expects to accumulate.

6.2.2 *Asset Accumulation*

6.2.2.1 *In Germany*

Asset accumulation is by far the most compelling factor for Turks desiring to go abroad; thus, it is largely to this end that they devote their earnings.[3] This process obviously varies from worker to worker, depending on earning capacity and desired asset balance. Moreover, the composition of the imported assets is not well documented but is generally believed to be in the form of foreign exchange (which by law must be converted to Turkish lira) and in goods such as automobiles, consumer durables and tools, the latter being included in the Turkish import statistics category labelled "imports with waivers." Asset accumulation in Germany consists of cash savings to be used for establishing a business in Turkey or acquiring consumer goods for sale there with the proceeds intended for investment or consumption purposes. It is assumed that many workers view temporary emigration as a means of paying off past debt accumulation and/or establishing a retirement fund for themselves and possibly their extended families as well. Consequently, after an acceptable standard of living has been attained, asset accumulation in Germany presumably becomes the major objective in the distribution of earnings. Moreover, the desired asset accumulation balance at least partially determines the standard of living in Germany, especially if the worker intends to remain there for only a relatively short period of time. As will be verified in Section III below, this asset accumulation fund is usually "remitted" to Turkey only upon the worker's return and represents, therefore, an accumulation of savings from the stock of past income rather than savings from a remitted yearly income flow.

6.2.2.2 In Turkey

It is further assumed that only after a worker has accumulated a desired stock of assets in Germany and achieved his standard of living maintenance in both Germany and Turkey is he then able to remit out of his yearly income (flow) for savings and investment purposes in Turkey. Consequently, this type of asset accumulation may well have a two to five year lag before funds are remitted to Turkey. Asset accumulation in Germany and in Turkey therefore differ in terms of end use and gestation period.

A complicating factor may arise in that money market differentials, either in exchange rates, interest rates, or general investment terms, may

---

[3] In this analysis it is assumed that emigrant workers have or could obtain employment in Turkey, even if in the form of disguised unemployment in the agriculture or service sectors. Therefore, the determination to emigrate is not for the most part a function of employment opportunities; rather, as elaborated later, it is a function of the real wage differential between Turkey and Germany.

induce workers to devote part, if not all, of these funds for savings and investment in Germany during the period they are in residence there. Thus, official transfer data do not necessarily represent an accurate statement of the emigrant workers' transactions in foreign exchange.

Schematically, the above can be presented in terms of a country and purpose matrix as follows :

Country

Purpose	Germany	Turkey
Standard of Living	S_1	S_2
Asset Accumulation	A_1	A_2

S_1 = the standard of living maintenance purpose in Germany, A_1 = asset accumulation in Germany, and S_2 and A_2 are the same factors in Turkey. This scheme is also useful to understand more clearly the actual remittance process since remittances made while the worker is abroad can be represented by S_2 and A_2. Finally, as a first step in deciding the relevant variables to be studied, the following model is presented which model summarizes the hypothesized relationships expected to explain remittances : [4]

$$R = Nr_{S_2} + Nr_{A_2} + Nr_{A_1}$$

R = the total remittances of Turkish workers from Germany in any one year, N = the total number of Turkish workers in Germany, rS_2 = rate of average remittances per worker for S_2 purposes, rA_2 = rate of average remittances per worker for A_2 purposes, and rA_1 = rate of average remittances per worker for A_1 purposes.

To make the model fully understandable, the following second order functions are presented.

---

[4] A somewhat similar model for Yugoslavia is under investigation by the IBRD (Hume, 1970). Additionally, the IBRD presents a migration flow equation as follows :
$$M_t = f (I_t, U_t, E_t, D_t, t)$$
M = the yearly flow of migrants, I = an index of economic growth of the recipient country, U = the level of unemployment in the recipient country, E = the real wage differential, t = the time trend, and D = a dummy variable to represent labor transfer institutional arrangements between the sending and receiving countries. The relationships shown by the model presented in this chapter are not expressed in a lagged form; however, further research may reveal a lagged relationship to be more accurate.

	In Germany	*In Turkey*
Standard of Living	$S_1 = f_1 (D_1, Y, A_1)$	$S_2 = f_2 (D_2, Y)$

	In Germany	*In Turkey*
Asset Accumulation	$A_1 = f_3 (L, W, I)$	$A_2 = f_4 (A_1, S_1, S_2, E)$

$D_1 =$ the number of dependents in Germany (including the worker himself),

$D_2 =$ the number of dependents in Turkey,

$Y =$ the domestic (Turkish) per capita income,

$L =$ the length of intended stay in Germany,

$W =$ the real wage differential between Turkey and Germany,

$E =$ money market differentials,

$I =$ an institutional arrangements factor to account for encouragement/discouragement/prohibition of imports from Germany (A_1), i.e., rearrangement of the Turkish import with waiver or tax system.

The expected relationships between these variables are presented below in the form of a set of hypotheses :

Hypotheses concerning S_1

H_1 — the more the dependents in Germany (D_1), the greater the distribution of earnings for German-based living. The actual level of German-based living is expected to be greatly influenced by the Turkish standard of living; in fact,

H_2 — it is presumed that Y represents a minimum level (floor) in the determination of S_1 balances, each calculated per worker or dependent. In other words, the worker will probably not desire to live much "worse off" than he did in Turkey but he may well desire to live somewhat "better off"; consequently, the lower the domestic per capita income, the less necessary are standard of living balances for German-based living.

Hypotheses concerning S_2

H_3 — the greater the number of dependents at home (D_2), the more the remittances for standard of living maintenance in Turkey (S_2); hence, the greater the rS_2.

H_4 — since it is presumed that emigrant workers do not emulate German standards of living (demonstration effect) for themselves and dependents in Germany and certainly not for their dependents at home, the lower the domestic (Turkish) per capita income (Y) as compared to other emigrant workers' domestic incomes, the lower the remittances for standard of living purposes.

Hypotheses concerning A_1

H_5 — the greater the desired A_1 asset balance, the lesser the amount of earnings available for S_1 purposes, at least above the minimum constraint of Y.

H_6 — the shorter the length of stay, the more rapidly the worker will attempt to accumulate his desired (ex ante) A_1 balance. Hence, L determines the rate of accumulation rather than the level of desired A_1 assets; however, the actual (ex post) level of A_1 may be influenced by the actual length of stay. Specifically, as L increases (decreases), the ex post A_1 balance may increase (decrease).

H_7 — the greater the real wage differential (W) at each skill level, the greater the amount of earnings devoted for A_1 purposes. Consequently, if the wage differential falls or if Turkey should send workers whose wage differential is relatively low (presumably highly skilled workers), then the desire for A_1 assets should decrease somewhat since these goods would no longer be as much of a luxury as before.

H_8 — the greater the ease of importing A_1 (hereinafter represented by the factor 1), the greater the A_1 balance. In fact, the composition of A_1 assets may well be determined by institutional factors of the Turkish import system. As long as the resale market in Turkey for automobiles and consumer durables remains buoyant, workers will shift the composition of the A_1 assets to reflect the demand in this resale market. Any adverse change (from the standpoint of the worker) in the import system may force workers to seek illegal or extralegal imports rather than increase A_2 remittances.

Hypothesis concerning A_2

H_9 — the greater the money market differentials, the greater the incentive to devote A_2 balances for savings and investment purposes abroad, where the incentives to invest abroad are greater than at home.

The fact that A_2 remittances are treated as a type of residual has important implications for labor migration policy formulation; moreover, to date most students of this labor migration phenomenon have tended to assume that remittances constitute a large share of earnings abroad and that most, if not all remittances are for investment purposes—i.e., they tend to equate R with A_2. If this analysis is correct, three major areas of research appear necessary : 1) estimation of the parameters explaining the marginal propensities to consume and save out of total income—i.e., attempts to calculate S_1, S_2, A_1, and A_2 coefficients; 2) investigation of the final use of accumulated assets, especially liquid assets; and 3) analysis of the implications of any change in the characteristics of migrants for the asset-remittance system—i.e., would an increase in relatively less educated, rural farm laborers drastically alter the levels and composition of assets accumulated and remittances sent. Although the severe lack of data vitiates present attempts to conduct such analyses, a survey of existing information and resultant policy implications is presented below.

6.3   Review of Survey Results [5]

Three areas of concern are addressed in this section. Although comprehensive data are not available, recent survey results are reviewed in an attempt to verify or abandon key assumptions of the model presented above. Of particular concern are (1) determination of which factors induce workers to migrate, (2) calculations of average propensities to consume and save and gross private rates of return in terms of increased earnings, and (3) tendencies of workers upon return with respect to utilization of earnings and employment.

The propelling force inducing Turkish workers to emigrate appears to be quite clear. According to Aker, over 75 percent go in order to accumulate greater wealth whereas only about one out of nine go due to unemployment or job dissatisfaction (Aker, 1972: 94). Similar low levels of unemployment are indicated in most other studies as well.[6]

---

[5] Data presented in this section are drawn almost exclusively from Aker, 1972. Although the authors would like to acknowledge the cooperation of the Bosphorus University Department of Economics staff for allowing use of their data, the authors alone remain accountable for any errors of omission or commission. The Aker study is based on a sample of 590 emigrants interviewed just prior to their departure from Turkey during 1970-71.

[6] Unofficial analysis of an unpublished State Planning Organization (SPO) survey of returned workers indicates levels of unemployment as low as three percent for urban

Since the Aker data represents workers in only one time period of the migration stream (before migration but not during the periods abroad and upon return), it cannot be used to statistically test the model above; however, it does yield valuable insights as to the underlying causal factors affecting the migration process. In order to quantify the emigrant workers' ability to accumulate assets, the data was disaggregated into the three monthly income groups 0-499, 500-999, and 1,000 TL and above (see Appendix Table 1 for mean values). Incomes for the period abroad are at the expected levels, and are corroborated closely by data obtained as part of independent surveys of returned workers.[7] The additional earnings for work abroad are discounted for five years at the eight percent Central Bank rate of discount and then divided by the before-migration annual Turkish salary to yield crude measures of private rates of return by income group.

Table 2

Income Differentials Due to Migration by Income Class

Income Group in Turkey		(Discounted Additional Earnings)/ (Annual Turkish Salary)
0-499	Low	130.6
	Median	67.1
	High	40.9
500-999	Low	44.6
	Median	22.3
	High	20.1
1000 and over	Low	16.5
	Median	9.5
	High	5.5

The above calculations do not include the necessary capital outlays to emigrate, estimated at an average of 1,670 TL (Aker, 1972: 98), nor income foregone due to possible advancement in Turkey, but they do

migrants and seven percent for rural migrants. These are low levels indeed given the 12 to 18 percent overt unemployment in Turkey, not to mention a very visual though immeasurable disguised unemployment in agriculture. For a review of employment trends in Turkey, see Miller, 1971 b.

[7] For instance, the Aker study reports average incomes before migration of about 9,120 T.L. yearly and 34,100 abroad whereas the unpublished SPO survey of returned workers indicates levels of 6,726 before and 27,980 while abroad.

reveal some highly significant private rates of return, especially at the lowest income levels. This is to say, in other words, that when income differentials are discounted at eight percent, emigrant workers earn from 10 to 70 times more than if they had not emigrated. Given reported estimates of marginal propensities to save of approximately 0.46, workers can save monthly amounts ranging from slightly greater than their total monthly income before migration to the order of magnitude of five times monthly income in Turkey.[8]

In an attempt to verify these income-expenditure-savings levels, the authors utilized consumption data for one medium sized and one large city in Turkey and estimated consumption requirements there (S_2 standard of living maintenance for Turkey). Furthermore, based on present estimates of expenditure levels of Turkish migrants in Germany, S_1 requirements were estimated for each income group. Thus, savings levels for each income group were calculated, the results of which are presented in Table 3.[9]

Table 3

Monthly Income — Expenditure — Savings
by Income Group in Turkey

	0-499		500-999		1000 and Over	
	Amount	%	Amount	%	Amount	%
Monthly Income	2486	—	3069	—	3278	—
S_2 needs	194	7.8	554	18.1	937	28.6
S_1 needs	917	36.9	1132	36.9	1171	35.7
$A_1 + A_2$	1375	55.3	1383	45.1	1170	35.7

Though admittedly crude, such calculations nevertheless appear to be consistent with earlier estimates. They indicate that the expenditures of Turkish workers abroad are low indeed and may even include purchases of some consumer durables (A_1 assets). While these estimates do not dis-

---

[8] G.E. Völker reports results of German studies which indicate a marginal propensity to save of 0.455 in 1967. He also reports that by German standards, 46 percent of Turkish workers are classified as either skilled or semi-skilled.

[9] Estimates of consumption by income level in Turkey are based on the State Institute of Statistics publication, Results of the Survey of Consumer Expenditures in Izmir and Eskişehir, 1972.

aggregate A_1 and A_2 assets, unofficial SPO estimates indicate that some 64 percent of all savings are brought to Turkey by the worker himself (A_2) with relatively few being remitted through the banking system while the worker is abroad (A_1).

The employment impact of migration in terms of skill acquisition and increased mobility are difficult to assess. Nevertheless, estimates of German and Turkish-based learning curves by Monson in this volume indicate that learning, especially experience generated on the job, was much more rapid in Germany than Turkey. In terms of skill utilization and mobility, Aker found that only 11.6 percent of the workers reported being employed in the same occupation before, during and after migration whereas 48.8 percent indicated the same occupational status before and after but not during migration. (Aker, 1972). The data in Table 4, disaggregated by employment sector and income class, exhibit similar trends. The only perceptible trend in terms of mobility appears in the highest income group where those who were predominantly wage earners before emigration show preferences for a more balanced distribution in services and as artisans upon return.

Table 4

Employment Before and After Emigration by Income Groups

Employment Before Emigration		Preferred Employment Upon Return:				
		Agriculture	Artisan	Services	Wage Earner	Undecided
Income Group : 0-499 (TL)						
Agriculture	33.3	28.3	—	20.0	—	46.7
Artisan	12.8	4.3	39.1	13.0	—	30.4
Services	5.0	11.1	—	55.6	—	22.2
Wage Earner	27.8	4.0	14.0	28.0	8.0	42.0
Income Group : 500-999 (TL)						
Agriculture	8.8	27.3	13.6	18.2	—	36.7
Artisan	11.6	—	51.7	10.3	—	31.0
Services	4.8	—	—	50.0	—	25.0
Wage Earner	61.0	3.9	8.5	23.5	17.0	42.5
Income Group : 1000 and Over (TL)						
Agriculture	7.5	16.7	—	25.0	—	50.0
Artisan	15.1	4.2	50.0	8.3	8.3	16.7
Services	5.0	—	12.5	50.0	—	37.5
Wage Earner	66.0	4.8	14.3	22.0	24.9	24.8

The purported benefits of massive inflows of foreign exchange to Turkey are also less than obvious. Clearly, there has been some inflationary impact, but examination of the magnitude and incidence of this phenomenon are beyond the scope of the current inquiry. Existing data do indicate that, contrary to the commonly-held view, relatively few of the workers devote A_1 or A_2 assets to create new investment or industrial capacity. In fact, only slightly over 26 percent of workers residing in urban areas invested in work ventures, and the mean amount declared was just over 25,000 TL. Ministry of Labor data indicate the following distribution among work venture types : craftsmen-services (electrician, plumber, welder, painter, etc.), 12.3 percent; entertainment and other services (cinema, restaurant, hotel, tea house, etc.), 17.2 percent; retail trade (overwhelmingly reputed to be grocery stores) 45.0 percent; production facilities (furniture making, shoes, textile and clothing, etc.) 15.4 percent; and other unclassified types 10.1 percent. (İş ve İşçi Bulma Kurumu, 1969).

It is also widely reported that migration relieves the chronic unemployment problem within Turkey. Again, though clearly some unemployment is alleviated, this situation too is less than obvious. The proportion of emigrants unemployed at time of emigration was less than half of the national average and declared skills were quite high; moreover, as shown in Table 5 the educational level of migrants was significantly higher than that for the nation as a whole.

Table 5

Educational Attainment of Migrants and Domestic Labor Force

	Migrants[a]		Domestic[b] 1965 Economically Active
Graduates of	TES	AKER	Population — Males
Primary	60.5	63.7	39.1
Secondary	2.5	3.2	3.4
Vocational	1.4	4.7	2.0
Lise	0.6	1.2	1.4
Higher	n.a.	n.a.	1.6

Sources :

[a] Turkish Employment Service, 1969: 11; Aker, 1972: 35.

[b] Miller and Çetin, "Regional Variations in Educational Attainment in Turkey", United States Agency for International Development, 1973, *Economic Staff Paper No. 12.*

Thus, educational attainment and skill data imply more of a brain than a brawn drain, especially in terms of those who might be upgraded by domestic training.

These observations generally reflect a situation which might lead one to conclude that, at the micro level, private returns to individual migrants are quite sizeable; yet, at the same time private entrepreneurs in Turkey are undoubtedly incurring higher costs and/or lower marginal productivity due to increased labor turnover and skilled labor losses. The macro impact, in terms of the widening and deepening of human and physical capital, is less clear but does not appear as optimistic as popularly reported. In the event Turkey continues to send large numbers of skilled workers to foreign labor markets, a comprehensive policy review may be warranted, especially in light of her forthcoming partnership in the European community.

Predictions as to the characteristics of future emigration from Turkey are fraught with difficulties; however, if Turkey attempts to meet increasing demands for skilled workers in Western Europe, she will do so only at greater costs to her own industrial development. Turkey's prospects for economic development may well hinge upon her utilizing the nation's scarcest resource (skilled labor) more effectively. That over 46 percent of her emigrant workers are, by German standards, classified as skilled or semiskilled would seem from this point of view a rather startling phenomenon and one inconsistent with Turkey's long range development goals.

REFERENCES

1. Aker, Ahmet, 1972, İşçi Göçü. Istanbul, Sander Yayınlari.
2. Livi-Bacci, M., 1971, *Report on the Demographic and Social Pattern of Migrants in Europe, Especially with Regard to International Migrations.* Strasbourg, Council of Europe.
3. Hume, I.M., 1970, *Migrant Workers in Western Europe.* Washington, D.C., International Bank for Reconstruction and Development.
4. İş ve İşçi Bulma Kurumu, 1969, *Yurt Dışındaki Türk İşçileri ve Dönüş Eğilimleri.* Ankara.
5. McLin, Jon, 1972, *International Migrations and the European Community.* New York, American Universities Field Staff.
6. Miller, Duncan, 1971a, "Emigrant Turkish Workers—A Framework for Analysis". *Studies in Development*, Fall, 529-541.
7. Miller, Duncan, 1971b, "Emigrant Turkish Workers : A Socio-Economic Analysis". In D. Miller, (ed.), *Essays on Labor Force and Employment in Turkey.* Ankara, United States Agency for International Development.

VII

INTERNATIONAL LABOR MIGRATION
AND TURKISH ECONOMIC DEVELOPMENT

Tufan Kolan

ABSTRACT

For determining the manner and extent to which migration assists or hinders economic development in a labor-exporting country, the case of Turkey is studied as a model of a developing economy with a large labor surplus. The adoption of a migration policy by the Turkish government is viewed as an effort to simultaneously relieve unemployment pressures and build up foreign exchange reserves.

Due to the unavailability of sufficiently detailed data with which to carry out a formal cost-benefit analysis of the effects of migration upon Turkish economic development, an assessment is made of the actual or anticipated impact of migration upon (1) gross national product and gross domestic product, (2) capital formation, (3) employment, (4) labor productivity, and (5) per capita income. Each of these five indices of economic development is treated first with regard to theoretical considerations followed by empirical investigations.

The favorable movements of the indicators imply that, at the very least, migration policy has not had adverse effects on Turkish economic development.

7.1 Introduction

For determining the manner and extent to which migration assists or hinders economic development in a labor-exporting country, this chapter studies the case of Turkey as a model of a developing economy with a large labor surplus.

Turkey is one of the major suppliers of labor to western Europe and it appears this condition will continue to prevail for some time. Whereas the specific factors giving rise to Turkey's large scale export of labor are numerous, they can generally be grouped under structural unemployment.

The years 1950 to 1970 represent a period of unprecedented economic change in modern Turkish history.[1] During this time span the country experienced a population boom. Agriculture was modernized, and the extensive use of the tractor and other mechanized agricultural implements

---

[1] Tevfik Çavdar, "Türkiye'de Şehirleşme Hareketleri" (manuscript, June 1965), pp. 55-64.

began to displace manpower. Significantly larger investments were made in highways and other infrastructure, resulting in increased mobility of the population. These factors all contributed to rapid and premature urbanization.

During the period 1955-59, employment showed a sharp increase. Due to low foreign exchange reserves, imports had been curtailed in 1954. Consequently, import-substituting industries mushroomed and created job slots for many unemployed, particularly those who had migrated to the cities.

In 1958 after devaluation of the Turkish lira, import doors were re-opened and the small manufacturing industries, which could not meet foreign competition, gradually closed down. The displaced labor force was sizeable and became a burden for the economy. As a result, employment policy for the decade following had to be directed largely towards meeting this development problem.

Turkish development policy attempted to meet the unemployment problem in two ways. The Five Year Plans—beginning in 1963—were oriented toward developing employment opportunities within the country by encouraging and stimulating industrialization. The second thrust was to enter into bilateral agreements with labor-scarce countries to enable Turkish workers to migrate and thus relieve the unemployment pressure.

The choice of migration as a policy tool was largely fortuitous. The burgeoning demand for labor in western Europe drew migrants from all the periphery countries, including many Turks—the latter initially on an informal basis. In 1961 the Turkish government endorsed this continuing movement by formal policy agreements with Germany. The number of Turks abroad increased year by year (except for the recession year 1967) until the number stood at 654,467 at the end of 1972, over 4 percent of the Turkish domestic labor force.

The magnitude of this movement has caused polarization of opinion in the Turkish parliament, among decision-makers, trade unions, employers' associations, and the general public regarding the wisdom of sending labor abroad.

Migration, like most policies, is a mixed blessing. Both the size of the migrant stock already in Europe and the backlog of applicants awaiting recruitment—each numbering in the hundreds of thousands—indicate that despite the personal costs of leaving one's country and living abroad, often at sub-standard levels and under social tensions, the potential for saving and realizing other objectives promises an even greater pay-off. However, without further evidence it is not possible to make either a similar or opposite claim for the national economy from which the migrants depart.

It is apparent that migration will yield benefits and accrue costs to the sending country, but the extent to which one exceeds the other is by no means obvious and constitutes a subject for investigation. Since labor-exporting countries have, for the most part, developing economies with fewer cushions to withstand the negative effects of migration than a developed economy, it is particularly important that a balance sheet of the assets and liabilities of the movement be made. The concern of this chapter is primarily with this need—namely, the effect of migration policy upon economic growth and development.

One method for assessing the effects of migration on a nation's social and economic well-being is formal cost-benefit analysis. However, supporting data from Turkey are not sufficiently detailed to conduct such formal analysis. Even if better data were available, it would be difficult in assessing effects at the national level to avoid double counting the costs and benefits measured in other spheres—e.g., government, business enterprise, the individual. A complete analysis would also reflect social and hidden economic costs, many of which are difficult to estimate and price.

Rather than set forth a formal cost-benefit analysis, the discussion will attempt to assess the actual or anticipated impact of migration upon five generally accepted indices of economic development : (1) gross national product (GNP) and gross domestic product (GDP), (2) capital formation, (3) employment, (4) labor productivity, and (5) per capita income. Each will be treated first with regard to theoretical considerations followed by empirical investigations.

7.2 *Effects of International Labor Migration upon Economic Development : Theoretical Considerations*

7.2.1 *Effects on GNP and GDP*

GNP is defined as the total value, at current market prices, of all goods and services produced in the country during the year. Subtracting net factor payments to foreigners yields GDP.

The effect of migration on GDP is the net of the following effects :

(a) There is an initial loss in domestic output (or opportunity cost of output foregone). Domestic output presumably would have been greater had the migrants remained working in Turkey. If the general labor market condition is one of labor surplus, this loss may be slight. The relevant consideration is a qualitative one. If the more efficient workers leave first, there is a net loss equal to the difference between the output they would have produced and the output of those who are recruited from the residual labor force to replace them. If unemployed workers migrate, the output loss is nil.

(b) Some marginal rise in service output might occur in transportation and government sectors as migrants prepare to leave the country. Moreover, there might be a small net gain or loss, plus a shift in geographic distribution, in consumption expenditures of those dependents who do not accompany the worker abroad but return to parents, in-laws or other relatives.

(c) In the medium term, one must consider any increment in production (and the timing of it) which results from the difference in output of returned migrants over what these same workers would have produced had they never migrated. Migrants who have received training abroad and hence are more efficient upon their return than they would have been after an equivalent stay in Turkey, produce a net gain which offsets losses described in (a) above. This, of course, presumes that their skills are utilized upon return; if newly acquired skills are not or cannot be put to productive use, there will be no offsetting gain.

(d) In the long term, the product lost from those working outside the country is offset also by increases in output generated by workers' remitted and repatriated capital. This effect might include government investment made possible by increased income from remittances and captured by the government through taxation.

(e) GNP would be augmented to the extent that remittances from migrants are greater than any foregone output which would have reduced GDP.

7.2.2   Effects on Capital Formation

Capital formation depends on the rate of saving or surplus—i.e., on the amount of the year's product not consumed. There are two related concerns : the gross amount of capital formation, and its distribution among uses with different productive potentials. Widely different uses of a given amount of saving can be made, with vastly different implications for the future output of the Turkish nation.

(a) The primary effect of migration is on the aggregate amount of savings. The amount of remittances, and savings temporarily held abroad but not remitted, is large and indicates generation of considerable non-consumed surplus. A certain amount of this surplus goes for domestic consumption when remittances are received by the worker's dependents. Another fraction is presumably converted to forced savings by the Turkish government through income or other forms of taxation. The remainder will remain as private savings. In any event, whether saved or spent, most of the money eventually reaches Turkey in the form of hard currency which provides medium for imports.

(b) To the extent that surplus captured by the government is used for capital investment purposes instead of current government expenditure items, capital will be developed. Moreover, conversion of hard currencies through the central bank gives the government the use of these currencies for capital purchases abroad.

If used as seed money for industrial development, this government investment might in the long term prove the most important benefit from the migration program even though over the short-to-medium term its effect on GNP might be small. On the other hand, if remittances are dispersed or dribbled away in private or public expenditures which do not improve infrastructure or capital investment of Turkish industry, the long-range benefits will be small or nonexistent. Policy-wise, while it would be the migration program which would provide the wherewithal, it would in fact be the private and public investment programs which would determine the kind and amount of benefits to be derived.

Repatriated savings are often used by returning workers to establish their own businesses. Such small businesses could dilute the productivity of Turkish industry by reducing its scale and by giving those workers with skills suitable for use in large combines the opportunity to work in lower-yielding self-employment.

(c) Human capital formation can be discussed in much the same way, but as investment capital formation its measurement is much less precise. The increase in human capital represented by foreign training and experience would have negligible effects on the Turkish economy if it were not put to use, and indeed might prove negative if highly trained workers were to return to find insufficient jobs which would employ their skills. For those workers who remain abroad, the Turkish government's investment in their training represents a net loss unless their remittances exceed the excess of what they would have produced in Turkey over what they would have consumed. Over the short run, this effect could be positive, but it cannot be assumed that they would continue to remit at present high levels for the duration of their working lives.

(d) Capital formation is meaningless without a skilled labor force.

Migration could thus impede or restrict the potential quality of industry made possible by it if skilled persons remain away from Turkey too long or emigrate permanently.

(e) Possible uses of private capital suggest that the government might take steps to develop the capital market by establishing savings banks or associations to assist the pooling of privately held capital. These associations would be able to invest in government or private bonds and thus facilitate the transfer of private capital to productive uses. As indicated above, the size of the benefit would depend primarily on the nature of investment policy, with the migration program providing the seed money.

7.2.3 Effects on Employment

Development depends in part on full use of a country's human resources. To a certain degree, employment levels depend on the extent of physical capital. This is more true the more fixed the capital-labor ratios are in the sense that there is little substitutability between capital and labor. To the degree that migration leads to increased capital formation, employment prospects will be improved.

In the short run, migration policy could reduce both employment and unemployment. Many unemployed will leave, but so will many employed. Because of their skills many of those who were employed before migrating may be very difficult to replace.

When vacated job slots are filled, training may often be a prerequisite. As replacement occurs it is possible that net employment might increase in the short run if it becomes necessary to employ less skilled replacements on more than a one-to-one basis to sustain the same output. Output might be lowered if hiring the necessary number of less skilled workers proved too expensive or available capital equipment did not permit it.

If given the choice, the receiving nation employing Turkish workers will recruit the most skilled and highly motivated. While the Turkish government is making an effort to control the skill mix of migrants and to encourage the emigration of the unemployed, the skill and motivation of the domestic labor force will inevitably be lowered while the migrants are abroad. Further, to the extent that types of labor are complementary and persons with skills in critical demand migrate, the complementary, lesser skilled workers may become unemployed or underemployed.

7.2.4 *Effects on Labor Productivity*

The growth of output per man-year is a critical element in economic growth and development. In a fully employed economy having a static labor force, this element represents the only potential source of economic growth. Productivity increases are complex phenomena resulting from increases in physical and human capital, innovation, and economies of scale.

(a) Increases in physical capital have been discussed above under capital accumulation. As far as growth of human capital in concerned, the question is one of the quality of the migrant and his pattern of migration. As many of the more highly qualified workers move to take advantage of higher wages in the labor-importing countries, an initial drain in skills will occur. If returning workers possess greater skills than before their departure, a reverse flow will then take place. Productivity, however, will depend upon the migrant's ability to use these new skills in Turkey. To the extent that these skills permit greater output per man-year than would otherwise have been possible had the migrant remained in Turkey, a net gain accrues. In the final analysis, it is a question of who stays and who returns.

(b) Innovation in the form of technological change could be adversely affected if the most innovative groups leave and do not return. On the other hand, such groups could return better trained after an experience abroad. Technology can also be imported to the extent that it is embodied in capital goods. In this case innovation depends upon the availability of the necessary labor skills to complement capital imports.

(c) In the short run, economies of scale could be reduced by the departure of skilled workers. In the long run, however, capital formation resulting from migration together with the presence of returned workers possessing augmented skills acquired abroad might allow greater economies of scale. Again, much would depend on who leaves and who returns, and how domestic businesses adjust to their absence.

Generally it might be said then that as the cream of the labor force migrates, migration policy would have the effect of reducing output per man. Only as these workers return and their augmented skills are effectively employed would productivity rise above what it would have been in the absence of migration. Again, the realization of increased productivity depends upon the appropriate combination of the new skills and capital investment to make their utilization possible.

7.2.5   *Effects on Per Capita Income*

One measure of economic development is the level of per capita income. The essence of the following analysis is the distinction between working and dependent populations within the country, and how migration can affect the status and income of people within these populations.

For purposes of the present analysis, any person producing less than the average national per capita income is considered among the dependent population. This includes all unemployed children, wives not employed outside the household, the aged, disabled, unemployed, and those who work but earn less than the average per capita income. By definition, it should be clear that the dependent population must be supported by the economically active population. Depending upon individual circumstances, support will derive from the extended family, government, or private charitable agencies.

The effect of migration on this process is illustrated in its most general form by Chart 1. It is assumed that the average per capita income level in real terms is shown by the line aa′ which rises over time to indicate presumed increases in the living standard. Line bb′, which also rises over time, represents the annual real wage the worker could earn in Turkey. The difference between the two lines is the amount of "surplus" he earns—i.e., the amount which he contributes to the per capita income of those who do not work.

In the case of the average, economically active migrant, his departure to the labor-importing countries contributes to the lowering of the average per capita income level by the amount of surplus he generates in his job in Turkey—i.e., the distance between aa′ and bb′. Should he make no remittances while abroad, the amount of the lost surplus represents an opportunity cost to Turkey resulting from his emigration. In the case of a migrant who was unemployed, his departure in and of itself contributes to raising the per capita income level since it represents his withdrawal from the dependent population. Similarly, the migration of a person earning less than aa′ per year would also represent an "opportunity gain" for Turkey.

Presumably the migrant would earn more in Europe than in Turkey as indicated by the broken line cc′ covering the period spent abroad (t_2-t_3). If during that time period he makes remittances shown by the shaded area between aa′ and bb′, the country neither gains nor loses from his migration. Should his remittances exceed that amount, then the per capita income in Turkey is increased during the period of his absence. The latter observation applies *a fortiori* in the case of a migrant unemployed before departure.

[Chart 1]

Earnings of Economically Active Worker in Turkey and Abroad
Compared with Typical Earnings and Per Capita Income
Paths in Turkey

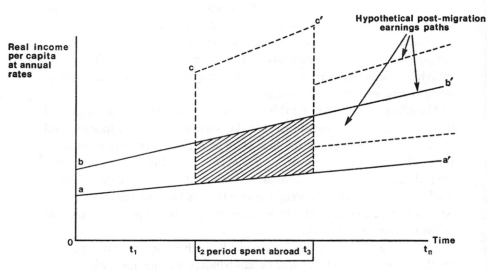

aa': Average per capita income in Turkey
bb': Typical earnings path of migrant if he remains in Turkey
cc': Earnings of worker while abroad

Upon his return to Turkey, the effects of migration on per capita income levels will depend on the relation between his actual earnings path and line bb' (the presumed earnings path had he never migrated). Should his post-migration earnings follow the lower path aa', the difference between aa' and bb' represents an opportunity cost and must be substracted from any gains which accrued during his period abroad. Should they follow a higher path, the country would stand to gain twice—both by remittances while abroad (if higher than the shaded area) and by higher post-migration earnings.

This analysis ignores the out-of-pocket costs involved in migrating, the effects of interruptions in earnings occasioned by shifting from a job in Turkey to one in Europe and back. In effect, out-of-pocket costs should be adjusted by deduction from net earnings (cc' or bb') during the relevant period.

For Turkey the most cogent concern undoubtedly lies in the height and shape of the post-migration earnings path. Present fragmentary evidence indicates that migrants earn proportionately more after returning from Europe than they did in their pre-migration jobs. Considering the training and skills acquired in Europe, this is not surprising. The task incumbent upon the Turkish government is to take such actions as will enable savings accumulated by migrants to be properly mobilized to the end that newly-acquired skills are productively combined with appropriate capital equipment. Should this occur in the future, the post-migration earnings curve will both lie above bb' and diverge from it as earnings both start out higher and grow faster.

By concentrating on the migrant, this analysis ignores some effects which are difficult to portray in a single graph. For example, if types of labor are complementary, the departure of migrants may reduce the productivity of other workers with whom they previously had worked. Moreover, migration could create labor shortages in critical sectors, cause workers in other sectors to become unemployed or underemployed and the scale of some operations to be reduced. Any such reductions in productivity should be included as opportunity costs. On the other hand, if the migrants' job slots are filled by workers previously unemployed or underemployed thereby reducing the size of the dependent population, the opportunity cost of migration is lessened and per capita income increased.

7.3   *Effects of International Labor Migration upon Economic Development : Empirical Investigations*

7.3.1   *Effects on GNP and GDP*

The theoretical effects of migration on GNP or GDP have been discussed above. Whether the theoretical effects are observed in practice will depend on two factors : the quality of the data and magnitude of migration. On both counts the prospects do not seem good for detailing precisely what effects, if any, migration has on these aggregates. However, the available evidence does suggest that these effects have not been unfavorable for Turkey, at least in the short term.

The basic evidence on real GDP is given in Table 1. GDP has the advantage of showing output attributable to the domestic labor force.

It is here rather than in GNP that output decreases resulting from erosion in the quality of the domestic labor force would be manifested.

Table 1 may be viewed in two parts—the first representing the pre-migration period (1953-61), and the second encompassing the migration years (1962-70). In the first period, real GDP grew at an average rate of 3.7 percent per year as compared to 6.1 percent during the migration period. Because of the size of the agricultural sector, and the fact that fluctuations in agricultural product are for the most part not dependent on the quantity or quality of labor input, the inclusion of this sector can conceal the effects of migration on GDP. It is useful, therefore, also to compare non-agricultural product for the two periods. Here the differences more dramatically favor the migration policy.

During the first period, average growth in non-agricultural product was 5.3 percent per year; in the second, 8.0 percent per year. The first period saw non-agricultural growth averaging 2.4 percent per year between 1953 and 1955, and rising to almost 8.0 percent per year between 1955 and 1959, then slowing to 3.5 percent between 1959 and 1961. Since then, growth has risen to about 9.0 percent per year each year after 1965. The same general picture is shown in the individual industrial sectors. Manufacturing and construction, two sectors in which labor migration might ordinarily cripple output by creating skill shortages, have grown faster since migration policy was implemented. Infusions of capital, made possible by migrants' hard currency remittances, could have offset the drain of human capital.

The preceding discussion indicates that migration seems to have been associated with no measurable slackening in the rate of growth of GDP. This growth is attributable to such factors as population expansion, capital accumulation, migration itself, and general growth in the other economies.

Effects of migration on GNP are treated below in the discussion of GNP per capita. In general it may be said that migration helps GNP directly by improving the balance on net factor payments to foreigners. This holds true, however, only so long as GDP is not reduced as a result of the outflow of productive workers. Table 1 has shown that in fact GDP is not reduced by migration, and that the additions to GNP represent net gains (and, indeed, may understate the true gains).

Effects of migration on the balance of payments—and hence indirectly on GNP—may be inferred from Tables 2 and 3. They show, from the international balance side, the three phases of Turkish economic growth

Table 1

Turkish National Product at Constant Producer's Values, 1953-70

(in thousands of 1968 Turkish Liras)

	1953	1955	1958	1959	1960	1961	1962	1963	1964	1965	1966	1967	1968	1969	1970
Agriculture, forestry, hunting, and fishing	22.8	20.0	26.3	26.3	26.3	25.6	27.1	29.2	29.2	28.1	31.5	31.7	33.7	33.7	34.2
Mining and quarrying	.9	.9	1.1	1.0	1.0	1.1	1.0	1.1	1.3	1.3	1.6	1.6	1.8	2.2	2.2
Manufacturing	6.1	6.7	7.8	8.3	8.3	8.6	9.3	10.2	10.9	12.1	13.3	15.1	16.3	17.7	18.2
Construction	3.9	3.4	4.5	4.8	4.8	4.3	4.6	4.9	5.4	5.6	6.3	6.8	7.5	8.1	8.5
Electricity, gas and water	.3	.3	.5	.5	.6	.7	.7	.7	.7	.7	.7	.8	1.0	1.2	1.2
Transport, storage, and communication	2.8	3.7	4.1	4.9	5.0	5.2	5.7	6.1	6.5	7.0	7.4	7.9	8.6	9.3	9.9
Wholesale and retail trade	3.7	3.4	4.4	4.8	4.7	4.7	5.1	5.5	6.0	6.4	6.9	7.6	8.2	8.7	9.4
Banking, insurance, and real estate	1.2	1.5	2.1	2.2	2.3	2.2	2.4	2.4	2.7	2.7	3.0	3.3	3.8	4.1	4.4
Ownership of dwellings	1.3	1.5	2.3	2.7	3.1	3.6	3.7	3.9	4.2	4.7	5.0	5.5	5.9	6.4	6.9
Public administration and defense	4.0	4.2	5.0	5.4	5.6	6.1	6.3	6.9	7.3	7.8	8.5	9.2	10.1	10.9	11.7
Services	1.8	2.3	2.8	2.8	2.9	3.2	3.4	3.7	4.0	4.2	4.5	4.9	5.3	5.7	6.1
Gross domestic product at factor cost	49.4	48.3	61.3	64.0	65.6	66.0	70.2	75.4	79.0	81.8	90.1	95.7	102.1	107.0	112.7
Nonagricultural products	26.6	28.3	35.0	37.7	39.3	40.4	43.1	46.2	49.8	53.7	58.6	64.0	69.7	75.7	78.5

Sources : 1953-61 : United Nations, Yearbook of National Accounts Statistics, 1965 (New York : U.N., 1966), p. 369.
1963-70 : United Nations, Yearbook of National Accounts Statistics, 1971 (New York : U.N., 1973), p. 475.

Table 2

Selected Turkish Balance of Payments Data, 1956-71

Items	1956	1957	1958	1959	1960	1961	1962	1963	1964	1965	1966	1967	1968	1969	1970	1971
Imports [a] (c.i.f.) (million US $)	-387	-375	-306	-468	-462	-509	-637	-688	-537	-572	-718	-685	-764	-801	-948	-1171
Exports (f.o.b.) (million US $)	304	330	249	362	335	365	399	368	411	464	490	523	496	537	588	677
Other current account items (net) (million US $)	58	11	-27	-21	5	24	3	64	37	88	133	48	37	43	189	372
Current account balance (million US $)	-25	-34	-84	-127	-122	-120	-235	-256	-89	-20	-95	-114	-231	-221	-171	-122
Worker remittances (million US $)	—	—	—	—	—	—	—	—	9	70	115	93	107	141	273	471
Balance without remittances (million US $)	-25	-34	-84	-127	-122	-120	-235	-256	-98	-90	-210	-207	-338	-362	-444	-593
Remittances as percentage of																
Exports	—	—	—	—	—	—	—	—	1.98	14.92	23.51	17.81	21.63	26.20	46.39	69.67
Imports	—	—	—	—	—	—	—	—	1.52	12.20	16.06	13.59	14.05	17.56	28.81	40.26
Composition of imports																
Capital goods	—	—	—	—	52.1	44.8	45.0	45.8	45.7	42.2	47.5	47.2	48.0	43.8	47.1	43.7
Raw materials	—	—	—	—	38.3	45.2	47.7	48.8	49.4	53.5	47.5	47.9	47.2	49.4	47.9	51.3
Consumer goods	—	—	—	—	9.6	9.9	7.3	5.4	4.9	4.3	5.0	4.9	4.8	6.8	5.0	5.0

Sources : Imports, exports, and other current account items :

    1956-60 : International Monetary Fund, *Balance of Payments Yearbook*, Vol. XIII (May, 1962), p. 1, Table 1.

    1961-62 : International Monetary Fund, *Balance of Payments Yearbook*, Vol. XIX (June, 1968), p. 5, Table 2.

    1963-71 : Data provided by the Turkish Ministry of Finance.

Composition   1960-62 : Data provided by the Turkish State Institute of Statistics.
of Imports :   1963-71 : Data provided by the Turkish State Planning Organization.

[a] Figures for 1956 to 1962 converted from f.o.b. to c.i.f. to make them consistent with the Turkish data for 1963 to 1971.

Table 3

Turkish Central Bank Reserves 1950-71

(in Millions of U.S. Dollars)

	1950	1951	1952	1953	1954	1955	1956	1957	1958	1959	1960	1961	1962	1963	1964	1965	1966	1967	1968	1969	1970	1971
Gross reserves (Central Bank)	214	217	191	213	205	211	230	315	297	269	203	194	189	178	141	141	131	119	123	245	431	761
Gold	150	151	143	144	144	144	144	144	144	133	125	133	140	115	102	116	102	97	97	117	127	130
Foreign exchange	65	66	47	69	62	67	86	172	154	136	78	62	50	63	40	25	29	22	26	128	304	626

Sources : 1950-59 : International Monetary Fund, *International Financial Statistics*, Vol. XIII, No. 12 (December 1960), pp. 256-57.
1960-66 : International Monetary Fund, *International Financial Statistics*, Vol. XX, No. 11 (November 1967), pp. 302-03.
1967-71 : International Monetary Fund, *International Financial Statistics*, Vol. XXV, No. 12 (December 1972), pp. 352-53.

Note. — The sudden jump of foreign exchange from $26 million in 1968 to $626 million in 1971 is to a great extent due to the Turkish devaluation in August 1970.

Table 4

Savings and Investment in Turkey — 1953, 1955-71

	1953	1955	1956	1957	1958	1959	1960	1961	1962	1963	1964	1965	1966	1967	1968	1969	1970	1971
GDP market prices (billions of current TL)	19.9	21.1	24.4	30.7	38.7	48.0	51.3	54.0	60.6	69.2	74.4	79.8	93.0	103.7	114.5	127.5	138.0	173.6
Gross investment as percentage of GDP[a]	12.1	14.4	13.8	12.7	12.7	14.0	14.7	14.5	14.4	14.6	13.3	14.8	16.3	16.7	17.8	18.4	20.7	18.7
Machinery and nonresidential construction as percentage of GDP	6.5	6.7	6.5	5.4	5.9	7.3	7.8	8.0	8.3	8.4	7.9	7.1	8.4	8.4	9.3	9.1	—	—
Imported capital goods as percentage of gross investment	—	—	—	—	—	—	—	—	—	—	—	—	—	19.8	14.3	13.5	25.0	23.7
Savings as percentage of GNP	—	—	—	—	—	—	—	—	—	11.7	14.0	15.4	16.0	19.0	19.0	19.4	19.4	20.3
Private savings as percentage of total	—	—	—	—	—	—	—	—	—	61	64	67	56	52	52	52	48	—

Sources : GDP, gross investment, and investment component :

    1953-69 : United Nations, *Yearbook of National Accounts Statistics, 1965* (New York, 1966), p. 369.

    1970   : United Nations, *Yearbook of National Accounts Statistics, 1970* (New York, 1972), p. 1246.

Capital goods imports : Data provided by the Turkish State Planning Organization.

Savings, GNP, and GDP data :

    1970-71 : Organization for Economic Cooperation and Development, *Economic Surveys : Turkey, 1972* (Paris : OECD, 1972), p. 40, Table II.

[a] Excludes stocks.

since 1956. As indicated earlier, imports were restricted up to 1958. Total reserves of the central bank (gold plus foreign exchange) were high averaging about $210 million during each year between 1950 and 1958. After 1958, imports rose from an average of $356 million per year between 1956 and 1958 to $468 million in 1959 and $688 million in 1963. The current account balance deteriorated and reserves began to slip. At the same time, non-agricultural GDP, which had grown at an average of over 7.0 percent per year between 1955 and 1959, declined to 3.5 percent per year in the following two years as import-competing industries were curtailed because of competition from abroad.

During the period migration policy has been in effect, imports have continued to grow. From 1962 to 1971 they increased by 84 percent while exports increased by only 70 percent. However, largely due to worker remittances the current account deficit fell from $235 million in 1962 to $122 million in 1971. As Table 2 indicates, Turkey has increasingly become a country which exports labor services to pay for imports. Between 1964 and 1971 remittances comprised 18 percent of imports. They have allowed Turkey's current account balance to remain almost unchanged ($89 million in 1964 versus $122 million in 1971) while allowing imports to increase by 118 percent, from $ 537 million to $ 1,171 million. At the same, Turkey's foreign exchange holdings rose from $ 40 million to $ 626 million (see Table 3).

7.3.2   Effects on Capital Accumulation

The primary nexus between migration policy and capital accumulation is that the remittances and savings of migrants can provide the country with the means to accumulate capital if the correct conditions are met. Migrants' remittances and savings enter the country net in the sense that they are resources from which the migrants' consumption needs do not have to be met. Whether they are spent by dependents, or saved, or collected as taxes will depend on a variety of factors and institutions.

It has already been shown in Table 3 that remittances, especially after 1967, have helped to restore Turkey's gold and foreign exchange reserves. In Table 4, the historical record of saving and investment is presented for the period 1953-71 except for 1954. Data on imported capital goods from Table 2 have been converted to percentages of GDP and entered in Table 4.

Gross investment as a percentage of GDP has shown an upward trend during the period of high migration. After reaching a six-year low of 13.3 percent of GDP in 1964, it rose steadily to almost 21 percent in

1970. Investment had never exceeded 14.7 percent of GDP before 1965, but has surpassed that every year since. Investment in primarily productive items (for which the categories of non-residential construction and machinery are used here) has also surpassed the averages for the pre-migration period shown. Although the available record is a short one, imported capital goods as a percentage of total gross investment stood at almost 20 percent in 1967. After declining to about 14 percent in each of the two succeeding years, the statistic averaged 24.4 percent during 1970-71, the period of highest remittances.

The ability to invest derives largely from domestic saving. Here again even though the record is not as long as might be desired, it is still indicative. During 1963, when there were few remittances, gross savings stood at 11.7 percent of GNP. In subsequent years the rate of domestic saving increased and has not fallen below 19 percent since 1967. It is unlikely that all increases in savings can be attributed to remittances. When in 1967 remittances fell to $ 93 million from the previous year's $ 115 million, savings as a percentage of GNP rose from 16 to 19 percent. Nevertheless, the overall trend is not inconsistent with the contention that remittances can strongly encourage saving. Available data also show that an increasing portion of total saving is attributable to the public rather than the private sector. Since 1965 the government's share has risen from 39 to 52 percent.

7.3.3 Effects on Employment

In the short run, migration would seem to have a negative impact on employment. Quantitatively, even if potential replacements are available as in Turkey they are, it takes time to search out and fit replacements to jobs. The departure of certain skilled personnel could cause others with dependent related skills to become unemployed. In the long run, however, increased investment generated by remittances could lead to greater employment than would otherwise have been possible.

Available labor market statistics make it difficult to evaluate these possibilities with much confidence. The basic source of information is the general census of population taken at five-year intervals. For the intervening years, employment estimates are made by projecting planned output in the various industrial sectors together with planned investment and rates of productivity increase. These figures are then revised when the results of the next census become available.

Table 5 indicates the level of employment by five-year intervals using the results of the 1955, 1960 and 1965 censuses and the State Planning

Organization's estimates for 1966-71. The domestic employed labor force grew by approximately seven percent between 1955 and 1960, five percent between 1960 and 1965, and eight percent between 1965 and 1970. There is considerable danger in comparing rates of change between points, since beginning and end years can have a disproportionate influence. Nonetheless, it can be safely assumed that domestic employment did not decline nor its rate of expansion decrease during the migration period. The one sectoral exception to this trend is agriculture, a labor-surplus area but one which is declining. Among other major sectors which might have expected to see either employment declines or reduced rates of increase, only construction exhibited a slowing rate of increase. Apart from construction, employment increased 45 percent between 1955 and 1960, it slowed to 21 percent in the next five years and then moved to a 20 percent increase in the period of heaviest migration, 1965-70. Employment in both manufacturing (including mining and public utilities) and transportation and communication accelerated during the last half of the 1960's.

Based on the data available, it is reasonable to assume that Turkish domestic employment would not be larger in the absence of migration policy than with it. If so, over 650,000 workers abroad represent a net increase in employment.

7.3.4 *Effects on Labor Productivity*

Since sub-sectoral data do not permit any conclusive results on productivity changes due to migration, an aggregate level of analysis can be done by taking the change in sectoral output per employed worker between the census periods. Table 5 compares the changes in output (real sectoral GDP) per worker by major sectors for the periods 1955-60 and 1965-70. For the domestic economy as a whole, output per worker increased at about the same rate, 27 percent, during both periods. However, when agriculture is removed and the average growth rate for all remaining non-agricultural sectors calculated, it is seen that real output per non-agricultural worker rose 13 percent during 1955-60 but only nine percent during 1965-70. This decline in over-all growth rates is attributable to the disproportionate growth in the service sectors—trade, government, finance—and to their increasing weight in the computations. The same phenomenon produces the peculiar result of total growth in GDP per worker being about 27 percent while agricultural growth was 19 percent and non-agricultural growth only nine percent. The shift over time from agriculture to non-agricultural occupations gives greater weight

Table 5

Gross Domestic Product per Worker in Turkey, 1955-70

Sector	1955			1960			
	GDP (in millions of 1968 Turkish Liras)	Employment (in thousands)	GDP per Worker (in 1968 Turkish Liras)	GDP (in millions of 1968 Turkish Liras)	Employment (in thousands)	GDP per Worker (in 1968 Turkish Liras)	Percentage Change 1955-60
Agriculture	20,030	9,446	2,120	26,446	9,737	2,716	28.1
Mining, power, and manufacturing	7,930	805	9,853	9,968	977	10,202	3.5
Construction	3,369	200	16,845	4,807	290	16,576	-1.6
Transportation	3,711	190	19,531	5,036	247	20,390	4.4
All nonagricultural	28,284	2,187	12,933	39,115	2,680	14,595	13.1
Total economy	48,314	11,633	4,150	65,561	12,417	5,273	27.1

Sector	1965			1970			
	GDP (in millions of 1968 Turkish Liras)	Employment (in thousands)	GDP per Worker (in 1968 Turkish Liras)	GDP (in millions of 1968 Turkish Liras)	Employment (in thousands)	GDP per Worker (in 1968 Turkish Liras)	Percentage Change 1965-70
Agriculture	27,056	9,750	2,775	32,305	9,750	3,313	19.4
Mining, power and manufacturing	17,500	1,074	16,294	27,403	1,407	19,476	19.5
Construction	5,638	351	16,036	8,164	421	19,392	20.7
Transportation	5,094	287	17,749	7,393	404	18,300	3.1
All nonagricultural	60,387	3,303	18,282	87,595	4,388	19,962	9.2
Total economy	87,443	13,053	6,699	119,900	14,138	8,481	26.6

Sources : GNP : 1955-60 : United Nations, *Yearbook of National Accounts Statistics, 1965* (New York : U.N., 1966), p. 369.
1965-70 : Data provided by the Turkish State Planning Organization.
Employment 1955, 1960, and 1965 : Organization for Economic Cooperation and Development, *Labour Force Statistics, 1959-70* (Paris : OECD, 1972), p. 370.
1970 : Data provided by the Turkish State Planning Organization.

to the higher-productivity sectors, and even though they may be increasing at a slower rate than agriculture, the shift by itself raises overall output per man-year.

Evidence for the short term would seem to indicate that migration has not slowed the rate of output per man-year—at least not in the manufacturing and construction sectors—two of the main sources of blue-collar workers of the type most desired in labor-importing countries. In agriculture, where some migrant workers have come from, productivity has risen over the migration period. However, because productivity in agriculture is so largely dependent upon weather conditions, it is difficult to attach any significance to this rise. A decline in the rate of growth in transportation and communications has been counterbalanced by growth spurts in manufacturing and construction.

An indirect index of productivity is output per capita in real terms. According to United Nations computations, this index increased by twelve percent between 1961 and 1965 and 20 percent between 1965 and 1969.[2]

There is, of course, no substantive evidence available as yet on the long run effects of migration on productivity. Such effects will depend upon the degree to which the added resources at Turkey's disposal are invested for capital accumulation and upon utilization of the skills brought back by migrants.

7.3.5   Effects on Per Capita Income

The net effect of migration for the country as a whole is shown in Table 6 where the measure of general income used is per capita GNP.

Migration will have two types of effects on per capita product. First, there is a population effect equal to the number of migrants abroad together with their accompanying dependents. Thus, migration reduces population in the sending country (column 1) from what it would have been in the absence of migration policy (column 5). Secondly, there is an output effect. Here the main consideration is the effect of migration on domestic output.

It has been shown above that real domestic output (real GDP) did not decline during the migration period nor did it grow at less than the pre-migration rates. If anything, it seems to have increased faster. Thus it seems fair to assume that GDP would be the same with or without

---

[2] United Nations, *Yearbook of National Accounts Statistics, 1970*, Vol. II (New York : U.N.), p. 113.

migration policy. It follows that the net output effect for the country as a whole is to be seen in the differences in GNP occasioned by migration policy. These differences are positive because net remittances increase GNP to its present level over what it would have been without a migration policy. This fact is clearly reflected in a comparison of actual GNP (column 2) with a hypothetical, non-migration GNP which excludes the value of workers' remittances (column 6).

The effects of this two-fold phenomenon can be seen by comparing actual per capita GNP (column 3) with hypothetical per capita GNP (column 7) and even more directly by examining column 8. The latter column shows that the estimated effects of migration on per capita product were small for the first years but have increased steadily. By 1971 migration had increased per capita GNP by seven percent over what it would have been without migration.

Conclusion

This chapter has examined the evidence of five indicators of Turkish economic development to evaluate the effects of migration policy. Although they cannot establish a causal relationship between migration of workers and the country's economic development, the results of the study are indicative of favorable effects.

The breadth of these indicators should be stressed, however. Other indicators should be examined which will reveal the impacts of migration—at finer levels of analysis—on particular classes of people, occupations, and industries, and by smaller geographic regions within Turkey. In this way it will be possible to be much more definite about the gains and losses involved.

Two broad kinds of recommendations are implied by this chapter. The first relates to the future of migration policy. Exporting labor should be viewed as a temporary solution to development problems. For the last dozen years or so, it has ameliorated the unemployment and foreign exchange problems. The future challenge is for the Turkish government to use its resources to build a base for domestic employment opportunities. The remittances of migrants—increased foreign exchange reserves—properly utilized, could provide the seed money for such efforts.

The second relates to information. This study has shown that migration can be, at the very least, a useful adjunct to development policy; at the most, a very significant and integral component of it. To optimize the benefits of migration, however, reliable information about its effects is essential. Turkish data are clearly inadequate for a complete assessment in the kind

Table 6

Per Capita GNP With and Without Migration Policy in Turkey, 1962-1971

(in 1968 Turkish Liras)

Year	With Migration Policy			Without Migration Policy				Ratio
						Hypothetical GNP [b]		
	Actual Population (in thousands) (1)	Actual GNP [a] (in millions of 1968 Turkish Liras) (2)	GNP Per Capita (2)÷(1) (in Turkish Liras) (3)	Migrants and Families Abroad [a] (4)	Total Population (1)+(4) (in thousands) (5)	Total (in millions of Turkish Liras) (6)	Per Capita (6)÷(5) (in Turkish Liras) (7)	Ratio of Per Capita Income (3)÷(7) (8)
1962	28,933	69,987	2,419	21,000	28,954	69,987	2,419	1.000
1963	29,655	76,800	2,590	71,000	29,726	76,761	2,581	1.003
1964	30,394	80,883	2,661	184,000	30,578	80,799	2,642	1.007
1965	31,391	84,284	2,685	271,000	31,662	83,571	2,640	1.017
1966	32,207	94,835	2,944	319,000	32,526	93,724	2,881	1.022
1967	33,109	101,397	3,063	304,000	33,413	100,532	3,008	1.018
1968	33,970	109,014	3,212	371,000	34,341	108,051	3,146	1.021
1969	34,740	114,931	3,308	539,000	35,279	113,742	3,224	1.026
1970	35,667	121,278	3,400	747,000	36,414	118,562	3,256	1.044
1971	36,559	132,050	3,612	886,000	37,445	126,840	3,378	1.066

Source :   Cols. 1 and 2 : Data provided by the Turkish State Planning Organization.
Col. 4 : Data provided by the Turkish Employment Service.

[a] Calculated by determining from data provided by the Turkish Employment Service the percentage of migrants with families abroad, and the number of dependents per migrating family. Total dependents were then added to total working migrants. Also, assumes that the number of dependents per returning migrant is the same as per migrant abroad.
[b] Equals actual GNP less remittances from migrants.

of detail required for many policy decisions and plans. Intensive surveys of the migrants—before, during, and after migration—are required for proper evaluation and decision-making. Further survey work is needed to assess the primary and secondary impacts on domestic areas, industries, and occupations.

Because of the paucity of reliable data and the fact that international migration in its present form is a relatively new field for economic analysis, this chapter has inevitably raised more questions than it has provided answers. Nevertheless, it is hoped that some of the more pertinent areas for investigation have been identified and that other students of the subject will continue theoretical and empirical research in this general field.

VIII

EFFECTS OF INTERNATIONAL MIGRATION UPON OCCUPATIONAL MOBILITY, ACCULTURATION AND THE LABOR MARKET IN TURKEY

RONALD E. KRANE

ABSTRACT

For Turkey, the formal opportunity which developed in 1961 to supply manpower to European labor markets was without historical precedent. By year's end 1972 approximately one of every 13 Turks in the 20-39 year age cohort had had first-hand exposure to West European culture in a working environment. Another 1.4 million Turks had applied for placement abroad.

In the broadest sense, the objectives of the field study were two-fold : (1) to define demographic characteristics and motivations of the migrant and to determine what socio-economic and socio-cultural effects the migration experience has upon the lives of returned migrants; (2) to learn what discernable effects the migration movement had had upon the Turkish labor market, particularly with reference to the three selected regional markets of Izmir, Kocaeli and Zonguldak.

Within each of these provinces, the applied methodology was three dimensional : (1) to obtain from official archives demographic data on one-time residents of the province who had been placed in positions abroad through official auspices; (2) to interview persons once employed abroad but since settled, or re-settled, in the province; and (3) to interview management in a cross-section of industries present there in order to define from this primary empirical source the characteristics of the regional labor market and to measure possible effects of emigration upon the regional economy.

Contrary to what is sometimes assumed, research disclosed that a substantial majority of international migrants are town or city dwellers who have already migrated internally at least once during their lifetimes and who possess important industrial and craft skills. Financial and educational considerations are predominant in motivating the decision. At least 90 percent of the returnees interviewed had achieved their purposes for going abroad, and an equal percentage claimed satisfaction with having made this decision. Acquisition of occupational expertise, work discipline and material gains were most often cited as important benefits realized. On the average, returned migrants earned one-third more than non-migrants and clear indications of upward occupational mobility between pre- and post-departure positions were evidenced in nearly 20 percent of all cases studied.

Other data revealed noteworthy perceptivity to cultural differences on the part of the returnees and observations of attitudinal changes and work discipline by industrial management employing them. Indications are that among the now quite sizeable contingent of returned migrants Turkey possesses manpower resources which, with improved coordination and incentives, could be re-directed to satisfy needs for skilled labor as they currently exist. It is nevertheless conceivable that in the foreseeable future government restrictions may be advisable to regulate a movement whose economic liabilities could eventually outweigh its assets.

8.1 *Introduction and Methodology*

For Turkey, the formal opportunity which developed in 1961 to supply manpower to foreign labor markets was without historical precedent. Unlike certain other nations of the eastern Mediterranean region where emigration for reasons of work had long been customary, though largely if not wholly on an informal basis, large-scale labor emigration from Turkey had no established tradition.

In October, 1961, Turkey concluded with the Federal Republic of Germany her first international agreement for supplying manpower to foreign labor markets. Since that time, similar agreements have been signed, in chronological order, with Austria, Belgium, the Netherlands, France, Sweden and Australia. Among these nations, West Germany has from the beginning been the major employer of Turkish manpower, attracting approximately 90 percent of all Turkish labor at work abroad.

While statistical methods applied by the various countries under consideration are by no means uniform and do not permit dealing in precise figures, it would nevertheless be reasonable to estimate that between October, 1961 and year's end 1972 approximately 775 thousand Turks have had first-hand exposure to West European culture in a working environment. Of these, perhaps 210 thousand had permanently returned to Turkey after up to eleven years of residence abroad. Moreover, so much in demand are positions abroad that approximately 1.4 million Turks have applications on file with the official Turkish government employment agency for placement abroad alone. A substantial number seek foreign positions through informal channels.

In the belief that the potential socio-economic and socio-cultural consequences of a movement of these dimensions constituted a topic worthy of detailed study, the author devoted a 16-month period during 1967-68 to pursuing the topic in Turkey. After establishing liaisons and gaining official cooperation, the bi-national research staff was given access to the necessary archival data and was able to conduct interviews with top-level industrial management and with returned migrants themselves in three carefully selected regions of the country.

In the broadest sense, the objectives of the study were two-fold : in the first instance, it sought to define demographic characteristics and motivations of the migrant and to learn what socio-economic and socio-cultural effects the migration experience has upon the lives of migrants who return to settle in their home country; in the second instance, it sought to learn what discernable effects the migration movement had had as of the summer of 1968 upon the Turkish labor market, particularly as it pertained to economic and demographic trends in three selected regional markets. In fulfilling this two-fold purpose, the study sought to investigate both in deph and in breadth areas which hitherto had not been systematically explored.

When the population falling within the stated scope of a study is potentially quite large, as it was in this case, the researcher is inevitably confronted with the problem of determining what may legitimately be termed "representative" or "typical". Statistical methodology lays down the rules for drawing a representative sample, but inherent in statistical method are presuppositions the realization of which may be impossible to attain or even approximate when basic data sources are non-existent or of inconsistent quality.

One prerequisite to drawing a representative sample is that the researcher know with a high degree of certainty the dimensions of the population falling within the scope of his stated definitions. Applied to the case at hand, the drawing of a representative sample would require that he know with relatively great precision not only the total number of migrants who had resettled in Turkey after employment abroad but also their location within the country. The empirical fact which confronts the social scientist in Turkey is that statistical procedures currently applied by that country allow for only a very rough estimate of total numbers of returned migrants and give virtually no indication of their whereabouts in the country.

Turkish sources which document the movement of citizens into and out of the country are basically two in number—border statistics and employment service statistics. Upon leaving, each citizen is asked at the portal of exit to declare his reasons for departure, country of destination, and province of residence in Turkey. Counterpart information is requested of citizens re-entering the country. By examining the compilation of this data, one can determine for a given year the number of citizens who left or re-entered Turkey for reasons of employment by a foreign firm. However, due to the manner in which the data is processed for publication, it is not possible to derive from this source the number of citizens departing or re-entering for reasons of foreign employment by province of residence. Neither is it possible to differentiate which are first-time departures and which represent exits after temporary return visits of persons already currently employed abroad. The specific internal destination of entering citizens is, of course, not requested. Furthermore, because a large number of departing and entering persons do not supply the full information as asked, data from this source is by no means complete.

Beginning in 1965, Turkish Employment Service statistics show the number of workers officially sent abroad by province of origin. Prior to 1965, it is possible to determine from these statistics only the general region from which the worker was sent. Since the Service does not operate at border stations, it has no independent means of systematically monitoring re-entries, domestic location and activities of returned migrants. The Service does from time to time in certain locations collect data on workers departing after temporary returns.

In summary, it follows that demographic data can be obtained from the above sources only for that group of workers who have been officially sent abroad under the auspices of the Turkish Employment Service in cooperation with counterpart agencies of the European governments involved. This data is contained in the archives of the regional Employment Service offices in Turkey where a separate dossier is maintained for each worker placed abroad through official channels. Using European work permit statistics as an index, it is estimated that those workers officially sent abroad constitute approximately 75-80 percent of all Turks who have emigrated from Turkey since 1961 to work for a foreign firm abroad.

Faced with these circumstances, the researcher has two options : either with rigid adherence to scientific method he realizes the futility of the task and abandons his investigation, or he gathers what data he can, where he can and how best he can, and with discriminating reason sensitized insofar as possible to cultural characteristics, formulates hypotheses which hopefully the accumulated experience of future decades will prove to have been reasonably accurate. Thus, to the degree that the following analysis purports to be "representative" or "typical" of the population under study, it does so not solely on the grounds of evidence derived from interviews, but also from observations contributed by other researchers and from whatever cultural insights five years of cumulative residence in the country under study might have afforded the writer.

With these and other restrictive factors clearly in mind, the staff sought to determine how the dual objectives of the study could best be realized within the limits of the resources at their disposal. The decision was reached to isolate out on the basis of pre-established criteria several provinces of the country which appeared from all available evidence to provide optimum conditions for fulfilling both objectives. Within each province finally to be selected the specific goals would be threefold: (1) to gather from the archives demographic and other vital data on one-time residents of the province who between 1961 and 1968 had been placed in positions abroad through official channels; (2) to interview persons who had been employed abroad but who had since returned to Turkey and settled (or re-settled) in the province; and (3) to interview management in a cross-section of industries present there in order both to define from this primary source the characteristics of the regional labor market and to measure possible effects of emigration upon the regional economy.

Criteria finally applied in selecting three specific areas for detailed field study were as follows :

(1) that the area be located within a general region comparatively high in total volume of emigration,
(2) that a balance in rural-urban relations continue to prevail within the area not unlike that within the nation at large,
(3) that the area have within it a rather wide diversification in types of basic industry.

With these criteria in mind, all of what are normally considered to be industrially advanced provinces were analyzed and Table 1 drawn up. Being an area largely urbanized with only about eleven percent of its population engaged in the agricultural sector, Istanbul province was eliminated as being highly atypical even though it would rank quite favorably according to the first and third criteria above. Ankara province was excluded due to its being primarily an administrative center with a relatively low degree of industrial diversification.

Once Table I was complete, two observations became apparent: (1) that the great majority of the industrially advanced provinces had textile, food, beverage, cement and ceramics establishments employing 50 or more persons, and (2) that of those provinces analyzed, Izmir and Kocaeli had by far the greatest diversification of industry. All 15 provinces analyzed had relatively strong rural-urban relations existing between the provincial center and surrounding rural areas. Finally, Zonguldak proved exceptional in that it alone was the center for the coal mining and basic iron and steel industries of Turkey. Too, in Zonguldak a relationship between industry and the agricultural sector manifested itself wherein the mining industry allows the villager to work part of the year in the mines and part in his village.

Table 1

Industrial Workplaces Employing 50 or more Persons
in 15 Provinces by Branch of Activity
1968

Province	Mining	Iron and Steel	Metal Products	Cement, Cement Products	Construction Materials	Ceramics, Glass	Chemicals, Chemical Products	Rubber, Plastics	Paper, Paper Products	Machine Tool Industry	Electrical Appliances, Equipment	Automotive Assembly, Parts Production	Textiles	Food, Beverages	Tobacco Processing, Tobacco Products	Cotton Processing	Wearing Apparel
Adana			×				×						+	+	×	#	
Aydın	×			×									×	×		×	
Balıkesir	×			×			×	×					×	×			
Bursa	×						×						#	×			×
Denizli													+				
Eskişehir		×	×				×							×			
Gaziantep				×									+	×			×
Izmir			#	×	×	×	#	+	×	×	×	×	#	#	+	+	×
Kayseri						×							+	×			
Kocaeli			#	×	×	×	#	×	×	×	×	×	×	×			
Konya	×						×						×	×			
Manisa							×	×					×	×		×	
Sakarya									×	×		×		×			
Sivas	×			×													
Zonguldak	+	×		×			×							×			

\# = ten or more workplaces.
\+ = five to nine workplaces.
× = less than five workplaces.

1 Because the Turkish Chambers of Industry, a relatively new establishment, had not yet organized the required data for the respective provinces, the information was gleaned from the sources indicated as well as from empirical observations in the field. Due to the nature of the data sources, omissions may unavoidably have occurred. This chart, therefore, is only intended to reflect general trends.

2 Here in all cases but one, the city which serves as the provincial center has the same name as the province itself. The exception is Kocaeli (pronounced Kojaeli) whose center is the city of Izmit. With certain important exceptions, major manufacturing industries are usually located in or near provincial centers. The table attempts to include all major industries in a province regardless of location.

Sources : Records of : (1) U.S.A.I.D., Ankara. (2) Turkish Employment Service.

The decision was thereby reached that Izmir, Kocaeli and Zonguldak would constitute the three provinces for field study. More specifically, it was decided that the study would concentrate on (1) the city of Izmir within Izmir province, (2) the industrial belt of Kocaeli province which extends along the Marmara Sea from the city of Izmit northward to the Istanbul province line, and (3) the industrial foci of Zonguldak province where Turkey's coal mining and basic iron and steel industries are centered. Each of the three areas was then visited and mapped and the preliminary data on industrial establishments refined.

Meanwhile, in the spring of 1968 the Turkish Employment Service conducted a survey in all 67 provinces among establishments employing ten or more persons (in Istanbul, Ankara and Izmir 20 or more) to learn where returned migrants were working. The results of this survey showing 1,300 returnees were available as were data on returnees who had applied to the Service for job placement.

With the number of interviews to be made distributed in approximate proportion to the volume of official out-migration from (and hence hypothesized return migration to) each of the three areas, the final sample of 228 workers was located on the basis of the Employment Service data as well as by random contact in the field. When possible, worker interviews were obtained in the same firms where management interviews were conducted since variety in types of positions held would thereby be ensured. The cross-section of 54 business establishments finally selected for study was chosen with a view toward diversification in such variables as branch of industrial activity, employment level, age of the establishment and predominance of either foreign or Turkish interests in the firm. If any one industrial sector such as the textile industry in Izmir and the mining industry in Zonguldak was especially predominant in the over-all composition of the regional labor market, the sampling was weighted accordingly.

The questionnaires were designed to serve as self-generating data sources for locating returnees not necessarily involved in the industrial sector. Each worker interviewed was asked to provide addresses of other returnees known to him in the community. On this basis, self-employed persons were located who were engaged as small businessmen, drivers, craftsmen and service workers. Given the distinguishing characteristics of the three areas studied, by far the greatest number of self-employed returnees were most likely to have been present in Izmir. Thus, the Izmir sample was weighted with this factor in mind.

When the quality of statistical data available precludes selecting the sample on more precise scientific bases, unwanted biases inevitably enter in. Among the most obvious of these is that there is no way to be sure to what degree returned migrants become self-employed. Census figures make it doubtful that it is to any lesser degree than shown by this sample, but on the other hand it could be to a considerably higher degree. Because the Employment Service survey located in major workplaces so few from among the then more than 100 thousand returnees, one might suspect that a much larger percentage may have been self-employed than the sample indicates. On the other hand, since this survey was restricted to establishments employing ten or more persons (in Istanbul, Ankara and Izmir 20 or more) a significant number of returnees may have been omitted because of their being associated with smaller establishments than these. Moreover, while the sample did include a few unemployed persons, its methodology would inevitably tend to omit persons not yet having established employment relations.

Too, because interviews were conducted only in cities, towns and at industrial sites either in or in the proximity of cities and towns, returnees solely associated with village type occupations were excluded. While a significant number of villagers were incorporated in the Zonguldak sample, these represented persons who were jointly dependent upon agriculture and industry for their livelihood. Yet another bias is that women in the sample were fewer in number than the proportion of women workers who emigrate. This anomaly arises due to the relative inaccessibility of women once they arrive back in Turkey where they often return to domestic situations.

In spite of these and other limitations, it is nevertheless believed that data derived from the interview sample does bring into focus general trends which would in all likelihood be upheld were a larger sample supported by more reliable statistical data made possible. This belief is strengthened by the fact that the randomly selected archival data involving 1,433 cases covering seven years, together with certain German Employment Service data, so often supported the general trends noted in the sample. When adjustments were made allowing for the fact that the interview sample included persons going abroad unofficially as the archival sample did not, the slight variations that did occur between the two sources seemed all the more plausible.

Lastly by way of introduction, mention should be made of four other research efforts which relate either directly or indirectly to the present study. The pioneering investigation was designed and conducted by Professor Nermin Abadan of Ankara University in late 1963 when under sponsorship of the Turkish State Planning Organization she interviewed in Germany 494 Turks then employed there. The scope of Professor Abadan's interest was broad, and from the point of view of the present work, among the more pertinent elements contained in the study was her concern with acculturation. Since, however, her work was done at such an early stage in the migration movement and since it was totally confined to the German context, it now serves primarily as a point of departure for studies completed since that time both in Germany and Turkey.

In 1965, the Institute for Empirical Sociology, Saarbrücken, under agreement with the German Ministry of Labor and in cooperation with Istanbul University, launched a study both in Turkey and Germany to measure the impact of industrialization on the value structure of Turkish workers. In Turkey, the 774 persons interviewed were composed of (a) industrial workers never having been abroad, (b) unemployed persons, (c) persons registered for placement abroad and (d) returnees from work abroad. In Germany, on the other hand, all 163 Turks interviewed were workers in industry.

Somewhat more than a year before the present research got under way, Professor Orhan Tuna of Istanbul University, again under sponsorship of the Turkish State Planning Organization, directed a study which included 280 returned workers in provinces surrounding the Sea of Marmara. In a number of respects, Professor Tuna's results helped to document certain findings here especially with respect to demographic variables and geographic mobility.

Finally, during 1970-71 Professor Ahmet Aker of Bosphorus University, Istanbul, interviewed 590 workers just prior to their departure for West Germany from Istanbul. Many persons interviewed were in process of returning to positions in Germany after temporary visits in Turkey. Professor Aker's data is of particular interest because it traces the employment and residential history of the respondents and furthermore studies wage differentials between Turkey and Germany. Because the aim in one part of the present study was to develop a complete profile of the migrant's employment history encompassing all positions held before departure, abroad and after return, certain of its data and those from the Aker study are seen to be complementary to but not overlapping with one another. However, no known research completed to date has undertaken to explore in a comprehensive manner the interrelated effects of Turkish migration both upon the nation and the individual, the most salient findings of which are herewith being reported for the first time.

Primary attention will be given to elaborating findings which supplement and/or empirically reinforce material presented elsewhere in this volume, which appear to be of enduring significance for the future as well as the past, and which in certain important respects are unique to the present investigation. Accordingly, the first section following will be concerned with the effects of international migration upon the occupational and socio-economic mobility of the returned migrant, the second with its effects upon processes of acculturation and the third with its effects in the labor market.

8.2   After several preliminary observations, the discussion will proceed to a detailed analysis of occupational mobility at all stages in the migration cycle. Subsequently, the subject of self-employment will be treated followed by a comparative analysis of earnings and savings in the various positions held both in Turkey and abroad. The section will conclude with an examination of the remittance practices of migrants and the uses to which accumulated cash savings are put after return.

At the time of their initial departure from Turkey it was necessary for 82 percent of the persons in the interview sample to sever employment relations. Eleven percent had been employed at some previous time but were not employed at time of departure. The remaining 17 percent had never held jobs. Consequently, contrary to what is sometimes thought, the great majority of migrants are not drawn from the ranks of the unemployed. Data to be introduced below will further show that in a high percentage of cases, they derive from the ranks of skilled labor whose deployment abroad would not necessarily appear to be in the best interests of a developing economy. On the other hand, assuming that replacement personnel with the requisite skills are available, their vacated positions presumably do provide employment opportunities for others in the labor market who are either unemployed or underemployed.

Seventy-three percent of the interview sample departed initially from Turkey with a one-year contract in hand arranged by the Turkish Employment Service. Twenty-seven percent located positions abroad either on their own initiative or with the assistance of friends or relatives already there. Due to tightened restrictions on entry and work permits in recent years, it is assumed that a somewhat greater percentage is currently departing under contract than before. It is of some interest to note with respect to first jobs abroad that in cases where a contract existed, as many persons reported terminating their jobs prior to the contract expiration date as quit after fulfilling the contract. Apparently, few contracts existed in jobs subsequent to the first.

Occupations in which respondents were engaged at all three stages in the migration cycle—before departure, abroad and after return to Turkey—were analyzed not only to provide an overview of the occupational stratification of the sample but also to trace occupational mobility patterns where possible. Table 2 is designed to depict changing distributions among occupational categories at all three stages in the migration cycle. Moreover, it shows the average level of formal education associated with each category. In organizing the table, three principles were applied as follows : (1) The classifications are listed in what might very generally be considered a descending order of occupational prestige. Since no occupational prestige scales for Turkish society at large are known to exist, the order applied here is speculative rather than definitive. (Thus, professional-technical occupations are in first position and unskilled occupations in last position). (2) Because of dissimilar levels of technological development between Turkish and West European societies, certain specific occupations (not shown here) were classified under different headings as the geographical location under consideration shifted from Turkey to Western Europe. Similarly, certain occupations pursued in the home country obviously would not be open to migrant labor in the European country of destination. (3) Since any one emigrant might have been involved in multiple occupations either in Turkey or abroad, data was gathered for "first" and "last" positions in each case under the assumption that the total range of mobility, if any, would tend thereby to be reflected. To allow for persons who had only one position either at home or abroad as well as for those having multiple positions, the term "last" includes (a) in cases of multiple positions, the *most recent* position, and (b) in cases of only one position, that *one* position which by definition would at the same time be the most recent position.

For occupations abroad the largest occupational category was that encompassing "assemblyline workers, fitters and craftsmen in industry" (22 percent). Next largest was that of "machine operators" (17 percent). Of approximately equal size were the categories of "metal workers," (11 percent), "miners" (13 percent) and "factory workers not elsewhere classified" (14 percent). All other categories were significantly smaller than these.

When mobility between "first" and "last" jobs abroad is analyzed from the subtotal figures, the following patterns emerge : (1) Classifications which attracted personnel were "administrative-clerical," "driver-operators" and "factory workers (n.e.c.)." (2) Losses were recorded for "automotive and machine maintenance personnel" and particularly for "miners." (3) All other classifications remained essentially in equilibrium.

With respect to occupations in Turkey, it is possible to observe from the table mobility patterns not only *within* each individual time period— *i.e.*, "before departure" and "after permanent return"—but also *between* these two time periods. Within the range of first and last occupations before departure, significant gains were recorded in the "administrative-clerical" and "machine operator" categories. Conversely, noticeable losses were visible in the "shopkeeper-retail sales," "miner" and "agricultural worker" classifications. A fairly steady equilibrium prevailed among all other groups.

No significant patterns of upward mobility were noticeable with respect to the range of first and last occupations after permanent return. There was, however, a very small amount of evidence that the "professional-technical" and "administrative-clerical" classifications were beginning to grow slightly, thus repeating the pattern for pre-departure occupations. Decreasing in size, on the other hand, were the "driver-operator" and "shopkeeper-retail sales" groups.

The downward trend which occurs for "driver-operators" over time between occupations held subsequent to their return is accounted for as follows: Many purchase automobiles while abroad which they later drive back to Turkey. For some, the automobile licensed as a taxi becomes a permanent type of occupation whereas for others it provides only an initial source of income until another, more preferable position is located and the automobile sold. Of the 62 automobiles imported by the respondents, all but five had already been disposed of by the time of interview. Moreover, perhaps somewhat indiscriminately, the emigrant while still abroad will often consider self-employment in any form as the ideal goal for the period following his return to Turkey. If achieved, self-employment frequently will be in the form of a small service or retail sales shop. However, actual experience in small business often proves that the financial advantages are not so favorable as previously anticipated. Accordingly, over an extended period of time, mobility tends to be away from shopkeeping toward jobs in industry which, at the expense of personal freedom, nevertheless often do provide greater financial security.

When pre-emigration occupations are compared with those pursued after return to the home country, mobility is shown to be in the direction of the following classifications : "driver-operator" "assembly line worker and fitter," "factory worker (not elsewhere classified)", "automotive and machine maintenance personnel", and to a certain limited extent, toward "shopkeeper and retail sales". Conversely, mobility is seen to be away from "machine operator", "services and entertainment", "craftsmen in construction trades" and "miner."

Table 2 also shows the average number of years of formal education persons in any one occupational category had received. While those in "professional-technical" type occupations had had an average of ten, those in mining had had only 4.1 years of schooling. All other categories fell between these extremes as indicated in the table. Of the 65 persons who reported having had specific occupational training, electricians, fitting machine and lathe operators were by far the most predominant.

One important concern for which empirical evidence was sought was the degree to which work experience obtained abroad was being transferred back to and applied in the country of origin. Sixty-three persons, mostly miners, machine operators, metal workers and electricians, were consistently engaged in the same occupation at all stages in the migration cycle—prior to departure, abroad and after return. In addition to these 63, another 16 took up the same occupation after returning that they had engaged in abroad—an occupation they had not previously pursued in Turkey. Furthermore, 13 persons were currently involved in occupations in Turkey related to but not identical to those pursued abroad. Apart from those already mentioned, another 33 respondents who were factory workers abroad also entered factory work in Turkey. In summary, in 125 or 55 percent of all 228 cases studied, relationships prevailed between the type of occupation engaged in abroad and that currently being pursued at the time of interview in Turkey.

Any attempt to assess the significance of such occupational change in terms of socio-economic mobility becomes especially difficult when the range of occupations represented among the migrant population is primarily composed of production process workers, craftsmen, construction workers, miners and service workers—i.e., of a relatively homogeneous stratum. Five culturally relevant distinctions which were considered when attempting to identify sub-strata within this broad overall stratum and to which distinctions certain subtle significance may often be attached are : (1) skill levels, (2) performance of supervisory or clerical roles in contradistinction to performance of manual labor; (3) degree of mechanization involved in performance of the task; (4) whether the task is performed within or outside the industrial context, and (5) whether self-employment within the given occupation ordinarily connotes preferential status.

Table 2

Occupational Distribution and Formal Education
(Percent)

Occupation	Before Departure		Abroad		After Permanent Return		Av. Yrs. Formal Education
	1st	last*	1st	last*	1st	last*	**
Professional, technical	6.2	6.6 ↓	1.3	1.3	6.4	6.8	10.0
Administrative, supervisory, clerical	4.3	9.0 ↓	0.5 ↑ 1.3		8.2	9.1	6.8
Machine operators	16.1	19.9	17.1	16.2	13.2	13.6	6.0
Driver operators	5.2	6.6	1.3	3.5	12.3	10.5	5.4
Assemblyline workers, fitters, craftsmen in industry	5.7	4.7	21.5	22.4	5.9	6.8	5.6
Factory workers (n.e.c.)	4.7	3.3	12.3	15.8	9.1	8.2	5.6
Automotive and machine maintenance personnel	7.1	7.1	5.7	4.0	8.2	9.1	6.4
Shopkeepers, retail sales	5.2	3.3	0	0	5.9	4.6	6.1
Services	6.2	6.2	1.3	1.3	2.3	2.7	6.0
Craftsmen in construction trades	10.0	11.0	4.0	4.4	7.7	7.7	5.2
Metal workers	8.5	7.6	11.8	11.4	7.7	7.7	5.4
Miners	13.7	11.9	14.9	10.9	10.4	10.5	4.1
Gardeners, fishermen, agricultural, and other unskilled workers	7.1	2.8	8.3	7.5	2.7	2.7	5.6
Percent	100	100	100	100	100	100	
Average education							6.3

Note :

* "Last" occupation is considered same as first occupation if respondent was engaged in only one occupation.

** Calculated in conjunction with last occupation after permanent return.

Seventeen respondents were unemployed before departure from Turkey and eight were unemployed after permanent return.

Listed in ascending order, six culturally relevant sub-strata, composed of the specified occupational groups, were established as follows : (1) unskilled manual labor, (2) miners, (3) persons in metal-working trades (outside industry), craftsmen in construction trades; (4) persons in the service sector, mechanics, small shopkeepers, (5) driver-operators, assemblyline workers and machine operators (within industry); and (6) administrative, clerical and technical personnel. In assessing mobility in each individual case, not only was transfer between the various sub-strata themselves considered but also where applicable the five distinctions outlined in the preceding paragraph.

Thus, movement between occupations which form part of the same sub-stratum is considered "horizontal" mobility, whereas movement between occupations which form parts of different sub-strata is viewed as "vertical mobility." For example, a person who was a machine operator in his first occupation but a metal worker in his second, would have changed his status horizontally. The machine operator who subsequently took an administrative job would be involved in upward vertical mobility, while the later movement of the same machine operator to work as a craftsman in construction trades would be characterized as downward vertical mobility.

When pre-migration and post-migration positions were compared applying this stratification schema, upward mobility was visible in 16 percent of the cases and horizontal mobility in 20 percent. Sixty-one percent of the sample remained essentially immobile, and three percent appeared to be downwardly mobile. Mobility tended to be away from positions as miners, craftsmen in construction trades, and service workers, and toward positions as mechanics, small shopkeepers, factory assemblyline workers and driver-operators.

Another potential indicator of mobility would be comparative skill levels applied in jobs held at the various stages in the migration cycle—prior to departure, abroad and after permanent return. Table 3 shows that (1) skill levels in most recent jobs after return are generally higher than those in last jobs held prior to departure, and (2) skill levels reported in jobs abroad are appreciably lower than for any job in Turkey. A number of factors may be responsible for the latter observation. First, for an emigrant worker to hold a supervisory or clerical post abroad, foreign language ability would presumably be a prerequisite. Even if the position abroad entailed supervision of Turkish nationals alone, opportunities would be quite limited. Secondly, an occupation in which foreign manpower is in great demand abroad is that of assemblyline production. In the classification used here, assemblyline positions were considered "semi-skilled". Thus, many persons who had worked as skilled personnel in Turkey became "semi-skilled" abroad simply as a result of technological differences in the respective production processes. Finally, a difference in classification standards prevails between the two systems under study. Work which is considered "skilled" by Turkish standards is often viewed as "semi-skilled" by West European standards.

In terms of specific figures, the table indicates that relatively more persons were in administrative, supervisory, technical and skilled positions after return to Turkey than prior to departure, while comparatively fewer occupied semi-skilled, apprentice and unskilled positions. Whereas prior to departure 58 percent of the sample worked as "skilled" personnel or at a higher level, abroad only 36 percent did so. This compares to a figure of 68 percent for the period after permanent return. If very fine individual distinctions were made, by Turkish standards it could be said that in 20 percent of the cases at most, some evidence of increased skill was present after return.

Table 3

Skill Levels

Level	Last Job Before Departure		Last Job Abroad*		Most Recent Job After Return	
	No.	%	No.	%	No.	%
Administrative	0	0	0	0	2	0.9
Clerical	8	3.8	0	0	7	3.2
Supervisory (headmaster**, foreman, head of shift)	9	4.3	6	2.7	21	9.5
Technical	30	14.2	13	5.7	36	16.4
Skilled (master)***	75	35.5	62	27.2	83	37.7
Semi-skilled (including assemblyline workers)	39	18.5	90	39.5	37	16.8
Apprentice	2	0.9	1	0.4	0	0
Unskilled	28	13.3	55	24.1	18	8.2
Undeterminable	20	9.5	1	0.4	16	7.3
Total	211	100.0	228	100.0	220	100.0

* Last job abroad is considered first job if only one position was held abroad.
** Supervisory positions abroad were as foreman only.
*** "Master" applies in Turkey only.

Note : 17 persons were unemployed prior to departure from Turkey and eight unemployed after return.

A factor potentially related to advancement of skills is on-the-job training. It was originally hoped by many in Turkey that employment abroad would afford migrants major opportunities for advanced training which upon their return to Turkey would contribute to a general up-grading of the nation's skilled manpower resources. If the number of first and last jobs held by the 228 respondents abroad is combined, a total of 352 jobs results. According to the information reported, 80 or 23 percent of these 352 jobs had some measure of in-plant training opport-unities associated with them. From among these 80 positions, the majority were in mining, assembly line and related factory work. In these occu-pations, the average duration of the training was between six and seven weeks compared to an over-all average of seven weeks.

As already indicated, self-employment seems to constitute a much sought-after ideal among Turks abroad and one which brings with it when attained some degree of higher status. Table 4 shows self-employ-ment status according to the time period in question :

Table 4

Self-Employment Status

Period	Persons	Percent
Before and after migration	18	7.9
After migration only	53	23.2
Before migration only	7	3.1
Never self-employed	150	65.8
Total	228	100.0

Thus, at the time of interview 71, or 31 percent, of the respondents were self-employed. Of these 71 persons, 53 were newly self-employed presumably as a direct result of capital savings and/or occupational exper-tise derived from the emigration experience. Prior to work abroad, 25 persons had been self-employed, and of these, seven did not resume self-employment status after returning to Turkey.

No satisfactory method exists for comparing self-employment ten-dencies among returned migrants to those applicable among the nation's population at large. The census categories make two distinctions for self-employed persons : (1) *işveren* (employer) and (2) *kendi hesabına çalışan* (persons working for themselves). Distinctions are not made, however, by economic sector, occupation or province. Agricultural workers are thus included in the census figures. When both the above two categories are combined, the 1965 census showed that 30 percent of Turkey's economically active population was so employed. Unless the census statistics can be corrected for specific occupations, which in fact they cannot be, no norm exists on the basis of which to judge the degree self-employment patterns noted among returned migrants are typical or atypical of the nation at large.

As for the branch of economic activity in which self-employed persons were participating at the time of the interview, the largest single portion, 32 percent, were in transportation, primarily as taxi drivers. Twenty-one percent were in services and 15 percent involved with the production of metal goods in small, privately established machine shops. Significant numbers were in furniture production and retail sales, the former occupation being primarily a handcraft industry in Turkey.

Basic to any study of socio-economic mobility is reliable data on income. To this end, interviewers inquired about wages received during all phases of the migration cycle in order to make possible comparative income analysis. So that a common denominator would be present, wages earned in foreign currencies were uniformly converted into Turkish lira, including in the formula for conversion the 27 percent premium established by the Turkish government on July 22, 1964. At this rate, in 1968 one German mark was worth approximately 2.85 Turkish lira, and one United States dollar 11.45 lira.

Thus, according to 1968 conversion rates, the average net monthly wage received in first jobs abroad was 1,928 T.L. This figure compares with 2,364 T.L. for last jobs abroad. Thus, the migrant's earning power in his last job was on the average 23 percent higher than in his first. On the basis of 300 T.L. gradations, initially more migrants were in the 1,600-1,899 T.L. income bracket than any other, while subsequently the largest group was in the 1,900-2,199 T.L. bracket. Cumulative percentages show that in the first jobs 54 percent received below 1,900 T.L. monthly and that wages above 3,100 T.L. were quite uncommon. In first jobs 95 percent of the sample received below 3.100 T.L. monthly, while in last jobs the 95th percentile ranged up to 3,700 T.L.

In contrast to net average earnings of 1,928 T.L. for first jobs abroad, first jobs after return to Turkey netted 949 T.L. monthly. The 40 persons having had more than one job since their permanent return reported an average net income of 1,026 T.L. in these subsequent positions. If 2,146 T.L. is taken as the average between first and last positions abroad, then the 949 T.L. average received for the first position after return represents a decrease of 56 percent in earning power. Another manner in which to express this comparative relationship would be to say that the first wage received after return constituted 44 percent of the average wage received abroad.

Going back to the initial phase of the migration cycle—namely, to the last job held prior to departure from Turkey—the average net monthly pre-departure wage was 604 T.L. Nearly half the respondents were receiving between 400 and 700 T.L. per month prior to emigrating. If 988 T.L. is taken as the average net wage for post-emigration jobs, then a 64 percent increase prevails between average wages received prior to departure and those earned after return. Between the last pre-departure job and the first job *abroad*, however, a 319 percent average increase occurred. Because of significant increases in German wage scales since 1968, differentials currently in effect are undoubtedly somewhat greater than reported here.

Quite apart from official government statistics, it was learned from interviews with industrial management that during the five-year period 1963-68 wages in Turkey rose an average of 50 percent and that the rate of increase was a steady rather than sporadic one. Wages in the mining industry, however, rose much more rapidly than in most other industries.

Due to the effects of the 1967-68 European recession, the average duration of residence abroad for the interview sample was just slightly more than 2.5 years. During this period, average wages in Turkey would then have risen approximately 30 percent except in the mining industry where a 35 to 45 percent rise was recorded. The conclusion then follows that the persons interviewed experienced a positive increment (64 percent) in wages between pre- and post-emigration positions which was considerably in excess of that experienced by non-migrants during the same time period (30 percent). This differential would seemingly be largely attributable to the following factors surrounding the emigration experience: (1) a large percentage of the migrants became self-employed upon their return—a factor which ordinarily augments earning power to a limited degree, (2) increased skills contributed to higher earning potential, (3) migrants reportedly demand and receive higher wages than personnel having only domestic work experience, and (4) since a significant number of miners were included in the interview sample, and since as noted above wages in mining rose more rapidly than in most other industries, the excess increment of 34 percent experienced by migrants as compared to non-migrants tends to be somewhat more pronounced than would otherwise have been the case.

It should be pointed out, however, that even though wages in Turkey rose approximately 50 percent between 1963 and 1968, the cost of living index also rose substantially. While the Central Bank did not compute such an index for the nation at large, it nevertheless did do so for the cities of Ankara and Istanbul. According to the Bank's *Monthly Bulletin*, if 1963 is used as base 100, the 1968 cost of living stood at 130 in Ankara and 143 in Istanbul. If an average is taken, it becomes apparent that the increase in wages managed to keep ahead of the increase in cost of living by only a slight margin. Be this as it may, relatively speaking, returned migrants were still at a distinct advantage over non-migrants from the point of view of earning power.

It should further be noted that while in most instances Turks earn abroad at least three times their pre-emigration wage, their living standards there are often not any higher from what they had been in Turkey, and in a goodly number of cases perhaps even lower. For workers without accompanying dependents, housing and meals are often provided by the foreign firm in a dormitory type arrangement at a minimal charge to the worker. To the extent that it allows him to retain significantly larger proportions of his wages as savings than would otherwise be possible, the migrant worker tends to be satisfied with such an arrangement. His objective while abroad is usually not to seek the same standard of living as the permanent resident population, for if he did so, his earnings would often not exceed maintenance expenses.

As long as the worker is willing to tolerate this type of living situation, he is at a distinct advantage wage-wise from what he would have been had he remained in Turkey. Moreover, mass-produced consumer items— particularly automobiles, home appliances and electronics equipment— can usually be purchased for considerably less in Europe than in Turkey, and to the extent that he may import the item into Turkey tax-free or recover any customs payment by resale, he remains at an advantage. Thus, given the anomalous situation in which the migrant worker finds himself while abroad, and considering too his motives for being present there, the higher cost of living in Europe does not necessarily affect him in the same manner or to the same degree as it affects a resident citizen of Western Europe.

Table 5 analyzes comparative earnings in ten specific occupations pursued by migrants both in Turkey and abroad. It was only in these particular occupations that sufficient cases existed in the sample to allow a comparative analysis to be made. Thus, the discussion following pertains only to Table 5 and not to the sample of 228 respondents as a whole.

Table 5

Comparative Net Average Earnings in Ten Selected Occupations (T.L.) 1968

Occupation	Jobs Abroad				Average F & L	% Difference Jobs Abroad	Jobs in Turkey						% Difference Jobs in Turkey	Increase F over Pre-Dep	% Decrease Post-Mig. under Av. F & L
	First		Last				Pre-Dep.			Post-Mig.					
	No.	T.L.	No.	T.L.	T.L.		No.	S	T.L.	No.	S	T.L.			
Miner	33	2321	10	3028	2675	+ 30.5	28	0	393	23	0	657	+ 67.2	+ 490.6	— 75.4
Metal worker	6	2347	3	2328	2338	— 0.8	9	0	470	6	3	700	+ 48.9	+ 399.4	— 70.1
Factory worker (n.e.c.)	25	1655	20	2273	1964	+ 37.3	10	0	410	16	0	629	+ 53.4	+ 303.7	— 68.0
Textile mach. operator	5	2009	2	2323	2166	+ 15.6	13	7	520	7	0	638	+ 22.7	+ 286.4	— 70.5
Assemblyline worker	28	1926	12	2226	2076	+ 15.6	1	0	500	5	0	762	+ 52.4	+ 285.2	— 63.3
Welder	15	1851	8	2416	2134	+ 30.5	7	0	492	9	1	892	+ 81.3	+ 276.2	— 58.2
Electrician	6	1820	4	2615	2218	+ 43.7	10	1	548	10	0	988	+ 80.3	+ 232.1	— 55.5
Machine operators	26	1886	12	2199	2043	+ 16.6	22	0	590	20	0	845	+ 43.2	+ 219.7	— 58.6
Auto mechanic	8	1737	1	1995	1866	+ 14.9	6	0	796	7	0	784	— 1.5	+ 118.2	— 58.0
Driver	1	—	3	2090	2090	—	12	1	774	27	17	1388	+ 79.3	—	— 34.0
Averages =					2090	+ 20.4							+ 52.7	+ 290.2	— 61.2

S = self-employed persons among the total number.   T.L. = Turkish Lira
F & L = first and last jobs abroad   Pre-Dep. = last pre-departure job   Post-Mig. = average of all post-migration jobs

With respect to the earning differential between first and last jobs abroad, it will be observed that income in last jobs was 20 percent higher on the average than in first jobs for the ten occupations being considered. Occupation-wise, the largest increments were reported by electricians and factory workers. Moreover, the average differential between last job before departure and jobs after return was an increase of 53 percent. In this instance, welders, electricians, drivers and miners apparently experienced the most sizeable increments, while auto mechanics and textile machine operators profited least.

Simply by leaving his job in Turkey and going abroad to work, the average worker in these occupations experienced an immediate increase in income amounting to nearly 300 percent. While the average was 290, for miners it was an unparalleled 490 and for metal workers about 400 percent. Auto mechanics reported an increase of only 118 percent, however, which would seem to reflect both a proportionately high income standard prior to departure as well as a proportionately low standard abroad.

In comparison to what he had been accustomed to earning abroad, the average worker in these vocations suffered an immediate reduction of 61 percent in his income upon return to Turkey. This is to say, in other words, that his earning power in Turkey was only 39 percent of what it had been abroad. Miners endured the most drastic cut—75 percent—while drivers, mainly due to their high level of self-employment, the least—34 percent. Metal workers and textile machine operators experienced decreases amounting to 70 percent in each case, and factory workers trailed closely behind with a 68 percent cut after return.

Monthly savings in jobs abroad averaged 808 T.L. for first jobs and 1,060 T.L. for last jobs. In computing these figures, cases reporting no savings were included. Whereas in first jobs 18 percent of the workers reported inability to save, in last jobs only nine percent said they were unable to do so. Average savings increased 31 percent between first and last jobs whereas earnings rose only 23 percent.

In jobs after permanent return to Turkey, on the other hand, 73 percent reported inability to save in first jobs and 57 percent in subsequent jobs. Including as above cases where no savings were reported, average savings for first jobs after return stood at 137 T.L. and for subsequent jobs 309 T.L.

Table 6 shows the figures which resulted when monthly earnings and monthly savings in jobs abroad were cross-tabulated. Here as elsewhere the figures would seem most reliable for those income brackets composed

of the largest numbers of respondents. Starting with the 700-999 T.L.
income bracket, a steady increase in savings is observed up through the
3,400-3,600 bracket with one slight exception in the 2,800-3,099 range.
Similarly, with minor fluctuations this same increase is noted when wages
saved are computed as percentages of wages earned. Beginning already
with the 700-999 income bracket, 27 percent of earnings were converted
into savings, and when the 2,800-3,099 level is reached, savings constituted
half of earnings. The progression continues through the 3,400-3,699 income bracket at which point 62 percent of wages earned were saved.

Table 6

Net Monthly Wages by Monthly Savings in Jobs Abroad
1968

Monthly Wages (T.L.)	Total Jobs (First and Last)	Average Savings for Income Group	Percent of the Average Wage Saved
100- 399	1	100	40.0
400- 699	4	0	0
700- 999	6	233	27.4
1000-1299	22	300	26.1
1300-1599	48	567	39.1
1600-1899	68	649	37.1
1900-2199	48	817	39.9
2200-2499	48	1075	45.7
2500-2799	41	1220	46.0
2800-3099	19	1495	50.7
3100-3399	6	1450	44.6
3400-3699	13	2208	62.2
3700-3999	5	1780	46.2
4000-4299	3	1267	30.5
4300 and above	1	2300	51.7

Note : Due to no answer *or* incorrect answers, 19 cases were undeterminable.

This section will conclude by briefly examining remittance patterns
and investment of savings. In all, 82 percent of the sample remitted funds
at some time during their stay abroad. Eighty-five percent of those who
remitted did so in order to support family or relatives, 16 percent to pay
for the purchase of real estate, nine percent to cancel debts, and ten
percent to add to savings accounts in Turkish banks. Since multiple re-

sponses were possible, percentage figures here as below do not total 100. The extent to which worker remittances have contributed hard currency exchange to the Turkish economy is discussed elsewhere in this book.

By the time of their return to Turkey, 181 respondents, or 79 percent, reported having accumulated at least some cash savings. Of these 181, 23 percent chose to invest in a business enterprise, 41 percent in real estate, and 20 percent in consumer items. Another 20 percent retained at least some funds as cash savings. Post-emigration expenditures for customs tax and marriage were cited in six and nine percent of the cases respectively. Twenty-four percent of those who purchased real estate invested in an apartment or house and the remaining 76 percent in lots, business property and/or agricultural land.

Only 39 persons, or 17 percent of the sample, reported importing job-related tools or machines for which Turkish customs exemptions are available to returning workers. Paradoxically, the item most frequently listed—automobiles by one in every four migrants—is an item for which no customs exemption exists.

Radios were imported by two out of every three persons, and phono-graphs, tape recorders, and cameras by about one in three. It was not uncommon for multiple units of these items to be brought in by the same person. In such cases, one unit was often intended for retention by the worker and the others for sale or gifts. Like automobiles, these items are not, for the most part, duty-free. Eighty-one percent of the persons who imported radios, phonographs, television sets and tape recorders retained them for personal use. Nearly all household appliances imported were kept for private use.

8.3 In studying the socio-cultural dimensions of the migration experience, this section identifies some possible indicators of acculturation as manifested both in comparative cross-cultural observations made by returned migrants themselves and in comments describing their behavioral characteristics by the industrial managers employing them. Among the topics to be considered are managerial observations on differential performance and attitudes, the migrants' own assessment of both positive and negative aspects of their encounter with a previously unfamiliar culture, and lastly their views regarding readjustment problems engendered as a result of their dislocation from Turkish society.

It should be emphasized that the interviewing technique applied was that of the open-ended question. Interviewers recorded verbatim the respondents' replies and were not permitted to suggest possible answers. In

translating the responses from the original Turkish for classification purposes, a high degree of discretion was exercised to ascertain that the
originally intended meaning was preserved intact. The classifications
were formulated only after a careful content analysis was made of the
specific responses.

With respect to interviews with industrial management, 41 out of 54
establishments contacted employed returned migrants either at the time of
the interview or at some previous time. (Conversely, 46 out of the 54 reported having personnel terminate positions in the firm in order to accept
positions abroad). Of these 41 establishments, 20 or half were clearly of
the opinion, and were willing to so state, that noticeable differences in
attitudes and work habits prevailed between employees who had worked
abroad and those who had not.

When asked to describe these observed differences, management in 17
of 20 affirmative responses named attributes considered to be of a
positive nature. Most frequently mentioned was the general concept of
superior "work discipline." Other attributes cited, which could be viewed
as facets of this same concept, were more "productive", "industrious",
"orderly" and "use time more efficiently." Not unrelated to the concept
of superior work discipline were the observations that personnel with
European experience were comparatively more "bound" to and "interested" in their jobs, that they did not "leave their job sites as often as
others during the course of the work day", and they "observe work
hours more carefully" and "work to deserve the wages they earn."

Also frequently mentioned were attributes relating to superior knowledge and work techniques. Employees with European experience were
viewed as more "specialized in their skills" and more "willing and able
to assume responsibility." In the words of management, "they do not
begin work without first understanding it", "make less mistakes while
working" and "handle tools and materials more responsibly."

Regarding attributes related to the Turkish concept of *görgü*, variously
translated "demeanor", "experience" or "manners" but for which no
single equivalent exists in English, management described the worker
returned from abroad as more "understanding", "gentlemanly",
"refined" and "respectful." As one manager stated, "his manner of
conducting himself is different." Others observed that "when he is right
he stands up for it, but when he is wrong he does not argue to save face",
that "when he is provoked with his supervisor, he does not take revenge
by ruining his work." Also observed was the returnee's respect for cleanliness as manifested in his greater concern for proper work attire and in
his reluctance to eat while in work clothing.

Among comments intended with a negative connotation were that the worker with European experience had become a more "robot-like" person who preferred only a specific, specialized job and who preferred not to work exceptionally long hours nor on Sundays. In the experience of two firms, the returned worker was "less deferential toward his supervisors", and not unrelated perhaps in another firm's view, the migrant-come-home "saw himself as superior to others even though just an assemblyline worker abroad." Other managers viewed the returnee as "more prone to complain about work conditions and equipment" and "cold toward his work if paid less than he was paid abroad".

Half of the establishments interviewed expressed preference for a job applicant with European experience, 30 percent for the applicant with only domestic experience and 20 percent expressed no preference. Management's reasons for preferring personnel experienced abroad to personnel with only domestic experience closely parallel the positive attributes cited above with respect to attitudes and work habits of returned migrants. Better work discipline and the various attributes associated with this general concept were again most strongly emphasized followed by the observation that persons with foreign experience have usually acquired superior technical expertise which theoretically can be transferred in the form of innovations to the benefit of the firm in Turkey.

Because not all establishments responding to this question had actually employed personnel with European experience, it is interesting to correlate management's preferences with first-hand opportunity for empirical observation. Among establishments which had actually employed personnel with European experience, 59 percent, or well over half, preferred personnel with this background. Nineteen percent of these establishments preferred personnel with domestic experience only and 22 percent expressed no preference. On the other hand, among establishments which had *not* employed personnel with European experience, only 18 percent preferred employees with this background. Sixty-four percent of these establishments preferred personnel with domestic experience only, and 18 percent expressed no preference.

Finally, the many-faceted concept of *görgü* was mentioned at some length, but in addition to the aspects noted earlier in this regard, one firm described the employee with European experience as "easier to deal with because of his greater experience in human relations." Another manager viewed his personnel experienced abroad as more "mature with respect to their approach to work and the importance they attribute to work." Still a third manager noted that their "work morals are more in order" in the sense that "they recognize a direct relationship between earnings and work accomplished."

Table 7

Managerial Preferences for Personnel Experienced Abroad

Preference	Firms having employed personnel with European experience		Firms not having employed personnel with European experience	
	No.	Percent	No.	Percent
European experience preferred	24	58.5	2	18.2
Domestic experience only preferred	8	19.5	7	63.6
No preference	9	22.0	2	18.2
Total	41	100.0	11	100.0

It is of some interest to observe that attributes seen by some managers as working to the firm's advantage were viewed by certain others as working to its disadvantage. Thus, new methods and skills learned abroad were considered by some managers as advantageous innovations but by others as irrelevant and too highly specialized to satisfy needs in Turkey. Reasons given for no preference between domestic and European experienced personnel were in most instances not dissimilar to those above which were interpreted by some managers as advantages but by others as disadvantages. Seeing both sides of the matter simultaneously, some preferred to take a neutral stand.

Having examined acculturative influences as witnessed from the standpoint of industrial management, the discussion now turns to a consideration of the subject as viewed by the migrants themselves.

When asked to assess their degree of satisfaction with foreign work experience, 79 percent of the sample expressed unreserved satisfaction with having made the decision to go abroad, eleven percent partial satisfaction, and six percent regretted their decision. Correlations between degree of satisfaction and duration of residence abroad showed that persons expressing unreserved satisfaction remained abroad an average of 34 months, those only partially satisfied 23 months, and persons who regretted having gone 19 months. The average duration of residence abroad for the sample at large was 32 months.

In the interviews, respondents returned from positions in Europe were further provided with the opportunity to assess what, in their judgment, were the most significant consequences deriving from the period of residence abroad. They were also asked whether upon their final return to Turkey they found it in any way difficult to readjust to conditions of life and work in the home country. If difficulties were mentioned, an attempt was made to define them specifically and to determine their duration. Responses to these inquiries provide still further data for identifying possible acculturative influences affecting the lives of migrants.

Replies to the former question regarding significant consequences of the experiences abroad could, in summary, be categorized as follows. Those judged *most* relevant from the perspective of acculturation were : (1) realization of the importance of uniform standards and order in the social system; (2) realization of worker rights, of the dignity of worker status, and of basic human equality regardless of occupation; (3) acquisition of cross-cultural perspective of Turkish society in relation to other societies; (4) acquisition of occupational expertise including efficiency, discipline and integrity in work methods; (5) acquisition of *görgü* in its multiple dimensions, among them being culture, enlightenment, experience, strength of character, demeanor and etiquette; (6) acquisition of a knowledge of foreign language; and (7) acquisition of an understanding of human relations. Replies deemed *less* relevant to the subject of acculturation were (1) acquisition of material benefits, including such specifics as cash savings, occupational equipment and the realization of future security in the form of a private business or dwelling place, and (2) realization of a rise in domestic living standards.

From among the foregoing categories, material benefits were most frequently mentioned, followed by occupational expertise, cross-cultural perspective, knowledge of foreign language and *görgü*, in this order. Correlations between significant consequences and years of formal education disclosed that responses most closely associated with higher levels of schooling were (1) knowledge of foreign language, (2) appreciation for uniform standards and order in the social system, (3) occupational expertise including efficiency, discipline and integrity in work methods, (4) rise in domestic living standards and (5) understanding of human relations.

The learning of a European language was identified both as an important motivation for going abroad as well as an important result derived from the migration experience. Respondents were specifically asked in the course of the interviews about their ability to communicate with foreign supervisors in matters pertaining to the work in the last job held prior to permanent return. Although based on self-evaluation, the results obtained seemed to prove rather reliable when tested.

Table 8

Positive Results of Foreign Work Experience
(multiple responses possible)

Results	Responses	Percent of 228
I. — A. *Material Benefits* : savings, acquisition of occu-pational equipment	87	38.2
B. *Security for Future* : establishment of own business and/or home	19	8.3
II. *Rise in Domestic Living Standards* : change in "style" of life	14	6.1
III. — A. *Occupational and Industrial Expertise*	82	36.0
B. *Work Methods* : efficiency, discipline, integrity	43	18.9
IV. *Cross-Cultural Perspective* : view of own country and society in relation to other countries and societies	65	28.5
V. *Knowledge of Foreign Language*	43	18.9
VI. *Realization of Dignity of Worker Status* : basic human equality; worker rights	15	6.6
VII. — A. *Understanding of Life* (general)	13	5.7
B. *Understanding of Human Relations*	18	7.9
VIII. *"Görgü"* : acquisition of culture, refinement, enlightenment, strength of character, experience	52	22.8
IX. *Appreciation of Uniform Standards and Order in the Social System*	6	2.6
X. *No Important Results*	6	2.6
No answer	2	0.9

One test applied in an attempt to assess validity of the self-appraisals was a correlation between reported language proficiency and period of exposure to the language. Persons who estimated their degree of proficiency to be "good" experienced an average exposure of 41 months. Those who rated themselves in the intermediate range—that is, possessing the ability to speak "haltingly"—had been exposed an average of 26 months, and those who required an interpreter, only 14 months. It would thus appear that a minimum period of exposure to any one language approximating three years was essential for acquiring the ability to communicate in the language with any degree of fluency.

A further correlation would appear to exist between foreign language proficiency and years of formal education. Persons reporting "good" language ability also reported an average of 7.3 years of formal education. Respondents who mentioned either the ability to speak "haltingly" or the need for an interpreter had an average of only 5.3 years of education each. Correlations by educational institution attended supported the above—the higher the institution attended the greater the degree of proficiency.

When language ability was correlated with age at time of departure from Turkey, results showed that persons who departed at a younger age attained the better language proficiency. An intervening variable at work here is the tendency for younger migrants to remain abroad longer than others and thereby increase their period of exposure to the foreign language.

Correlations between language proficiency and important results achieved abroad showed further that those who reported "good" proficiency also mentioned "knowledge of foreign language" as among the most important benefits realized. High correlations also existed between "good" language proficiency and "understanding of human relations", "appreciation for uniform standards in the social system", and "occupational expertise." More than four-fifths of those reporting "no important results" cited low degrees of language proficiency.

Alongside important positive results derived from the experience abroad, respondents were encouraged to present a balanced perspective by mentioning any less desirable aspects as well. Out of 228 persons, 150 cited one or more negative aspects which individually covered a wide range but could nevertheless be grouped into three general categories : (1) aspects peculiar to the foreign country, (2) aspects peculiar to migrant workers resident in a foreign country, and (3) aspects manifested in or engendered by compatriots resident abroad. Specific points mentioned within each major category are shown in Table 9.

Within each of the categories, one and sometimes two perceived grievances stand out in particular. Among those constituting the first category, "non-national workers being viewed as inferior to nationals" is predominant followed by what were interpreted as "manifestations of immorality in the society." In the second category, "absence of customary food and drink" looms large as does "language problems." Most striking in the third category were perceptions of "lack of etiquette and obedience for law."

Table 9

Repugnant Aspects of Foreign Experience
(multiple responses possible)

	Persons	Percent
No repugnant aspects encountered	78	34.2
One or more repugnant aspects encountered	150	65.8
	228	100.0

Aspect	Responses	Percent of 150
I. *Aspects Peculiar to the Foreign Country* (as perceived by non-national)		
— Social relationships : role of women, family relations	6	4.0
— Manifestations of "immorality"	22	14.7
— Characteristics and values of the people	10	6.7
— General lack of religious beliefs	3	2.0
— Alien workers being viewed as inferior to nationals	41	27.3
— Lack of ample housing facilities to suitably accommodate migrant workers	6	4.0
II. *Aspects Peculiar to Migrant Workers Resident in a Foreign Country*		
— General hardships suffered by compatriots	3	2.0
— Difficulties arising from different religion and prayer methods	7	4.7
— Absence of customary food and drink	22	14.7
— Inability to take family abroad	6	4.0
— Homesickness	2	1.3
— Feeling of "foreignness"	7	4.7
— Language problems	11	7.3
— Imprisonment	2	1.3
III. *Aspects Manifested in or Engendered by Compatriots Resident Abroad*		
— Factory translators' misuse of authority	3	2.0
— Lack of etiquette and/or obedience for law	28	18.6
— Inter-personal hostilities : between compatriots and between them and other migrant groups abroad	6	4.0
— Ineffectiveness of official representation abroad	3	2.0

One out of four respondents saw fit to mention that, in their opinions, the guest worker was viewed by a significant number of West Europeans as someone of inferior skills and someone, therefore, to whom the less desirable positions were allocated. Consequently, a basic incompatibility was often felt to prevail between the local populace and migrant groups. The idea cropped up in a number of cases that while the older generation in Europe understood Turks and Turkey well for the most part, the younger generation knew Turks much less well. This lack of in-depth understanding, it was believed, often contributed to feelings of incompatibility. Interpreted by respondents as "manifestations of immorality in European society" were, among other things, what they saw as "the social freedom and independence of women", "unrestrained acts of emotional self-expression in public", "holidays characterized by large-scale consumption of alcoholic beverages," and, in contrast to their society of origin, the "relatively relaxed state of morals in European society in general."

Although comments of this nature were not solicited, of no small interest was the migrants' objectivity in being critical of themselves as well as of their foreign environment as shown in category three. When noting the negative impressions certain of their compatriots were, in their opinion, making upon European society, they suggested that such persons be screened out before departure from the homeland.

Specific responses to the inquiry regarding re-adjustment problems experienced upon permanent return to the country of origin, like those pertaining to the question of significant consequences, again covered a wide range. Classified generally and listed insofar as possible in order of apparent relevance to the topic of acculturation, they were as follows : (1) dissatisfaction with the "way" or "style" of life; (2) recognition of a need for more uniform standards and dependability in the social order; (3) dissatisfaction with traditional social relations and with the tendency both on the part of business management and society in general to hold worker status in low esteem; (4) recognition of a need for more efficient, disciplined work methods and for increased sensitivity toward associated values; (5) dissatisfaction with living standards, earning power and ability to save; (6) dissatisfaction with work conditions inclusive of long hours, physical environment, and degree of mechanization; and (7) difficulty securing employment related to past training and experience.

Though reluctance to mention such problems was felt to be present in many cases, in all, 53 percent of the sample nevertheless did cite one or more readjustment difficulties. Here again, the problem most frequently noted—and this by more than half of those who cited problems—was that of "lower living standards." "Recognition of a need for more uniform standards and dependability in the social order" was cited by one in four. Each of the remaining classifications listed above was mentioned with about equal frequency, this being, in each case, by approximately one out of every five respondents who noted problems.

Table 10

Readjustment Problems Reported upon Permanent Return
(multiple responses possible)

	Persons	*Percent*
No readjustment problems reported	105	46.1
One or more readjustment problems reported	121	53.1
No answer	2	0.8
	228	100.0
Problem	*Responses*	*Percent*
I. *Work Conditions*		
— Long hours, manual labor, physical environment	26	21.5
— Difficulty securing suitable employment	22	18.2
— General lack of efficient, disciplined work methods and appreciation for associated values	19	15.7
II. *Living Standards*		
— Low earning power, inability to save	63	52.1
III. *Social Relations*		
— "Way" or "style" of life	19	15.7
— General lack of uniform standards, orderliness and dependability in the social order	31	25.6
— Low esteem for worker status by management and society in general	23	19.0
IV. Specific problems not stated	5	4.1

When duration of residence abroad was correlated with readjustment problems, it was found that persons reporting no problems remained abroad an average of only 28 months while persons mentioning one or more problems were outside their home country an average of 35 months. Migrants who noticed upon their return an "over-all lack of uniform standards, orderliness, and dependability in the social order" remained abroad longer than any other group—namely, an average of 41 months as compared to the average for the sample at large of 32 months. In second position were persons who upon their return were aware of an "over-all

lack of efficient, disciplined work methods and values attached thereto"—
i.e, values which respect the potentialities of well-organized manpower and
the attribute of diligence. In third place were those returnees who were
sensitive to traditional social relations and the low esteem attributed to
worker status. As might be anticipated from the preceding analysis,
persons most proficient in foreign language ranked readjustment problems
in this same order.

Finally, it was found that persons reporting no readjustment problems
were far less disposed to go abroad again than were those who had experienced problems. Fifty-one percent of the former group asserted they
would not return abroad under any condition while only 23 percent of
the latter group took this position.

When asked about degree of satisfaction with current jobs in Turkey,
55 percent of those respondents who were employed at time of interview
expressed satisfaction, 40 percent dissatisfaction, and about five percent
did not reply. The most common reason for dissatisfaction cited in 75
percent of the relevant cases was inadequate wages. Approximately one
in every four dissatisfied respondents mentioned "inefficient work
methods", "low productivity", "unsatisfactory management-employee
relations", and/or "recurring trouble in the work."

In conclusion, the empirical data gathered would seem to suggest that
exposure to European industrial society had left its impressions upon
migrants in no small measure, that these impressions had remained con-
sciously present in the minds of migrants for significant periods of time
following their return to the country of origin, and that these impressions
were objectively discernible by others who themselves had not participated in the migration experience. Furthermore, it has been shown
that the types of acculturative effects and value orientations European
industrial society engendered in Turkish migrants were to a very high
degree viewed by a cross-section of industrial managers in the country
of origin as desirable effects.

8.4   As indicated in the introduction, a second major objective of the
field study was to determine what effects the migration movement had had
as of the summer of 1968 upon the Turkish labor market in general and
upon economic and demographic trends in three regional markets in
particular. The detailed results of the investigation were reported in
Emigration and the Labour Market in Turkey (MS/M/404/301), OECD,
1969 and *Manpower Movements and Labour Markets*, OECD, 1971. In
the present context, only the most salient findings emerging from that

investigation will be discussed—particularly those which are of enduring significance meriting further empirical inquiry in the future.

Four basic data sources relevant to labor market studies exist in Turkey : (1) general censuses of population taken each five years in years ending in "0" and "5", (2) general nation-wide surveys of industry and workplaces, (3) labor force surveys in selected main cities, and (4) various publications of the Turkish State Employment Service (İş ve İşçi Bulma Kurumu), the chief one of which is the monthly *Work and Manpower Bulletin*. The first three sources mentioned are all published by the Turkish State Institute of Statistics, and except for the census, have not in the past appeared on a regularized basis. The quality of the data varies and reconciling the respective sources is often problematic. Frequently, the data is categorized in ways which do not lend themselves to specific functional concerns with which the analyst may be confronted.

Since the objective in the field study was to measure the effects of international migration on three specific regional labor markets, it was felt that first-hand interviews with industrial management in these areas might be one of the most dependable empirical indices available. Accordingly, in each area an attempt was made to interview top-level management in a representative cross-section of industries present there.

Industry in all major branches of the Turkish economy was contacted with the exception of the wearing apparel industry which is largely confined to Istanbul. As shown in Table 11 management at a total of 50 firms, or 54 individual workplaces was interviewed. Thirty-four of these firms were in Izmir, 14 in Kocaeli and two in Zonguldak. Firms interviewed in Izmir employed 16,501 persons, in Kocaeli, 14,234, and in Zonguldak, 37,814—in all, 68,549 persons.

Defined in the broadest sense, industrial employment in Turkey as a whole in 1968 was estimated from the official statistical sources to be in the vicinity of one million. Thus, the establishments interviewed employed approximately seven percent of all persons then employed in Turkish industry. Firms interviewed in Izmir employed about 28 percent of all industrially employed persons in that city, firms interviewed in Kocaeli employed about half of all industrially employed persons in that province, and the two firms contacted in Zonguldak province employed approximately three-fourths of all persons engaged in industry and mining there. Almost without exception, all of Turkey's major industrial workplaces were included in the research design.

Table 11
Distribution of Firms Interviewed by Province and Industrial Branch

Branch	Izmir			Kocaeli			Zonguldak			Totals		
	No.	Employment	%	No.	Employment	%	No.	Employment	%	No.	Employment	%
Mining							1*	33,906	89.7	1*	33,906	49.4
Iron, Steel							1	3,908	10.3	1	3,908	5.7
Metal Products	5	1,341	8.1	2	822	5.8				7	2,163	3.2
Cement, Cement Products	2	1,038	6.3							2	1,038	1.5
Construction Materials	2	189	1.2							2	189	0.3
Ceramics, Glass				2	2,027	14.2				2	2,027	2.9
Chemicals, Chemical Products	2	410	2.5	4	1,097	7.7				6	1,507	2.2
Rubber, Plastics	2	218	1.3	2	1,346	9.5				4	1,564	2.3
Paper, Paper Products	1	82	0.5	1	5,912	41.5				2	5,994	8.7
Machine Tools	1	70	0.4							1	70	0.1
Electrical Equipment	2	260	1.6	1	1,633	11.5				3	1,893	2.8
Automotive Assembly, Parts	2	974	5.9	2	1,397	9.8				4	2,371	3.5
Textiles	7	7,460	45.2							7	7,460	10.9
Food, Beverage	7	2,861	17.3							7	2,861	4.2
Tobacco Products	1	1,598	9.7							1	1,598	2.3
Totals	34	16,501	100.0	14	14,234	100.0	2	37,814	100.00	50	68,548	100.0

* One firm having five workplaces.

In each interview industrial management was asked whether any personnel had severed employment relations with the firm in order to go abroad to work. Forty-six of 54 workplaces reported that some employees had terminated to go abroad, two reported that none had left for this reason, four had no way of knowing, and two did not reply. Of the 46 answering in the affirmative, eleven reported that at least some of the jobs vacated by workers terminating to go abroad were difficult to fill while 35 indicated that recruitment for these positions was not problematic.

Positions most frequently reported difficult to fill were of two types : (1) specialized types of machine operators peculiar to the textile industry, and (2) general types of machine operators required by many industries for maintenance purposes if not the production process itself. The latter category refers in particular to lathe, fitting, milling and planing machine operators. Also cited were electricians, welders, molders, blacksmiths and some types of skilled workers required for mining.

In all, management knew of 503 former employees who had quit jobs to go abroad. However, the mining and iron and steel industries, both the largest of firms interviewed, are not included in this figure since they reported having no way to estimate departures of migrants. If the same rate prevailed in these two industries as in all the others combined, it might be projected from employment levels that total departures were in the vicinity of 1200 rather than 500. One-half, or 253, of the 503 which were reported were in the textile industry, 95 in the electrical appliance, 34 in the food, 31 in the metal products and 23 in the chemical products industries. As far as positions then being held in these firms by workers returned from abroad were concerned, 375 were mentioned.

In the final analysis, it is the fluctuations in skilled personnel which are crucial. Unfortunately, management had no means to compare skills of departed migrants with skills of returnees. Among the latter, however, at least 68 percent possessed a skill of some type. Only 22 of the 375 were unskilled and five semi-skilled. Had one or two firms been able to report more precise information, the 94 whose skill level was unclear could have been classified. Due to the nature of the firms where they were employed, however, it is assumed that a sizeable proportion of these 94 would also fall into "skilled" or "highly skilled" categories.

To measure current demand for skilled labor in the three labor markets studied, firms interviewed were asked what job vacancies presently existed for skilled labor. A total of 364 positions were listed. Only the cement and tobacco products industries reported having no current vacancies. The paper, textile, and automotive assembly industries each had 50 or more vacancies, while the mining, iron and steel, food and beverage industries each had 30 or more. Of the 364 vacancies, 103 were for machine operators as follows: fitters, 44; lathe operators, 32; planing machine operators, 14; milling machine operators, 10; and press operators, three.

For the period 1963-68, the firms interviewed reported 47,825 jobs vacated and 55,031 persons hired. Had all firms been able to report and report for the entire five-year period under consideration, new jobs created would undoubtedly have been substantially higher than the 15 percent increment shown. However, the high rate of turn-over in personnel indicated by these figures is not uncommon in the Turkish labor market and, under any circumstance, is attributable to international migration only to a small degree.

A prerequisite to any assessment of the effects of emigration upon the Turkish labor market is perspective on that country's total manpower resources. The latter, in turn, is by definition closely associated with the structure of Turkish population.

During the last several decades, Turkey's population has experienced unprecedented growth. Between the 1950 and 1955 censuses a 14.7 percent increase occurred followed by another in the amount of 15.1 percent between 1955 and 1960. Only during the last two inter-census periods —1960-65 and 1965-70—has growth begun to diminish somewhat. A 13.2 percent increment was recorded in 1965 and approximately 13.6 in 1970. In October, 1970, Turkey's population stood at 35.7 million, up from 20.9 million in 1950.

It follows that the population of Turkey is a predominantly young population. In October, 1965, 51.2 percent of all Turks were under 20 years of age. Nearly four-fifths, or 79.1 percent, were under 40 years of age. The overwhelming majority of emigrant workers are between ages 20 and 39. In 1965, there were 8.8 million Turks in this same 20-39 age cohort, and they represented 62.2 percent of the nation's total labor potential between ages 20 and 65. Thus, the 775 thousand persons who are thought to have migrated abroad between 1961 and the end of 1972 comprised about four percent of the working-age population and two percent of the nation's total population. It may be surmised that from among the entire Turkish population in the 20-39 year age range, approximately one person in 13 has at some time during his working career migrated abroad for employment.

According to the 1965 census, approximately 72 percent (9.8 million) of the nation's economically active population was engaged in the agricultural sector where hidden unemployment is generally recognized to be quite extensive. Reasonably precise figures on unemployment or under-employment in Turkey are not available; however, Turkish estimates showing ten percent or more of the working age population as unemployed are not uncommon. It follows that, quantitatively in terms of absolute numbers, those Turks working abroad represent a rather small portion of the nation's total manpower resources.

This is the perspective as seen from a purely quantitative view. More important, particularly in the case of a developing nation, are qualitative considerations. Paradoxically, one of the most critical of all types of data is at the same time among the most difficult to obtain—namely, reliable information on skills of departing and returning migrants. No known large-scale research has as yet been undertaken in this highly crucial area. However, if the data from both the archival and interview samples of the present study may be taken as indicative of prevailing conditions, it is surmised that a significantly high proportion of all migrants are skilled and that the occupations they pursue in Turkey are in many cases crucial to the development of the economy.

It should be emphasized that the quality of the archival data varied considerably from one location to another and that the research staff had no means by which to refine it. Consequently, the figures cited must be taken as indicative only of very general trends. Be this as it may, when only the determinable cases (902 out of 1,433) are considered, 45.6 percent of persons sent abroad through official channels between 1961 and 1968 in the three provinces studied were shown to be personnel possessing skills which by Turkish criteria were skills at least equivalent to the "master's" level. The comparable statistic for the determinable cases in the interview sample (191 out of 228) was 44.1 percent. Additionally, the interview sample was composed of 15.7 percent technical and 4.2 percent clerical personnel which the archival sample was not. Presumably, if the same criteria applied in classifying the interview sample had been applied in the archival sample, many persons considered as unskilled in the latter case (53.1 percent) might instead have been classified as semi-skilled. In any case, that over 40 percent of all migrants in each sample had attained skill levels of "master" or higher is believed to be a significant observation as it relates to the qualitative profile of the Turkish labor force migrating abroad. Among the 50 industrial firms interviewed, 64.4 percent of returned migrants working in the firms were reported to be at the "master's" level or higher (again excluding technical and clerical personnel).

Table 12

Skill Levels before Departure

	Archive Sample Percent	Interview Sample Percent
1. Supervisory (headmaster, head of shift)	1.9	4.7
2. Skilled (master)	43.7	39.4
3. Technical	—	15.7
4. Clerical	—	4.2
5. Semi-skilled	1.3	20.4
6. Apprentice	—	1.0
7. Unskilled	53.1	14.6
Determinable Cases	902	191

Even though 70 percent of Turkey's population resides in villages, contrary to what is sometimes supposed the majority of Turks migrating abroad are *not* villagers. The data collected by Aker over a one-year period during 1970-71 indicated that 27.9 percent of all respondents in a sample of 590 were residing in villages at the time of their departure. City dwellers constituted 46.8 percent of all departures and town residents 15.3 percent. In the archival and interview samples percentages for village and town were somewhat lower than this. That at the most only about one in three departures appears to be from the village would seem to strengthen the plausibility of the hypothesized over-all high skill levels prevalent among migrants.

Data from the interviews indicated that industrial management in Turkey is for the most part quite keenly aware of the potential dangers uncontrolled migration could present for the economy in general and the labor market in particular. Some managers expressed regret at having trained skilled workers only to have them migrate sometime later. Others felt that the type of work a migrant does abroad is often too specialized to satisfy the more generalized requirements of Turkish industry upon his return. A concern quite commonly expressed was that a sharp recession in the European economy could send migrants home *en masse* and thereby generate a crisis situation in the Turkish labor market. Still other managers felt that already now difficulties prevail in securing adequately trained skilled labor and that migration abroad only tends to aggravate an already problematic situation.

Be this as it may, the same group of managers elsewhere in their interviews indicated that they had current openings for only 364 skilled personnel. When placed alongside an employment level of 68.5 thousand in these same firms and when considering too the rather large numbers of presumably skilled migrants already returned to resettle in Turkey, the figure of 364 would appear rather inconsequential. Evidence leads the analyst to hypothesize that among her now quite large contingent of returned migrants Turkey does in fact possess skilled manpower resources which, primarily for want of systematic recruitment and necessary incentives, are currently diverted outside areas of prime need. It is further hypothesized that this potential supply of skilled manpower could very substantially satisfy specific demands in the labor market as they presently exist. Wages have indeed risen as has the cost of living, but it is highly doubtful that any correlation could be drawn with certainty at the national or regional levels between emigration and wages. As observed above, a high degree of turnover in personnel is characteristic of the Turkish labor market under any circumstance and not one engendered by emigration as such.

8.5   Summary of Demographic Characteristics and Conclusions

At the outset, the dual objectives of the study were stated as follows : (1) to define demographic characteristics and motivations of the migrant and to learn what socio-economic and socio-cultural effects the emigration experience has upon the lives of migrants who return to settle in their home country; (2) to learn what discernible effects the emigration movement had had upon the Turkish labor market as of the summer of 1968, particularly with respect to economic and demographic trends in three regional markets. The following paragraphs will briefly summarize what would appear to be the most significant findings of the research.

First, with respect to the former concern stated above, it would appear probable that a comparison of the demographic data from the interview and archival sources discloses broad trends which in most instances are indicative of conditions applicable in the nation at large. Accordingly, from all available evidence it seems reasonable to characterize the most numerous group of Turkish migrants as being between 23 and 35 years of age at time of departure and having a median age in the vicinity of 29 years. Departures prior to age 23 and after age 35 are more the exception than the rule. While few women participated in the early stages of the emigration movement, at the present time approximately one in five workers abroad is a woman.

When departing, roughly four out of five migrants are married. More have two children as dependents than have three. Nearly all have been exposed to the equivalent of a primary school education (five years), but education in excess of eight years is rare. It is estimated that between five and ten percent have had at least one year of vocational training and that somewhat less than five percent attended the lycee or beyond. The majority are born in villages and towns (communities under 20 thousand population) but are residents of cities (communities over 20 thousand) at time of departure. About one in three migrants are village dwellers at time of departure.

It follows that for the large majority of workers going abroad, migration is not a new experience. In the interview sample, 70 percent of the respondents had changed their community of residence at least once prior to departure. Fifty-two percent had migrated across provincial boundaries, and another 28 percent had moved considerable distances either from what are now foreign territories or from remote regions within the Turkish Republic. Upon returning from Europe, the large majority of migrants would appear to re-settle in the community from which they originally departed.

While persons in the interview sample remained abroad an average of 32 months, economic conditions prevalent in Europe during 1967-68 were responsible in many cases for premature returns. Four to five years is believed to be the average preferred period of foreign residence. Moreover, there are indications that, conditions permitting, a substantial number of Turks at work in Europe would like to remain abroad indefinitely. This latter group, however, is at present thought to be a relatively small contingent of the whole.

Temporary returns to Turkey of about one-month's duration are quite common during the period of residence abroad. These seem to average approximately one return for each 18 months spent in Europe. About one in five migrants was accompanied by a spouse who also was employed in most instances. Nearly two-thirds of the respondents would be receptive to migrating once again under favorable conditions.

Persons interviewed were overwhelmingly successful in realizing the goals which motivated their original decisions to migrate. Only between four and nine percent were unable to attain their objectives. Multiple motives ordinarily underlay the emigration decision, but foremost among them were financial and educational goals. The former usually did not constitute an end in itself but rather a means to opening a private business, purchasing real estate or obtaining major consumer items in Turkey.

The latter most often pertained to acquisition of occupational expertise, foreign language skills and opportunity to travel.

Occupation-wise, at time of departure approximately 60 percent of migrants interviewed had worked as craftsmen, automotive equipment or machine operators, and production process workers. A similar percentage were, by Turkish standards, skilled workers. Averages for a nation-wide sample, however, would undoubtedly fall somewhat below this level. Nine out of ten migrants severed employment relations in Turkey in order to assume positions abroad.

Until now, there have been virtually no government controls placed on emigration. The prevailing philosophy seems to have been that domestic job vacancies created by emigration would provide others with the opportunity to secure employment. Emigration has often been viewed as a form of release for unemployment and under-employment pressures which inevitably come to the fore when rapid population growth offsets economic growth. Also, remittances and exchanges made by migrants serve to bolster the nation's hard currency resources in no small measure. As discussed in detail elsewhere in this volume, the export of labor has become in recent years Turkey's leading earner of foreign exchange.

If large-scale demand for Turkish manpower continues to develop in European labor markets, it would seem that in the best interests of the nation the Government of Turkey might seriously want to consider modifying its present manpower policy which permits virtually unlimited emigration. Guidelines for a comprehensive manpower policy which is in harmony with long-range economic development goals have already been laid down in Turkey's five-year development plans. As indicated there, quantitative projections of potential European demand for Turkish labor are only a minimal starting point. Maximally, a policy should be implemented which considers the qualitative dimensions of emigration and their implications for the domestic labor market—a policy which realistically weighs both the pros and cons of emigration and assesses what is in Turkey's best interests not only in the short run, but ultimately as well.

The experience of one decade is far too short a time span in which to assess cumulative evidence of acculturation in Turkish society at large resulting from the mass movement of Turkish citizens between different cultural spheres. Effects and influences of West European industrial society are indeed present and measurable in that restricted segment of Turkish society which has been exposed to life in Western Europe for extended periods of time, but "effects" and "influences" must not be interpreted as "acculturation" *per se*. Rather, acculturation at the societal level is a phenomenon which lends itself to analysis in historical time exceeding the confines of one decade.

Suffice it to say that the mass migration of manpower across cultural boundaries could well prove to be as it develops in the course of time one of the more important media that circumstances peculiar to the present century have produced for transmitting not only the accoutrements of western industrial society to Turkey, but also the values responsible for and surrounding these accoutrements as well. To what extent Turkish society may choose to assimilate or adapt these values as its own is, for the present, an intangible variable which can be brought into focus only with the passing of time. Continued European economic prosperity and projected large-scale requirements for manpower from abroad are expected to substantially intensify the potential for mutual cultural inter-penetration between West European and Turkish societies in the decade ahead.

IX

THE TURKISH BRAIN-DRAIN : MIGRATION TENDENCIES AMONG DOCTORAL LEVEL MANPOWER

TURHAN OĞUZKAN

ABSTRACT

This chapter is concerned with the migratory behavior of Turkish citizens holding the Ph.D. degree who are professionally employed outside Turkey. Its purpose is to examine selected characteristics of the migrants, to relate these characteristics to migratory behavior, and to identify the main motives for migration. Presumably, such information could be used in attempts to control or regulate the migration of talent from Turkey.

Comparisons with the annual production of doctorates in Turkey, the present stock of Ph.D.'s, the growth rate of this stock over time, and the current need for Ph.D.'s suggest that loss due to migration is substantial. The study showed that the greatest loss occurred in sciences and engineering which together represent crucial areas for economic development.

In addition to the Ph.D.'s who leave their jobs in Turkey for employment abroad, there are also graduate students who frequently do not return to their homeland after foreign study. The decision to migrate from Turkey, or to remain abroad if already there, was found to be related to professional, economic, socio-cultural, personal and political reasons. Of these, professional reasons consistently weighed by far the heaviest. As expressed by respondents, these professional reasons were closely related to the immediate environment of work such as "opportunity for advanced training","physical facilities" and the like.

Academicians constitute the largest proportion of migrant Ph.D.'s. Thus, it seems that the university is one of the more important types of institutions in which measures could be taken to control or regulate the migration of Ph.D.'s from Turkey. If Turkish universities are to increase their attracting and holding powers for talented staff, a review of personnel policies and practices may be advisable. Moreover, rules and practices governing the study abroad of Turkish graduate students might also be reviewed from the standpoint of controlling the drain of talent.

The international migration of talent is an old phenomenon but a new issue. One could cite numerous historical examples of scholars, writers and artists who sought their fortunes in foreign lands. It is interesting, however, that the movement has become an issue in many countries of the world only during the past ten to fifteen years.

Reasons underlying the attention given this phenomenon in recent times include the acceleration of the so-called "brain-drain" movement itself and an unprecedented concern with the problems of development all over the world. Obviously, development in an age of science and technology requires highly qualified manpower in the sciences, engineering, health, agriculture, and other areas. Therefore, it is natural that any large scale or continuous flow of such manpower across national boundaries should become a subject for discussion and careful examination.

Although statistical evidence at hand gives only a partial picture of the entire movement, indications are that it has been gaining momentum during the past years. No less important than the increase in volume is the general direction of the movement. The talent tends to flow from the less developed regions of the world where it is relatively scarce to more developed regions where it is already concentrated. Due to this fact, the movement becomes especially important from the standpoint of developing countries.

Even a cursory survey of the literature reveals that Turkey is frequently placed among the countries subject to serious brain-drain. Statistical evidence and whatever available research there is in the field suggest that those professionals most affected by the movement are physicians, engineers and scientists.

Among the most detailed immigration statistics available are those from the United States. According to the U.S. Immigration Office, a total of 512 Turkish physicians, engineers and scientists were admitted to that country as immigrants between the years 1962 and 1966 (U.S. House of Representatives, 1967). Another 195 Turks in these same professions gained immigrant status in 1967 (National Science Foundation, 1969). When Turkish professionals already employed in the United States but contemplating possible immigrant status are included, the actual volume of talent migrating from Turkey to the United States might very well exceed the totals mentioned here.

A study conducted jointly by Johns Hopkins University and the Ankara Health School in 1962-63 indicated that 2,248 or 18.4 percent of a total stock of 12,275 physicians graduated from Turkish medical schools were employed outside Turkey (Ferguson & Dirican, 1966). According to this study, West Germany attracted the most Turkish physicians at that time followed closely by the United States. Other nations where sizeable numbers were located included England, France, Switzerland, and the Scandinavian countries. A more recent survey concerning Turkish engineers and architects estimated that at least 975 or 5.6 percent of a total stock of 17,233 of these professionals were working outside Turkey in 1968 (Kösemen, 1968). In this case, the United States attracted the most. Other countries employing them were England, France, Switzerland and West Germany.

Hasan Üner (1968) attempted to estimate the investment which had been made in 203 Turkish physicians and other health personnel, engineers and scientists admitted to the United States as immigrants during 1967. Considering the investment per immigrant to be approximately $ 90,000 inclusive of maintenance, education, and earnings foregone during schooling and employment, Üner concluded that the total cost to Turkey of these 203 professionals migrating was $ 18,270,000 at 1965 prices.

The three studies mentioned above dealt mostly with the quantitative aspects of migration, and except for the study on Turkish physicians, little attention was given to the characteristics of migrants and the dynamics of migratory behavior. Consequently, the present study sought to explore the problem in sufficient depth so as to secure data concerning the nature and causes of the migration of Turkish elites. Sponsored by the Turkish Scientific and Technical Council, it was conducted during 1968-69 and selected as its subject Turkish Ph.D.'s employed abroad. The full report was published in Turkish by Middle East Technical University in 1971. What follows is a summary of the research design, major findings and policy recommendations.

9.1 Design

9.1.1 The Problem

Concerned with Turkish Ph.D.'s working abroad, the study investigated selected personal, social, educational and professional characteristics of this particular group of migrants, and especially the relationship between these characteristics and the patterns of migratory behavior. Since previous studies on the migration of high-level manpower from Turkey were limited with none having been done on the specific group selected for this study, an exploratory approach was used. The study sought to identify the socio-economic factors and personal motives responsible for the migratory behavior of the group under investigation so that those emerging as the more significant could be studied further. It was also believed that the information and insight gained from the study might have practical uses in attempts to control the loss of talent from Turkey.

9.1.2 Basic Assumptions

Two basic assumptions underlie the study. One is related to the significance of the brain-drain movement itself from the standpoint of development. The other is concerned with the interpretation of the essential nature of migratory behavior.

Assumption 1. The significance of the brain-drain movement from the standpoint of development is a controversial matter in the literature. Some writers react to the international migration of talent favorably by stressing the idea of service to humanity, the basic rights of the individual to work in the place of his choice, and the maximization of the marginal utility of talent through free movement under competitive market conditions (Grubel & Scott, 1966; Johnson, 1965). Other writers, who are concerned more with national interests and the effects of mal-distribution of talent throughout the world, react unfavorably to the movement. The latter argue that the migration of talent impairs development efforts in regions where such efforts are most needed (Kidd, 1964; Thomas, 1967 : 479-506; U.K. Committee, 1967). It is also pointed out that competitive market conditions do not fully exist in countries where the brain-drain occurs since migration policies are used as flexible instruments to protect national interests similar to policies on tariffs (Thomas, 1967: 495).

This author assumes that any large scale or continuous flow of highly qualified manpower from less developed to more developed regions of the world is undesirable. Sending countries are deprived of potential contributions that migrant talent could make to their economic development, and the nation's investment in the education of highly qualified professionals is lost. Moreover, emigrating weakens leadership potentials in the nation's professional and social life.

Therefore, the study assumes that searching for ways to control the migration of talent out of Turkey is desirable. It further assumes that any acceptable pattern of control should be harmonious with the natural desires of this talent to develop and be productive and with the established Turkish government policy of maintaining fruitful cultural ties with other countries.

Assumption 2. Assumptions regarding the essential nature of migratory behavior are again related to points of view in the literature. Although positions are not always clear-cut, some writers seem to emphasize objective conditions such as the supply of talent and the demand for it and the development of centers of excellence attracting talent. Others stress the subjective dimensions of migratory behavior such as personal motives, personality structure and the value system of the individual. Perhaps, a more balanced approach is one that takes into consideration both the objective and subjective dimensions.

One concept that is sufficiently broad as to encompass both is that of push forces in the sending country and pull forces in the receiving country. This concept was, for example, used effectively by the Pan American Health Organization (1966) as a framework for analyzing the migration of professionals in health, engineering and sciences from Latin American countries. The present study applies the push-pull theory in analyzing the migratory behavior of Turkish Ph.D.'s. It assumes that the migratory nature of talent is the result of an interplay of objective conditions which set the stage and of subjective motives which prompt the decision to migrate. It further assumes that since the decision of the migrant depends on his individual perception of the objective conditions, the key to understanding migratory behavior is to be found in the person who has made this decision.

9.1.3 Definition of Population

The population included all Turkish Ph.D.'s (or holders of an equivalent professional degree) who were working abroad full-time without any employment ties in Turkey during the period of the study. No limitations were set on fields of specialization except that doctorates in the medical sciences were excluded.

9.1.4 Method of Investigation

Since the study assumed that the key to understanding migratory behavior was to be found in the individual person who had made the decision to migrate, information was collected directly from migrants themselves. Specific variables which it included were as follows :

9.1.4.1 *Dependent variables* : (1) pull factors in the country of immigration at the time of the decision to migrate; (2) push factors in Turkey at the time of the decision to migrate; (3) factors holding the migrant in the receiving country at the time of the study; (4) migration routes to the country of residence at the time of the study; (5) continuing desire, if any, for professional contact with Turkey; (6) intention, if any, of returning to Turkey in the foreseeable future; (7) cooperation, if any, of individuals or agencies in Turkey with the migrant abroad; (8) the migrant's possible views on improvement of working conditions for his professional group in Turkey.

9.1.4.2 *Independent variables* : (1) age; (2) sex; (3) place of birth; (4) present citizenship; (5) marital status including number of children and citizenship of spouse before marriage; (6) father's vocation; (7) education of father and mother; (8) mother tongue and foreign languages known; (9) secondary and higher education; (10) field of specialization; (11) present country of residence; (12) professional experience including employment both in and outside Turkey; (13) income.

A pre-test of the questionnaire was administered to a group of Ph.D. returnees in Turkey. After corrections and improvements based on an analysis of their replies were made, the questionnaire was put into final form.

Names and addresses of migrants were obtained through (1) the Ministry of Education, universities and research institutions in Turkey; (2) selected scientists and other professionals in Turkey representing various fields of specialization; (3) migrant Ph.D.'s temporarily in Turkey during the survey; (4) lists furnished by known migrants abroad; (5) Turkish embassies, consulates, and cultural attachees in Canada, England, Germany, Italy, Sweden, Switzerland and the United States; (6) outstanding research institutions and scientific foundations in these countries; (7) statistical information; (8) scientific and professional journals; (9) catalogues of foreign universities; (10) membership lists of scientific organizations; (11) university alumni associations; (12) newspaper features in Turkey; and (13) names furnished by respondents to the questionnaire.

All these sources together produced a population of 217 potential respondents of whom 150 actually replied by March 31, 1969. The questionnaires were analyzed in the data processing laboratories of Middle East Technical University. In addition to simple computations, the chisquare test was used wherever possible to assess the significance of the relationships between selected variables. The level of significance acceptable was set at $p < .05$.

9.2 Major Findings

9.2.1 General Aspects of Migration

The country which attracts most Turkish Ph.D.'s working abroad is the United States. Out of 150 respondents, 107 or 71.3 percent were employed there followed by 10.0 percent in Canada, 8.0 percent in West Germany, 3.3 percent in France and 2.7 percent in England. All other countries combined employed the remaining 4.7 percent.

Specialists in a variety of fields were represented. Engineers and physical scientists were the two largest groups followed by social scientists. Engineers comprised 38.7 percent of the group, physical scientists 38.0 percent, social scientists 13.3 percent, agronomists 5.3 percent and persons in the humanities 3.3 percent. Within the first three general fields, civil engineers, physicists and economists predominated respectively.

As far as the employing organizations were concerned, it was found that 62 percent of the respondents were associated with institutions of higher education. This trend was especially apparent in the United States. Industry employed 19.3 percent of the respondents and all other sectors of the economy combined, a similar proportion. Of the 115 holding academic titles, 33 percent were at the rank of professor, 28.7 percent associate professor and 19 percent assistant professor. More were involved predominantly in research than in teaching.

9.2.2 *Significance of the Flow*

If as suggested earlier the average preparation cost per Ph.D. is assumed to be $90,000 at 1965 prices, the investment equivalent in the entire group of 217 Turkish Ph.D.'s working abroad at the time of this study would approximate $ 19,530,000. A more meaningful index with which to judge the significance of the flow abroad, however, would be a consideration of the production rate and stock of Ph.D.'s in Turkey.

Production in all fields averaged 111 per year during the period 1962 through 1965, the latest years for which statistics were available. If this yearly average of 111 is taken as the basis for comparison, then 217 migrant Ph.D.'s would be equivalent to approximately two years' production. Even more significant is the fact that the rate of production in engineering and the physical sciences is considerably slower than in the social sciences and humanities. If the former two fields which represented the great majority of Turkish Ph.D.'s working abroad are singled out for comparison, migrant Ph.D.'s in engineering were equal to seven years' production and those in the physical sciences 6.4 years' production.

As far as the existing stock is concerned, no definitive statistical data could be located. An estimate of Ph.D.'s in the physical sciences only produced during the period 1933-1968 indicated that those working abroad in 1968 constituted approximately 18 percent of the entire existing stock in this field.

The crucial question here might be the extent to which Turkey needs Ph.D.'s in the fields represented by the migrants. Reliable estimates or well-designed projections are lacking, but there are a number of indications pointing in the direction of a definite need. First of all, higher educational institutions have been developing in Turkey at an unprecedented rate, creating a growing need for qualified scholars in most fields. Second, the government has been trying since 1963 to implement a plan for educating 3,000 young people abroad in order to meet the needs of higher education. Finally, the Second Five-Year Development Plan which ended in 1972 contained a number of policies reflecting the increasing need for Ph.D.'s. Among these policies were the development of graduate programs at the universities, the implementation of special programs to prepare university staff, the encouragement of qualified people working in other sectors to join the universities, and the promotion of vital fields through research and training scholarships.

It is evident that the flow of Ph.D.'s out of Turkey is rather substantial when placed against a background of the country's need for such talent, the current production rate and existing stock. This exodus impedes inadequate efforts at increasing stocks to meet growing needs, especially in higher education. The flow not only results in the free transfer of investment value to other countries, but perhaps more importantly than this, leads to a denial of possible contributions that the highly educated might make in the development of their own country. Since talent in the fields of engineering and physical sciences is particularly scarce, Turkey, like any other developing country, needs to be especially careful in making full use of her human resources in these areas vital for development.

9.2.3 *Personal and Social Characteristics of the Migrants*

Analysis of the information concerning father's occupation and educational background of parents indicated that most Turkish Ph.D.'s working abroad came from homes which stood socio-economically far above the national average. Whereas according to the 1965 census only twelve percent of the entire employable population of Turkey was working in professional, technical, administrative, managerial, clerical, business, sales and military occupations, 82 percent of the respondents' were doing so. Again, although half of the entire population over age five was illiterate in 1965, 44.7 percent of respondents' fathers were university graduates and another 24.7 percent high school graduates. Forty-four percent of the mothers had graduated from institutions above the elementary school level.

A very significant proportion of migrants had attended private high schools in Turkey which use European languages as the medium of instruction. Admission to these schools is through competitive examination and payment of tuition. During the years the typical migrant was in junior high school, 5.7 percent of all junior high school students in the nation were enrolled in private institutions whereas 36.7 percent of the migrants were so enrolled. At the senior high school level, comparable statistics were 6.9 percent for the general population compared to 38.7 percent for the group under study.

Since the necessary data are non-existent, there is no satisfactory way to determine whether the foregoing observations on socio-economic status are peculiar to migrant Ph.D.'s or whether they apply to Turkish Ph.D.'s in general. The median age of the migrant group was found to be 40 years which would indicate a mature group well-established in their professions. Certain other findings such as those on academic titles, positions in employing organizations, and total years of work corroborate this. Thus, the information on migration presented in this study derives from a highly experienced group of people. Those who were married comprised 83.3 percent of the group and the typical family had two children. More migrants were married to foreign spouses than to Turkish ones.

The great majority, or 79.3 percent, of Turkish Ph.D.'s working abroad retained their original citizenship. This tendency could be interpreted in a variety of ways, but one probability is that although many had been working outside of Turkey for some years, they regarded their stay abroad as a temporary matter. This observation was reinforced by replies to the question on intentions of returning to Turkey. Nevertheless, even among those who intended to remain abroad, one of the ties most difficult to break was that of citizenship.

9.2.4 *Educational Background*

Although a relatively high proportion of migrant Ph.D.'s attended private schools teaching in European languages, there is no way to ascertain whether a relationship exists between this early exposure to a foreign culture and later migratory behavior. In any case, 26 percent went on to receive bachelors degrees, 34.0 percent master's degrees, and 81.3 percent doctoral degrees from foreign institutions. Most foreign studies had been carried out in the United States where 56 percent earned their doctorates.

The relationship between foreign study and migration often suggested in the literature deserves closer examination. There is no doubt that the foreign student goes through a process of adjustment to a new culture during his stay abroad, affecting each individual in a variety of ways. This is also a time when serious decisions about one's profession, future career, and often marriage must be made. The individual may find himself surrounded by a number of influences and alternatives as he advances through his higher education in the host country. These might include educational programs geared to the needs of the host culture, emerging professional interests which may be better fulfilled there, desire for success, the possibility of high earnings, demands for his skill and some-times offers of specific jobs. In addition, social ties develop in the course of daily life, and sometimes a family tie is established by marriage with a spouse from the host country. All of these factors influence the duration of the student's stay in the host country after graduation.

It seems that many Turkish Ph.D.'s working abroad fit this descrip-tion. For example, 30 percent of the respondents indicated that they had no work experience whatever in Turkey either before or after completing their doctorates. Those who were employed in Turkey before but not after receiving their doctorates constituted 58 percent of the group. These findings suggest a close relationship between foreign study and the migration of talent.

A clear relationship exists between education abroad and securing the *first* full-time job abroad in the sense that this was achieved with the help of university advisers in 26 percent of the cases under study. Other some-what less common routes to employment in order of frequency were personal initiative, initiative of the employing organization, and friends in the profession. Sixty-four percent reported being outside Turkey when their first full-time jobs were located abroad.

Below the doctoral level 51.3 percent bore their own expenses without scholarship aid whereas this percentage increased to 61.4 during doctoral studies. Those who received scholarships from the Turkish government comprised 31.3 percent of the group for levels below doctoral studies and only 10.7 percent during doctoral studies. On the other hand, support from scholarships administered by other governments or inter-national organizations increased from 14.0 percent for below doctoral levels to 26.7 percent during doctoral studies.

9.2.5 *Professional Experience*

Medians for total years of full-time employment stood at 4.4 years be-fore doctoral studies and 7.2 years afterwards. While many had no work experience in Turkey, the range for those who did have was one through 25 years. Because Turkish government scholarships carry compulsory service requirements, a significant relationship existed between years of work in Turkey and type of support during higher education.

Nearly half of those who had been working in Turkey before migration were associated with universities. Thus, the university served as the major launching pad from which migrant Ph.D.'s departed. This particular professional characteristic of the migrants is important in understanding certain aspects of their migratory behavior as well as specific motives or causes for their migration. It is also important from the practical stand-point of searching for ways to control the flow of talent out of Turkey at the Ph.D. level.

Annual incomes of the respondents ranged from $ 3,000 to $ 45,000 with the median being $ 15,900. The frequency of income above the $ 20,000 level was significantly greater in the United States than in any other country under consideration. There was a close proximity in income between Turkish academicians in the physicial, agricultural and social sciences working in the United States and their American counter-parts. This was, in turn, well above the professional income of their counterparts in Turkey, leaving no room for doubt that working abroad is by far financially more rewarding even after differences in purchasing power are adjusted out.

9.2.6 *Factors Affecting the Decision to Migrate*

Both pull forces in the receiving country and push forces in the send-ing country were studied as motives or causes for migration. In addition, since reasons for migrating in the past and for continuing to stay abroad at present are often somewhat different, "holding forces" were also analyzed. For example, a person might have migrated for financial reasons but once this need was satisfied he might have continued to stay abroad for professional or family reasons. In this instance, attractive pay abroad together with insufficient pay at home would respectively constitute the pull and push forces, whereas professional or family reasons would be the holding forces.

Generally speaking, the decision to migrate may be related to economic, professional, socio-cultural, political and personal or family reasons which may be variously defined. Some typical examples of definitions are as follows. In the case of economic reasons, the definition was simple, consisting of the single item of "professional income". Professional factors, on the other hand, included such specific items as "work available in the field of specialization", "physical facilities for work", "rapid promotion in the career", "opportunity for advanced training", and "close contact with great scientific centers". Socio-cultural factors com-prised such considerations as "satisfactory social relations in the work situation" and "desire to know a foreign culture". The political factor meant "freedom from political pressure or political unrest". Personal or family factors included "foreign spouse", "better educational oppor-tunities for children" and the like.

Since the decision to migrate or remain abroad might have been motivated by multiple considerations, respondents were asked to rank the primary, secondary and tertiary factors which affected their decisions. The results are summarized in Table 1. The last column shows the total over-all weighting of the various factors.

Regardless of whether push, pull or holding factors are considered, professional reasons far outweigh all other reasons for migrating or remaining abroad. This is apparent both in column "A" in each case as well as in the total column. As a push or pull factor, professional considerations weigh over-all between four and five times greater than the next strongest factor.

Both as a push factor and a holding factor, economic considerations rank next to professional considerations. Ranking second as far as pull factors are concerned is socio-cultural considerations followed very closely by economic considerations. Over-all, socio-cultural considerations rank third both as a push factor and a holding factor. As a primary holding factor, personal or family considerations weighed as heavily as economic considerations even though in the total weighting, it fell to fourth place.

The extent to which replies were biased by rationalization is, of course, indeterminable. Nevertheless, professional factors loomed so large in such a consistent manner that it seems beyond doubt that these constitute the most common reasons for migration. This fact is perhaps related to the personality make-up of these highly trained professionals, their strong need for achievement and their sustained motivation for professional satisfaction. It seems quite likely that they would tend to consider professional prospects foremost when faced with other critical decisions in their lives.

A significant relationship was found to exist between the present citizenship of the migrant, the citizenship of the spouse before marriage and specific holding factors in the receiving country. Those who fit this description tended to relate their migratory behavior to socio-cultural and family factors rather than to professional or economic ones.

In addition to the foregoing analysis, the relative strength of specific items within the five major categories was also assessed. Thus, under the general category of professional factors, opportunity for advanced training as a pull force and lack of such opportunity as a push force was predominant in the decision to migrate. Other specific professional reasons which had considerable strength as pull or push factors included "closer contact with great scientific centers", "physical facilities for

Table I

Push-Pull Factors Ranked by Effect on Decision to Migrate and Holding Factors Ranked by Effect on Decision to Remain Abroad

Factors	Primary (A)						Secondary (B)						Tertiary (C)						Total of (A), (B), (C)					
	Push		Pull		Holding		Push		Pull		Holding		Push		Pull		Holding		Push		Pull		Holding	
	No.	%	No.	%	No.	%	No.	%	No.	%	No.	%	No.	%	No.	%	No.	%	No.	%	No.	%	No.	%
Economic	20	13.3	13	8.7	19	12.7	13	8.7	17	11.3	22	14.7	15	10.0	16	10.7	26	17.3	48	10.7	46	10.2	67	14.9
Professional	70	46.7	94	62.7	78	52.0	77	51.3	87	58.0	71	47.3	60	40.0	64	42.7	36	24.0	207	46.0	245	54.4	185	41.1
Socio-cultural	12	8.0	14	9.3	18	12.0	13	8.7	14	9.3	17	11.3	15	10.0	23	15.3	20	13.3	40	8.9	51	11.3	55	12.2
Political	12	8.0	12	8.0	3	2.0	6	4.0	4	2.7	1	0.7	5	3.3	10	6.7	4	2.7	23	5.1	26	5.8	8	1.8
Personal or family	17	11.3	2	1.3	19	12.7	6	4.0	2	1.3	10	6.7	7	4.7	4	2.7	13	8.7	30	6.7	8	1.8	42	9.3
Others	2	1.3	2	1.3	—	—	1	0.7	—	—	1	0.7	—	—	1	0.7	6	4.0	3	0.7	3	0.7	7	1.6
Unknown	17	11.3	13	8.7	13	8.7	34	22.7	26	17.3	28	18.7	48	32.0	32	21.3	45	30.0	99	22.0	71	15.8	86	19.1
Total	150	100.0	150	100.0	150	100.0	150	100.0	150	100.0	150	100.0	150	100.0	150	100.0	150	100.0	450	100.0	450	100.0	450	100.0

work", "work available in the field of specialization", and "rapid promotion in one's career". Among holding forces, on the other hand, the most frequent professional factor was "physical facilities for work" followed by "satisfactory position in the profession". There is little doubt that such detailed information could be of value in developing policies to control the migration of talent.

9.2.7 Other Findings

In addition to learning the reasons for the decision to migrate, the research also inquired about the migrants' desire to keep in touch with professional developments in their fields in Turkey, their intentions to return to their native country in the near future, and the possible ways of co-operating with them while they were abroad. Their general comments and suggestions regarding the migration of talent out of Turkey were also solicited.

Three-fourths of the group reported a desire to keep in touch with professional developments in their fields of specialization in Turkey. This desire was significantly higher among those who intended to return to Turkey in the near future. Suggested as means to this end were publication in scientific journals, bibliographical work, bulletins containing information about employment opportunities for scientists in Turkey, and personal contact through visiting professorships, consultative work and conference activities in Turkey.

When asked their intentions of returning to work in Turkey in the near future, 35 percent expressed a definite or probable plan to do so, 33 percent were undecided and 27 percent said they would in all likelihood remain abroad. Because 68 percent were either positively inclined to return or undecided, a program for attracting migrants back to Turkey may be in order. In view of the high expenditures and long time required to train such talent, the country's need for them, and the valuable professional experience they represent, such a program may be worth serious consideration.

The statistical analyses indicated that the age, present citizenship of the respondent and original citizenship of the spouse were significantly related to the intention of returning to Turkey. This intention was weakest among the age group 50 and above, among those who adopted the citizenship of the receiving country and among those married to a non-Turkish spouse.

General suggestions most frequently made by respondents for retaining or attracting talent back to Turkey included the creation of suitable conditions for scientific work and research, satisfactory professional income, and a more rational employment and promotion policy for scientists, in that order. Respondents predominantly engaged in teaching tended to emphasize professional income while those whose main activity was research tended to stress the creation of suitable conditions for scientific work and research.

Because female migrants constituted only 13 out of 150 respondents or 8.7 percent, no attempt was made to analyze the relationship between the sex of migrants and patterns of migratory behavior.

9.3 *Conclusions*

The study was limited to a highly select group of Turkish migrants at the Ph.D. level. It investigated by use of a mail questionnaire a number of personal characteristics, related these to migratory behavior, and identified some of the main causes or motives for migration. The findings provide certain insights on a subject of growing interest in many countries of the world. If it is assumed that any large scale or continuous flow of talent out of a developing country to better developed regions of the world is detrimental to the former and therefore undesirable, efforts at controlling the flow would seem justified.

Surveys indicated that there were an estimated number of 217 Turkish Ph.D.'s working mostly in the United States, Canada and Western Europe during the time of the study. Comparisons with the annual production of doctorates and the existing stock of Ph.D.'s in Turkey suggest that the loss due to migration is substantial and that replacement of this talent is costly both in terms of time and financial investment. This loss is occurring at a time when Turkey needs to increase her stock of Ph.D.'s fast, especially in scientific and technical fields, in order to develop her system of higher education and to promote research in vital areas.

The fact that the heaviest loss occurs in the physical sciences and engineering deserves special attention. It is particularly in these fields that developing countries face a serious shortage and international competition for trained personnel is strongest. Developing countries such as Turkey which help supply talent to better developed regions need to formulate policies to cope with international competition in the use of their talent. Such policies should be based on reliable objective data.

In addition to leaving jobs in Turkey for employment abroad, another common channel of emigration is not returning to the homeland after study abroad. The decision to migrate was found to be related to professional, economic, socio-cultural, political, personal and family reasons. Professional reasons, however, weighed by far the heaviest both as push and pull factors as well as a factor causing migrants to remain abroad once there.

Academicians constitute the largest proportion of migrant Ph.D.'s. Thus, it seems that the university is one of the more important types of institutions in which measures could be taken to control the migration of Ph.D.'s from Turkey. If Turkish universities are to increase their attracting and holding powers for talented staff, a review of personnel policies and practices may be advisable. Moreover, rules and practices governing the study abroad of Turkish graduate students might also be reviewed from the standpoint of controlling the drain of talent.

REFERENCES

Ferguson, Donald C. and Dirican, Rahmi, 1966, The Turkish Medical Graduate in America : 1965—A Survey of Selected Characteristics, *The Turkish Journal of Pediatrics*, 8(3) : 176-177.

Grubel, Herbert G. and Scott, Anthony D., 1966, The International Flow of Human Capital, *American Economic Review*, 56(2):268-274.

Johnson, Harry, G. 1965, The Economics of the 'Brain Drain'—The Canadian Case, *Minerva*, 3(3): 299-311.

Kidd, Charles V., 1964, The Growth of Science and the Distribution of Scientists Among Nations, *Impact of Science on Society*, 14(1):5-18.

Kösemen, Cevdet, 1968, A Report Presented to the Education and World Affairs Committee Concerning Emigration of Engineers and Architects from Turkey to Foreign Countries for the Project 'International Migration of Talent', mimeo, 3(2).

National Science Foundation, 1969, *Scientists, Engineers and Physicians from Abroad : Fiscal Years 1966 and 1967*. Washington, D.C.:12.

Pan American Health Organization, 1966, *Migration of Health Personnel, Scientists, and Engineers from Latin America*. Washington, D.C.

Thomas, Brinley, 1967, The International Circulation of Human Capital, *Minerva*, 5(4).

U.K. Committee on Manpower Resources for Science and Technology, 1967, *The Brain Drain : Report of the Working Group on Migration*. London, Her Majesty's Stationary Office.

Üner, Hasan, 1968, *The Economic Impact of the Outflow of High-Level Manpower from Turkey to the United States*. (Unpublished thesis), The George Washington University.

U.S. House of Representatives, Committee on Government Operations, 1967, *The Brain Drain Into the United States of Scientists, Engineers and Physicians*. Washington, D.C., U.S. Government Printing Office : 17-90.

SELECTED BIBLIOGRAPHY

BOOKS, MONOGRAPHS AND BIBLIOGRAPHIES

Abadan, Nermin, 1964, *Batı Almanya'daki Türk İşçileri ve Sorunları* (Inquiries Regarding Turkish Workers in West Germany). Ankara, Turkish State Planning Organization.

Adams, Walter, ed., 1968, *The Brain Drain*. New York, The Macmillan Company.

Aker, Ahmet, 1972, *İşçi Göçü* (The Migration of Workers). Istanbul, Sander Yayınları.

Beyer, G., ed., 1973, *Brain Drain*. The Hague, Martinus Nijhoff.

Bingemer, K., et al, 1970, *Leben als Gastarbeiter*. Köln, Westdeutscher Verlag.

Böhning, W.R., 1972, *The Migration of Workers in the United Kingdom and the European Community*. London, Oxford University Press.

Bouvard, Margeurite, 1972, *Labor Movements in the Common Market Countries*. New York, Praeger Publishers.

Castles, S. and Kosack, G., 1973, *Immigrant Workers and Class Structure in Western Europe*. London, Oxford University Press.

Hoffmann-Nowotny, H.J., 1970, *Migration : Ein Beitrag zu einer Soziologischen Erklärung*. Stuttgart, Ferdinand-Enke Verlag.

——, 1973, *Soziologie des Fremdarbeiter-problems*. Stuttgart, Ferdinand-Enke Verlag.

Istanbul University, 1966, *Sosyal Siyaset Konferansları* (Social Science Lectures). Istanbul, Sermet Matbaası.

Kayser, Bernard, ed., 1971, *Manpower Movements and Labour Markets*. Paris, OECD.

Klee, Ernst, ed., 1972, *Gastarbeiter : Analysen und Berichte*. Frankfurt, Suhrkamp Verlag.

Miller, Duncan, ed., 1971, *Essays on Labor Force and Employment in Turkey*. Ankara, United States Agency for International Development.

Organization for Economic Cooperation and Development, 1969, *Bibliography : International Migration of Manpower*. Paris, The Organization.

Slotkin, James S., 1969, *From Field to Factory—New Industrial Employees*. Glencoe, Illinois, The Pree Fress.

Thomas, Brinley, ed., 1958, *Economics of International Migration*. London, The Mac Millan Company.

——, 1954, *Migration and Economic Growth*. Cambridge, Cambridge University Press.

Tuna, Orhan, 1966, *Türkiye'den Almanya'ya İşgücü Akımı ve Meseleleri* (The Flow of Manpower from Turkey to Germany and Its Problems). Istanbul, Sermet Matbaası.

Turkish State Planning Organization, 1973, *Third Five-Year Development Plan*. Ankara, The Organization.

Van Houte, Hans and Melgert, Willy, 1972, *Foreigners in Our Community*. Amsterdam, Keesing Publishers.

PERIODICALS

Ausländische Arbeitnehmer—Beschäftigung, Anwerbung, Vermittlung, 1961—present. Nürnberg, Bundesanstalt für Arbeitsvermittlung und Arbeitslosenversicherung.

International Migration, 1963—present. Geneva, Intergovernmental Committee for European Migration.

International Migration Review, 1967—present. Staten Island, New York, Center for Migration Studies.

İş ve İşgücü Bülteni (Work and Manpower Bulletin), 1962—present. Ankara, Turkish State Employment Service.

REPORTS, PAPERS AND THESES

Böhning, W.R., 1970, *The Social and Occupational Apprenticeship of Mediterranean Migrant Workers in West Germany*. Canterbury, University of Kent Centre for Research in the Social Sciences.

Hagmann, H.M. and Livi-Bacci, M.L., 1971, *Report on the Demographic and Social Pattern of Migrants in Europe Especially With Regard to International Migration*. Strasbourg, Council of Europe.

Hume, I.M., 1970, *Migrant Workers in Western Europe*. Washington, D.C., International Bank for Reconstruction and Development.

Kaupen-Haas, H., 1967, *Reintegration Problems Among Turkish Workers*. Paris, OECD.

Krahenbuhl, R.E., 1969, *Emigration and the Labour Market in Turkey*. Paris, OECD.

Mc Lin, Jon, 1972, *International Migrations and the European Community*. New York, American Universities Field Staff.

Neyzi, N.H., 1966, *Turkey Country Study on Migrant Workers Returning to Their Home Country*. Paris, OECD.

Organization for Economic Cooperation and Development, 1964, *International Joint Seminar on Geographical and Occupational Mobility of Manpower*. Paris, The Organization.

——, 1965, *International Joint Seminar on Adaptation of Rural and Foreign Workers to Industry*. Paris, The Organization.

——, 1967, *International Joint Seminar on Emigrant Workers Returning to Their Home Country*. Paris, The Organization.

Özşahin, Şener, 1969, *Turkish-European Manpower Movements*. Ankara, United States Agency for International Development.

Redding, David, 1967, *Turkish Workers in Western Europe—A Comparative Study*. Ankara, United States Agency for International Development.

Rodié, Raymond, 1967, *Les Travailleurs à l'Étranger et Leur Réintégration dans L'Économie Locale en Fonction du 2ème Plan Quinquennal de Developpement 1968-1972*. Paris, OECD.

Selcen, Iris, 1965, *Berufliche Wertmuster der Türkischen Gastarbeiter und die sich Daraus Ergebenden Anpassungsprobleme an die Deutsche Industriearbeiterschaft*. Köln, Universität Köln.

Tuna, Orhan, 1967, *Yurda Dönen İşçilerin İntibakı Sorunları* (Questions of Adjustment Among Workers Returning to the Homeland). Ankara, Turkish State Planning Organization.

Turkish State Employment Service, 1968, *Yurt Dışındaki Türk İşçileri ve Dönüş Eğilimleri* (Turkish Workers Outside the Homeland and Their Tendencies to Return). Ankara, The Service.

Üner, Hasan, 1968, *The Economic Impact of the Outflow of High-Level Manpower from Turkey to the United States*. Washington, D.C., The George Washington University.